THE MYTH OF THE *TITANIC*

To my good friend
Mike
(we share a quiet
mutual interest)

Don Reed
1999

The Myth of the *Titanic*

Richard Howells
Lecturer
Institute of Communications Studies
University of Leeds

St. Martin's Press
New York

THE MYTH OF THE TITANIC

Copyright © 1999 by Richard Howells

St. Martin's Press, Scholarly and Reference Division, 175 Fifth Avenue, New York, N.Y. 10010

First published in the United States of America in 1999

This book is printed on paper suitable for recycling and made from fully managed and sustained forest sources.

Printed in Great Britain

ISBN 0–312–22148–7

Library of Congress Cataloging-in-Publication Data
Howells, Richard Parton.
The myth of the Titanic / Richard Howells.
p.   cm.
Includes bibliographical references and index.
ISBN 0–312–22148–7 (cloth)
1. Titanic (Steamship)—History.   2. Shipwrecks—North Atlantic
Ocean—History.   3. Myth.   4. Great Britain—Social conditions—20th
century.   I. Title.
G530.T6H68   1999
910'.91634—dc21   98–53552
                                                                  CIP

For my parents

Contents

Acknowledgements

This book has been a long time in the making. Consequently, it would be impossible to acknowledge everyone who has contributed towards its completion. The following individuals and organizations have, however, been especially generous with their expertise, their thoughts or their support, both personal and financial. Their specific contributions are both known to them and valued by me.

Kate Alderson-Smith and the Brotherton Library, University of Leeds; Joanna Benn; Elaine Bradshaw; Olivia Brent; the British Newspaper Library, Colindale; Hamish Bryce and Thorn Lighting Ltd.; Colin Butterfield; the Cambridge University Library; the City of Stoke-on-Trent Museum and Art Gallery; Nicholas J. Cull; Henry Devlin; Henry Louis Gates, Jnr.; Jack Greenwood; Eva Hart; Charles A. Haas and Titanic International Inc.; Philippa Howells, Ray Johnson; Fred Inglis; Ida Leader; Don Lynch and the Titanic Historical Society; Graham McCann; Leonard McCann and the Vancouver Maritime Museum; Michael McCaughan and the Ulster Folk and Transport Museum; Brent MacGregor; the Marine Museum at Fall River, Massachusetts; the Master and Fellows of Emmanuel College, Cambridge; Robert Matson; the Mildmay Essay Club, Emmanuel College, Cambridge; Gregory Nagy; Michael C. Neitzel; Steve Rigby and the British Titanic Society; Geoff Robinson; Roger Simmons; the Southampton Maritime Museum; John S. Spong; Staffordshire County Library; Tiffany Stern; John R. Stilgoe; Ann Sutton; Philip M. Taylor and the Institute of Communications Studies, University of Leeds; John B. Thompson; Aruna Vasudevan; and Ruth Willats.

List of Plates

All photographs by the author.

Introduction

There are two *Titanic*s; this book is about the second of them. The first is the physical *Titanic*, the rusting remains of which can still be found at 49° 56′ west, 41° 43′ north, at a depth of 12,000 feet below the north Atlantic Ocean. The second *Titanic* is the mythical *Titanic*: the *Titanic* that emerged just as its tangible predecessor slipped from human view on 15 April 1912. It is this second *Titanic* which is the much more important, and infinitely more interesting, of the two.

The sinking of the *Titanic* is an event whose mythical significance has eclipsed its historical importance. Unlike, say, the Yalta Conference, as an historical event the *Titanic* is relatively unimportant. In the scheme of world affairs, it changed very little.[1] Even in terms of loss of life, the twentieth century has seen far greater disasters, both on land and at sea. In April 1980, for example, a tanker collided with a passenger ferry off the Philippines. The death toll was nearly three times greater than that of the *Titanic*, but the Philippines ferry disaster is little remembered outside the Philippines.[2] There can be few people in British and indeed Western culture, on the other hand, who have not heard of the *Titanic*. Hardly a week, it seems, passes without there being some reference to it: schoolchildren sing songs about it,[3] comedians tell jokes about it,[4] politicians make allusions to it,[5] and fictional characters have even gone down in it.[6]

This significance of the *Titanic* in the public imagination shows no signs of abating as the twentieth century draws to a close: Beryl Bainbridge set her 1996 Booker Prize short-listed novel *Every Man for Himself* aboard the *Titanic*,[7] while 'Titanic' the musical opened on Broadway in April 1997,[8] and James Cameron's blockbuster movie 'Titanic' was released that same year at an estimated cost of $200 million.[9] It was then the most expensive film ever made, and won 11 Oscars in the 1998 Academy Awards. Cameron's production is the sixth feature film to date to be set aboard the famous ship, and is the third to be called simply 'Titanic'.[10] The *Titanic* has entered the computer age, too. A computer game, 'Titanic: Adventure out of Time', challenges players to escape a 'virtual' re-creation of the ship before it sank,[11] while questions of taste were raised by publications such as *The Last Dinner on the Titanic*, which enabled the reader to re-create the last first class dinner on board.[12] Despite its antiquity, the sinking of

1

the *Titanic* is still front-page news: a theory about poor steel quality in the hull made page 1 of *The Guardian* over 80 years after the event, under the enticing headline 'Titanic Iceberg Is Innocent'.[13]

There has been no shortage of more or less serious books on the *Titanic*, the majority of which present the details of the building, sailing and sinking within a traditional, narrative and chronological structure. Books such as these have proved extremely popular with *Titanic* enthusiasts of which (interestingly) there is a growing number worldwide.[14] The best volumes are assiduously researched and contain vast amounts of information gleaned from contemporary documents, inquiry reports, survivor interviews and old-fashioned detective work. They remain, however, concerned substantially with the 'facts' about the first of my two *Titanics*: the actual, physical and considerably less fascinating of the pair.[15]

For an analysis of the second of the two *Titanics*, we need to turn our attention to a cultural approach to history which focuses on beliefs as much as it does realities. The French historians Robert Darnton and Roger Chartier have made an important contribution here: Darnton's *The Great Cat Massacre and Other Episodes in French Cultural History* of 1984[16] and Chartier's *Cultural History*,[17] published four years later, took an historical approach, which focused upon the importance of *mentalités* (attitudes) rather than simple events. In this way the 'facts' of the incidents they described were of secondary importance to the attitudes that such episodes were held to represent. Thus, Chartier was able to speculate (much, no doubt, to the dismay of traditional historians) that it did not really matter whether Darnton's 'Great Cat Massacre' ever actually took place:[18] The point was that people chose to *believe* that it happened, and invested the event with cultural value. In this way, the 'cat massacre' was able to take its place in French social memory. Social memory, which so often – for right or wrong – provides the basis for social action, needs therefore to be taken very seriously if we are to get to grips with a thorough understanding of why people behave the way they do.

The French have not had a monopoly on this approach, however. Paul Fussell in *The Great War and Modern Memory*,[19] for example, demonstrated how the First World War became imprinted upon British social consciousness by way of novels, diaries, poems, autobiographies and newspaper reports. It is these sources, rather than official records, which have contributed to 'the making of memory'.[20] As Fussell put it, the First World War was 'relying on inherited myth, it was generating new myth, and that myth is part of the fibre of our own lives.'[21] In just the same way, Beau Riffenburgh, in *The Myth of the Explorer*, was deftly able to echo Chartier's sentiments on the slaughter (or otherwise) of cats in France: 'Historians and geographers have argued that what is perceived to exist or happen is equally important as what actually exists or happens.'[22] As we shall discover, this is exactly the case with the *Titanic*.

To the social scientist, approaches such as these may equally be described as lying within the 'sociology of representation'.[23] Thus, it is not the physical *Titanic* itself which is the major object of concern. Rather, it is *representations* of the *Titanic* which occupy our attention. It is these representations which provide illuminating textual manifestation of the *mentalités* of the societies from which they arose. It is in this vein of research that the current analysis is offered, fully subscribing to Stuart Hall's belief that representation is 'an essential part of the process by which meaning is produced and exchanged between members of a culture'.[24]

This study seeks to present the first serious analysis of the *Titanic* as myth. It pays particular attention to a detailed textual analysis of previously neglected, non-canonical materials both to describe and interpret the myth of the *Titanic* as articulated in British popular culture from 1912 to 1914.[25] It begins with the launching of the 'unsinkable ship', and ends with the outbreak of the 'war to end all wars'. This constitutes a defining part of what I shall refer to as the 'late Edwardian' period. Edward VII himself had, of course, died in 1910, but culturally, the Edwardian period extended until at least the start of the First World War.[26] It is upon this final part of the Edwardian period that the current analysis focuses. It has a tripartite aim: first, to analyse the *Titanic* myth to provide an insight into the particular culture and values of late-Edwardian society; second, to demonstrate that late Edwardian culture was one in which myth was both produced and employed just as it was in ancient and 'primitive' societies; and third, to draw far greater conclusions about myth, mythogenesis, popular culture and society as a whole. I shall conclude by contending that myth is not limited to seemingly diverse societies divided from us by both time and space but is, rather, equally vibrant and extant in late twentieth-century Western civilization. In this way, this investigation marries theory and practice with the noumenal and the phenomenal to create a case study which not only relegates the physical *Titanic* to a supporting role, but which is also not even primarily about the *Titanic* at all.

Throughout this analysis, I shall not be using the word 'myth' lightly – and certainly not in any pejorative sense. Claude Lévi-Strauss claimed that pre-literate peoples were just as intellectually sophisti-cated as we are today. What I am doing, then, is reversing that equa-tion to argue that we are, therefore, just as likely as pre-literate peoples to think in terms of myth. Both ancient and modern myths encode abstract thought in concrete form. Further, these myths com-prise both temporal and universal elements. The temporal is revealing of the values and concerns of the particular people that made specific myths, while the universal dimension is common to myth-makers across both time and space. The temporal element can therefore be used as a 'psychoanalysis in reverse' of a particular society, while the universal element sees societies in general using myth to construct meaning out of an arbitrary universe.

The sinking of the RMS *Titanic*, as represented in late Edwardian popular culture, amply illustrates this argument. If we undertake a detailed analysis of contemporary newspaper reports and special edi-tions, hastily published books, commemorative sheet music, postcards, statues, records, memorial ceremonies and souvenir memorabilia, we can arrive at an understanding of both the temporal and the universal components of the *Titanic* myth. More than that, however, we shall see how late Edwardian society quickly reanimated the historical data surrounding the sinking of the *Titanic* to bring about a mythical trans-formation in which a triumph was made out of a tragedy. Universally, if we examine the commonly held belief that the *Titanic* had been hailed as the 'unsinkable' ship, we find that this was in fact an essen-tially retrospective invention: the *Titanic* only really became 'unsink-able' after it had in fact sunk. What happened in the popular culture of 1912–14 was that the historical data were, again, rapidly reanimated to create a modern myth of hubris and – inevitably – nemesis. In this way, cultural meaning was constructed out of an arbitrary event. This, it is contended, is a major function of myths both ancient and modern: they fashion meaning out of a seemingly meaningless world.

The pursuit of this argument involves taking popular culture seri-ously. T.S. Eliot observed: 'To understand the culture is to understand the people',[27] and few people today would deny the validity of culture as a legitimate field of research. Yet although many will think sum-marily of culture as literature, poetry, the fine and the performing arts, it is important to remember how much more to culture there actually is. As Eliot showed in his *Notes Towards a Definition of Culture*, it embraces all manner of things from a sports final and Wensleydale cheese to the music of Elgar.[28] Scholarship has tradition-ally occupied itself much more with the likes of Elgar than it has with football (or indeed cheese!), but as Colin MacCabe argued in 'Defining Popular Culture': 'Those who isolate themselves within the narrow and exclusive traditions of high art'[29] can only expect a narrow understanding of a breadth and complexity of culture – and, consequently, society – as a whole. An intelligent analysis of popular culture, then, provides us with a far wider understanding of culture and society than the élite and the avant-garde. Eugene Weber heeded this in his study *fin de siècle* France. Although sympathetic to avant-garde movements in both literature and fine art, he preferred to focus on the more popular cultural experiences of everyday life, be they going to the music hall or riding a bicycle. This was because no matter how much he personally admired the avant-garde, he believed such schools and movements were 'marginal and unrepresentative' and did not necessarily represent even 'the wider educated public'.[30]

Our attention turns, then, to cultural forms which, although we may not necessarily admire their quality, are nevertheless particularly valuable to us. Consequently, the most valuable work on popular culture is likely to be done by those who seek neither to praise nor to condemn it, but simply to understand it. Indeed, forms which may be poor in aesthetic merit may be correspondingly rich in cultural value. James Monaco, for example, personally preferred the 'art' to the 'popular' film, but nevertheless recognized the greater usefulness to the sociologist of mass-produced Hollywood products because 'they are often better indexes of public concerns, shared myths and mores than individually conceived, intentionally artistic ones are'.[31] Therefore, we need to incorporate the study of popular culture into the study of society, not simply to extend the range of our analysis, but also because there are some ways in which popular culture is actually more revealing to us than 'high' art.

This is due in part to the relative sincerity and unselfconsciousness of vernacular forms. Robert Warshow, for example, described the popular film as a kind of 'pure culture ... which has not yet altogether fallen into the discipline of art'.[32] J.B. Jackson made a similar point in continually urging scholars to focus on the 'vernacular' as opposed to the deliberately 'architectural', built environment, because that which we see in our vernacular landscape is 'the image of our common humanity'.[33]

Popular culture occupies an increasingly central position in society. It may be vernacular, but it is certainly not peripheral. Even those who disapprove of popular culture are coming increasingly to recognize its importance. Critical theorists such as Adorno and Horkheimer despised it both qualitatively and ideologically, but they nevertheless took it seriously enough to argue passionately that economics alone is not sufficient to explain social conditions.[34] Consequently, they held up popular culture to rigorous intellectual examination. They may not have liked what they found, but they knew that they could not afford to dismiss it. Adorno, in particular, intensely disliked much of popular culture, but he nevertheless understood that 'when, for the sake of humanity, you close yourself off from what has become of humanity ... you yourself approach the inhumane.'[35] One does not necessarily have to subscribe to Adorno and Horkheimer's somewhat polemical conclusions to be persuaded that popular culture is indeed both highly pervasive and ideologically saturated, and that, as such, it would be academically irresponsible to ignore it. If so, then we must surely agree with Fred Inglis that 'to study public communications is to study one of the most important topics of the day. Such study should be a compulsory part of every citizen's liberal education.'[36]

Research into popular culture, then, is not trivial but vital, for whatever qualitative judgements we may be tempted to make, there is too much at stake for it to be ignored. Consequently, the apparently frivolous nature of the subject matter should not be mistaken for frivolity on the part of the analyst. As Wittgenstein put it: 'For a philosopher there is more grass growing down in the valleys of silliness than up on the barren heights of cleverness.'[37]

Such studies, however, need not be as trivial as their subject matter might seem to suggest. Siegfried Kracauer observed: 'The films of a nation reflect its mentality.'[38] A study of German film from 1920 onwards, he said, could help in the understanding of Hitler's rise to power. For, 'Germany carried out what had been anticipated by her cinema from its very beginning.' When the battles raged after Nuremberg, 'It was all as it had been on the screen.'[39]

How, then, are we to investigate the myth of the *Titanic*? The analysis of popular culture is, as Graham McCann has pointed out, 'a messy business'. Just because popular culture may seem simplistic, it does not at all follow that it is going to be simple to understand. As with all cultural questions, therefore, we must be always aware of our methodological limitations in trying to understand them. As John Dunn has stated, there can be no 'specific methodology which, correctly applied, would yield descriptions which would never be false or always be true'.[40] This does not mean, however, that we should, or can, give up. If, as Geertz has argued, the culture of a people is 'an assemblage of texts',[41] what we need is a methodology for getting to grips with that component assemblage of texts which constitutes the myth of the *Titanic* in British popular culture from 1912 to 1914.

Scholarship has seen a strong tradition of 'scientific' or content-based examination of media, culture and society, and this has usually been quantitative in approach. This kind of analysis is at its most effective with the overt content of cultural forms, but the trouble is that the most valuable content of cultural forms is often latent. This is what scientific content analysis usually fails to account; it always runs the risk of merely scratching the surface, of failing to reach, as Adorno put it, 'the heart of the matter'.[42] We can end up, therefore, as Clifford Geertz said, going all the way round the world just to count cats in Zanzibar.[43]

The difference between the 'overt' and the 'latent' content of a work is crucial to us. In *The Origin of German Tragic Drama*, for example, Walter Benjamin sought to strip away what he called the 'material content' of the Baroque tragic drama (*Trauerspiel*) to arrive at the greater inner 'truth content', which was communicated through allegory. For Benjamin, this examination of the allegory represented the crucial progression from commentary, which concerned itself with the simple description of the information contained in the *Trauerspiel* (or any other work for that matter), to real criticism, which set itself to reveal the truth expressed within the work at hand.[44] Where Benjamin talked of allegory, Geertz was to talk about metaphor. Essentially, they were talking about the same thing. In his celebrated essay 'Deep Play: Notes on the Balinese Cockfight', Geertz claimed that the cockfight was a way of encompassing popular themes, issues and concerns as 'an image, a fiction, a model, a metaphor'.[45] Life was not literally a cockfight, but the cockfight eloquently represented important aspects of life by way of an almost aesthetic mystery through which something could have a quality that was not literally there.[46] It is here, on the borders of the inarticulable, that the real content lies.

What we need, then, is not a scientific but a hermeneutic approach to the interpretation of popular culture as modern myth. Hermeneutics is the project of interpretation; a human as opposed to scientifically objective approach to the understanding of human activity.[47] According to Geertz, the hermeneutic or interpretive methodology is like 'penetrating a literary text'. He argues that this methodology provides a kind of 'close reading' of cultural texts and concludes: 'societies, like lives, contain their own interpretations. One has only to learn how to gain access to them.'[48] For Geertz, therefore, the analysis of culture is 'not an experimental science in search of law, but an interpretive one in search of meaning'.[49]

The current analysis takes an unashamedly interdisciplinary approach. In doing so, it does not seek to defile existing disciplines but, rather, to enrich our understanding by forging connections between them. Terry Eagleton, in his Inaugural Lecture as Professor of English at Oxford University, went so far as to claim that 'much of the most interesting work in the humanities' now being carried out was 'constantly transgressing the frontiers between traditional subject areas'.[50] I have very much proceeded under that belief. As Henry Louis Gates, Du Bois Professor of the Humanities at Harvard has said: 'This is the wave of the twenty-first century – recombining our traditional notions of disciplines'.[51] An interdisciplinary approach is not only defensible but indeed essential in tackling such a wide-reaching and complex subject as the myth of the *Titanic*.

This investigation focuses upon material not usually consulted in an examination of the *Titanic*. It draws especially upon the following texts: commemorative editions of newspapers and magazines, advertising material, postcards, hastily published books, statues and memorials, memorabilia and souvenirs, records, songs and sheet music, and memorial events. It does not use ordinary newspaper reports. This is not simply because these were often frenetic, garbled or contradictory; rather, it is because the texts upon which I have chosen to concentrate are all active and deliberate forms of social memory. They were set down at more of a distance from events and attempted to view the story and lessons of the *Titanic* as a whole instead of on the basis of information which happened to be at hand in time for the next edition. It is these deliberate acts of social memory, my research has found, which prove to be by far the richer in social significance and, therefore, as social resources.

Similarly, although I have, of course, studied the published survivors' accounts, I have not drawn significantly upon these in this case-study. This is because survivors' accounts are first-person accounts, which purport to recount the sinking from an individual's point of view, and often have individual axes to grind.[52] More useful to us are the third-party accounts, which provide more of a collective and less of a personal perspective of events. Again, they emphasize social rather than personal memory. Where these survivor's accounts have been incorporated into third-party narratives, however, I have drawn more heavily upon them as they have been more thoroughly accepted by and absorbed into the social memory.

I have not drawn upon purely local texts, fascinating though many of these have been. Southampton, for example, was the city from which the *Titanic* set sail and which provided the majority of its crew, and so the local press provided a particularly well-focused reflection of their particular concerns. Similarly, Belfast was the city in which the *Titanic* was built, and Stoke-on-Trent was the city of the captain's birth. The local reactions from both areas are again revealing, but as I have chosen to concentrate on the general reaction to the *Titanic* in Britain as a whole, this has precluded the investigation of local and particular cases. One seeming exception to this may appear to be my use of statues and memorials as texts, but it will be understood that as these are inevitably local due to their only being able to occupy one site, I have chosen to draw upon them as general rather than local examples.

Official inquiries into the *Titanic* disaster were held first in the United States and then in London. The reports from these inquiries are, of course, invaluable to the study of the *Titanic*, but while I have naturally included them in this research, I have not used them as central texts because government reports should not be considered works of popular culture.

I have conducted an extensive personal interview with one of the survivors of the *Titanic* disaster,[53] but I have similarly elected not to use this as a central text. This interview has, of course, usefully informed my understanding of the whole *Titanic* discourse, but as it lies outside my remit of deliberate acts of social memory in the popular culture of Britain from 1912 to 1914, it has remained as background rather than foreground information.

Although this study seeks to examine the popular cultural reaction to the sinking of the *Titanic*, it has also proved necessary to take into account the material published on the *Titanic* before its maiden voyage. This, as will be seen from the ensuing chapters, has proved particularly important in getting to grips with the question of whether or not the *Titanic* had ever actually been publicized as an 'unsinkable' ship.

Finally, a word should be said about the expository tone of this investigation. In his 1990 novel *A Tenured Professor*, the economist John Kenneth Galbraith describes a meeting between a distinguished professor and a promising young scholar. 'Never forget, dear boy,' warns the professor, 'that academic distinction in economics is not to be had from giving a clear account of how the world works.' Indeed, she continues, anyone who 'cannot be understood at all will be especially admired.'[54] The scholar takes the professor's advice, and a glittering academic career ensues.

Sadly, economics is not alone here, and criticism of impenetrable prose is limited neither to that field nor to purely fictional characters. It is particularly rife in cultural and theoretical approaches to the humanities and social sciences. Perhaps some ideas are so complex that they are able only complexedly to be described. Maybe, on the other hand, some theorists really are much better at thinking than they are at explaining, and so their turbid style may simply be the result of expository ineptitude. Then again, perhaps – as Galbraith has intimated – there actually is what we might term a 'politics of obfuscation' at work in which some scholars, through insecurity or guile, deliberately write incomprehensibly in order to appear far more complex than they are. I do not aim to unravel such mysteries here; I do, on the other hand, feel it expedient to make it plain that in the following chapters I have taken great pains to explain myself as clearly and as concisely as possible at all times. My aim is to elucidate, not obfuscate. Galbraith's distinguished professor would, of course, have counselled me otherwise, but my hope is that if any point I make should strike the reader as obvious, it is because I have struggled long and hard to make it appear so.

My first chapter, 'A brief history of the *Titanic*', provides a narrative, historical background to orient the reader among the undisputed facts regarding the *Titanic*. In this way, the chapter serves as a solid outline against which the embroideries of the myth may be better examined, judged and understood. Readers who already have expertise in the *Titanic* story will (intentionally) find little to surprise them in this chapter; those new to the topic or who wish to refresh their memories will find it valuable as a grounding for the detailed and thematic analysis which is to follow.

Chapter 2, 'Myth and the *Titanic*', argues that a myth is not necessarily a falsehood, but rather a cultural device in which abstract values are encoded in concrete form. In this way, the case is made for the *Titanic* as a modern myth in that considered, anthropological sense.[55] It pays particular attention to the complex relationship between myth and history, and lays the ground for a consideration of the myth of the *Titanic* in the tradition of myths both ancient and modern.

Chapter 3, 'Women and children first!', initiates our close examination of the popular texts. It focuses upon that part of the *Titanic* myth that tells us that, as the ship was about to sink, men stood aside while women and children were given places in the few lifeboats. They chose to die rather than behave 'improperly'. Their actions were instantly mythologized in late Edwardian popular culture. This chapter therefore demonstrates how the *Titanic* myth articulately encoded late Edwardian assumptions about the different behaviours expected of men and women both in times of crisis and in society at large.

As the waves finally closed over the *Titanic*, one version of the myth has it that the captain's final order to his crew was: 'Be British, boys, be British!' The captain, of course, went down with his ship. But what did it mean to 'be British' in the face of death? Chapter 4, 'Be British', contrasts 'British' with 'foreign' behaviour in the *Titanic* myth. It reveals underlying assumptions about the innate qualities – and presumed superiority – of the Anglo-Saxon race.

Chapter 5, 'We Shall Die Like Gentlemen', takes its title from one of the most repeated elements of the *Titanic* myth. This is the story of the first class passenger who, along with his valet, changed into evening dress as the last of the lifeboats slipped away. 'If we are to die,' he is said to have told a steward, 'we shall die like gentlemen.' This chapter investigates the issue of social class in the *Titanic* myth. It discovers assumed connections between class and behaviour, investigates the correlation between class and survival, and analyses the myth's preoccupation with the upper-class minority in comparison with the emigrant majority on board.

The *Titanic* band, so the myth has it, played ragtime as the lifeboats were being lowered, but concluded with the hymn 'Nearer, My God, to Thee' as those who remained on board were about to die. Chapter 6 examines that belief, together with the perceived role of the divine in the sinking of the *Titanic*. It discovers deep ambiguities in the mythical response and argues that the myth of the *Titanic* reveals shifting relations between secular and spiritual values in late Edwardian society.

Chapter 7, 'The Unsinkable Ship', focuses upon perhaps the most enduring of all the *Titanic* stories: the belief that the luxury liner was believed to be the 'unsinkable' ship. This chapter, however, demonstrates that this is a classic case of retrospective mythogenesis: the *Titanic* was never really called 'unsinkable' until after it in fact sank. A 'control' comparison is made with the *Titanic*'s elder, yet identical 'sister', the *Olympic*, which preceded the *Titanic* into service yet has never attracted any form of myth. The chapter concludes that the *Titanic* was retrospectively dubbed 'unsinkable' to transform a random shipping accident into a tragic myth of both 'hubris' and 'nemesis'.

The conclusion contends that contemporary Western societies make and use myth, as do distant, ancient and 'primitive' societies divided from us by both time and space. It argues for the value of such case studies as the *Titanic* myth for a fuller understanding of both mythogenesis and ourselves.

* * *

Although this study concerns the second of my two *Titanic*s, I shall now proceed with a brief history of the first, against which the reader will better be prepared to observe the emergence of the second.

1 A Brief History of the *Titanic*

There can be no such thing as a definitive history, and this single chapter does not attempt to be one. Inasmuch, however, as facts can ever be established, here follows a brief history of the *Titanic*. It is, of course, a history of only the physical *Titanic*. Its purpose is simply to set the stage for my analysis of the much more important mythical *Titanic*; to provide a background – a perspective – against which that mythical *Titanic* can be better understood.

By the turn of the twentieth century, Atlantic crossings were very big business indeed. Western Europe and North America were social and economic power-houses, divided by a large and inhospitable ocean. The Atlantic liners provided, quite literally, 'the only way to cross'. If we think of the incalculable importance of international airlines in trans-Atlantic travel and communication today, we can begin to imagine the crucial position which the passenger liners held in the culture and economy of 1912. Between 1840 and 1890, trade between Britain and the United States had increased by 700 per cent.[1] Those crossing the Atlantic were not only the business and social élite; the 'huddled masses' in their millions were also making their way, inevitably by sea, from the reality of one continent to the hope of another. In 1907 alone, 1,285,349 immigrants had entered the United States. Although the great liners of the period are best remembered for their 'luxury' and their wealthy passengers, it is important to underline that immigrant traffic was in fact their greatest single source of income. In this way the *Titanic*, for all its reputation for opulence, was both economically and officially an emigrant ship.[2] All the major steamship companies competed energetically to win the trade of both wealthy and emigrant passengers.[3] Just because emigrant passengers were typically poor, this did not mean that they were not selective in choosing the ships in which they were to cross. Competition in terms of accommodation and price both resulted from and further contributed to the emigrant passengers' power to choose, and this further added to the competitive atmosphere among rival carriers in this potentially hugely lucrative trade.[4] For the shipping companies, the answer was size. This was true not only in terms of economies of scale, but also in terms of competition for passengers: passengers of all classes were attracted to the idea of big ships and spacious accommodation for what was still typically a 5–7 day passage over stormy seas.

It is in this competitive atmosphere that bigger and yet bigger passenger ships were planned and constructed by the rival companies. The size of Cunard liners, for example, grew from the *Umbria* (8,127 tons) in 1884 and the *Campania* (12,500 tons) in 1893 to the *Lusitania* and *Mauretania* (both approaching 32,000 tons) in 1907.[5] The rival White Star line competed with their 'big four' liners: the *Celtic* (20,904 tons) of 1901, the *Cedric* (21,035 tons) of 1903, the *Baltic* (23,884 tons) of 1904, and the *Adriatic* (24,541 tons) of 1907. The Germans, too, were strong competitors in the trans-Atlantic market. They were building increasingly large ships from the North German Lloyd line's *Kaiser Wilhelm der Grosse* (14,350 tons) of 1897 to the *Kaiserin Auguste Victoria* (24,581 tons) of 1906. It can easily be seen, however, from this that the ships 'to beat' in this increasingly competitive field were the enormous (by 1907 standards) Cunarders, *Lusitania* and *Mauretania*. The problem for their competitors, and especially the White Star Line, was not only that the Cunard duo were considerably larger than anything else afloat, they were also faster. The *Mauretania*, in particular, was not only the largest liner in the world but also held the Blue Riband Atlantic speed record for 22 years. Realizing that they were unlikely to beat the Cunard line for speed, White Star made the strategic decision to overtake them in size and luxury. In this way, White Star's opulence would not only counter Cunard's alacrity, but they would also have the all important financial advantage in payload. Fuel costs would be cheaper, too, for high speeds demanded a disproportionate quantity of coal to be consumed in the boilers of the Atlantic 'greyhounds'. A final advantage would be that the slower cruising speed of the new White Star ships would lessen vibration. Although the White Star liners would take one half-day longer from Southampton to New York than the Cunard pair, the passage, it was reasoned, would be considerably more comfortable.

In 1907, the Liverpool-based White Star Line[6] took the decision to build not one but three such Atlantic liners, each of which would be more than one and a half times bigger than the rival *Lusitania* or *Mauretania*, and carry twice as many passengers. By having three as opposed to two identical ships on the Atlantic run, White Star reasoned that they would be able to provide a regular, reliable, seamless, weekly service in both directions. The plan was agreed between the

Chairman of the White Star Line, J. Bruce Ismay, and Lord James Pirrie, a fellow director and also a partner in Belfast shipbuilders Harland and Wolff, the yard that traditionally built all White Star ships. The three ships – the *Olympic* class of liner – were to be bigger and more luxurious than any of the competition, even though they would never be capable of the top speeds of their Cunard rivals. Work on the first of the three liners, the *Olympic*, began in Belfast in December 1908, while work on the second, the *Titanic*, started on the adjacent slipway in March 1909. Work on the third, the *Gigantic*, was scheduled to begin when the *Olympic*'s slipway became clear. The *Olympic* was duly launched on 20 October 1910; the *Titanic* the following 31 May. As the first of the class, it was the *Olympic* that gained the lion's share of White Star ceremonial and public attention. The launch of the *Titanic* only made page 9 of *The Times*: 'The launching arrangements for the *Titanic* were similar to those in the case of the Olympic last October', their correspondent reported.[7] The *Olympic* had a gross tonnage of 45,324, while the *Titanic* underwent some additions and improvements in the light of experience with the *Olympic* and so, at 46,328 tons, became, technically, the largest liner in the world. In terms of length, width and height, however, the *Titanic* was not an inch larger that its elder and, at the time, better-known 'sister', the *Olympic*.

It is worth briefly putting the size of the *Olympic* and the *Titanic* into context here. While both were indeed the biggest liners in the world, they held this status for only a brief period. The *Olympic* was, of course, succeeded by the slightly larger *Titanic*, but the *Titanic* would only have been the world's largest for a few months even if it had not sunk. The Hamburg-America Line's *Imperator* of 1913 was, at 52,117 tons, significantly larger than either of the White Star 'sisters'. By way of further comparison, the *Titanic* at 46,329 tons was considerably smaller than the 83,673 ton *Queen Elizabeth*, which was built in Scotland between 1936 and 1940, and less than half the size of the 109,000 ton *Grand Princess*, which P&O put into service in 1998.

The launch of both the new White Star liners was followed by ten months of 'fitting out' with engines and interiors. Economy was the priority of neither builder nor owner, with the *Olympic* class, in common with other White Star/Harland and Wolff collaborations, being built on a 'cost plus' rather than a tender basis. The *Olympic* and the *Titanic* were both 882 feet 9 inches long, 92 feet 6 inches wide, and 104 feet high from the keel to the navigating bridge. Coal-fired,

steam-driven reciprocating engines powered two large outer propellers, while a turbine engine drove the smaller, inner propeller. The
operating speed was designed to be 21 knots.

The hulls were divided by 15 transverse, watertight bulkheads,
each starting at the double bottom and extending above the water-
line. The bulkheads were connected by 12 watertight doors operating, as was 'usual'[8] in White Star steamers, on a drop system, which
could be operated either from the doors themselves or by remote
control from the captain's bridge. Publicly proud though White Star
were of these features, Vernon Gibbs, in his history of British passenger liners, has noted: 'Watertight subdivision was not as good as
in the Cunarders.'[9]

In terms of life-saving facilities, the *Titanic* carried 14 conventional
lifeboats, two 'emergency cutters' and four Engelhardt collapsible
lifeboats, a number in excess of British Board of Trade regulations.
Additionally, there were 3,560 lifebelts, approved and inspected by the
Board of Trade. There was also a five kilowatt Marconi radio system,
staffed by two Marconi-trained operators.

White Star publicity for the new liners concentrated, however, not
upon the safety features but upon the size and luxury of the *Olympic*
class. A publicity brochure of October 1911 declared:

> Their surpassing dimensions – exceeding those of any other ships –
> have made possible the utmost liberality in planning the passenger
> accommodations, which are upon a scale of greater magnificence
> than those of any other steamers.[10]

White Star publicity must, of course, be viewed as such.
Nevertheless, it is true that the *Olympic* class of liner was designed to
be particularly luxurious – for sound economic reasons. The first-class
dining saloons, with seating for over 500 passengers, were panelled
and furnished in oak in the style, it was claimed, of a Jacobean country
house. The reception rooms featured Aubusson tapestries, while the
bronze ceiling and bracket lights were designed to 'reflect their
hundred lights upon the glittering jewels of women in brilliant evening
frocks ...'[11] The à la carte restaurants were of Louis XVI design, lit by
large bay windows and featuring 'ample accommodation for an
orchestra'.[12] The entrance halls and grand staircases were also well-
publicized features, topped by iron and glass domes which shed
natural light on the stairs and landings. On the top landings were
clocks supported by female figures, said to symbolize Honour and
Glory crowning Time. The effect, claimed the publicists, was that: 'we

at once lose the feeling that we are on board a ship, and seem instead to be entering the hall of some great house on shore.'[13] Three passenger lifts provided for those who would rather not take the stairs. The lounges were declared to be in Louis XV style, while the smoke rooms were *faux* Georgian. Turkish baths were done in 'oriental' style, while the *Olympic* class also featured a gymnasium and an indoor swimming pool 'of splendid size' (actually 32 × 13 feet), a then unusual – but not unique – feature for a ship.[14]

The first-class suite rooms were decorated in different styles or 'themes': Louis XVI, Empire, Adams, Italian Renaissance, Louis XV, Louis XIV, Georgian, Regency, Queen Anne, Modern and Old Dutch. Each of the first-class state rooms was furnished with beds rather than bunks, the majority of which were four feet wide. 'This is a feature which will be greatly appreciated by passengers,' declared a brochure.[15] Of the two ships, the *Titanic* alone was fitted with four particularly spacious parlour suites, which each comprised two bedrooms, a sitting room, private bath and WC. Two of the four had an additional 50 foot-long private promenade deck. The majority of first-class accommodation, however, was less splendid, with many rooms having only shared bathrooms and WCs.

The White Star Line claimed that the second-class accommodation on the *Olympic* and *Titanic* was much higher than was usually the case. The dining rooms were oak-panelled, while passengers sat on swivel chairs which were fixed to the linoleum-tiled floors. Pianos were provided. The second-class 'libraries' (actually, they were much more like lounges) were panelled in sycamore and boasted Wilton carpets. The smoke rooms were 'a variation of Louis XVI'[16] with oak and Morocco chairs and, like the dining rooms, had linoleum-tiled floors. There was one second-class passenger lift in each ship. The second-class state rooms (White Star did not like to use the word 'cabins') were finished in enamel white with mahogany bunks and linoleum floors.

The third-class dining rooms were painted in enamel white and divided by bulkheads. The ceilings were supported by metal pillars between the long tables, while the walls were decorated with coat hooks and shipping posters. The oak-panelled smoke rooms were fitted with teak chairs and slatted benches. 'Here, under the soothing influence of the fragrant weed, many a thought will be given to the homeland and those left behind', declared a White Star brochure, betraying an unspoken assumption about its third-class passengers.[17] The third-class lounges (known as 'general' rooms) were panelled in pine, finished in enamel white and furnished with teak chairs and benches. The brochure claimed that this would prove 'one of the liveliest rooms in the ship'. Indeed:

> The friendly intercourse, mutual helpfulness and bonhomie of third class passengers is proverbial, and, remembering that many of them have arrived at the most eventful stage in their career, we realize that 'touch of nature that makes the whole world kin.'[18]

Third-class accommodation was generally in the lower decks, with men and women segregated at opposite ends of the ship. Families were able to take small rooms amidships, with sleeping accommodation in bunk beds. Two bathtubs served over 1,000 third-class berths. As the *Titanic* provided far better than average accommodation for its lowest fare-paying passengers, the White Star Line felt justified in calling this 'third' rather than 'steerage' class.[19] The term 'steerage', however, remained common in popular usage.[20]

Although it is the *Titanic*'s first-class passengers and accommodation that have attracted by far the greatest popular attention, it is important again to stress the importance of the third class aboard the *Titanic*. Of the *Titanic*'s 2,566 passenger capacity, 1,034 was made up of first class, 510 second class and 1,022 third class.[21] In terms of planned capacity, therefore, the number of third-class passengers was more or less equal to the first. Additionally, the ship provided accommodation for 945 crew.[22] These figures, however, reflect the maximum capacity of the *Titanic*. On the *Titanic*'s maiden voyage, the ship was considerably less than full: 325 in the first class, 285 in the second and 706 in the third. There were 885 crew. In other words, on its famous maiden voyage, the *Titanic*'s third-class passengers outnumbered the first by a ratio of more than two to one.[23]

Fares for a one-way crossing on the *Titanic* began at £7 9 shillings in third class[24] and rose to £870[25] for a suite for one or two passengers (and a servant) in high season. The first-class accommodation was marketed towards American passengers; the British, apparently, considered the *Olympic* class to be rather ostentatious and preferred the rather more understated Cunard competition. The majority of the well-known passengers for the *Titanic*'s maiden voyage were, therefore, American. Among the best-known millionaires were J.J. Astor and Benjamin Guggenheim. Astor was one of the richest men in the world, and had recently divorced his wife and remarried a younger woman, Madeleine, amid some social scandal. They had gone to Europe and Egypt on honeymoon, and with Madeleine now five months pregnant, had chosen to return on the *Titanic*.[26] Guggenheim, meanwhile, had something of a reputation as a playboy, and was travelling without his wife.[27] Politics were represented by Archibald Butt, Aide-de-Camp to President Taft, and trade by Mr and Mrs Isador Straus, who had made the department store Macey's an American institution. Three of the (subsequently) most prominent British men aboard were there in their official capacities: Thomas Andrews was the designer of the *Titanic*, and J. Bruce Ismay was the managing director of the White Star Line. Edward John Smith was the commodore of the line and its senior captain. As such, it was his customary responsibility to take new ships out on their maiden voyages, and his skills as the head of a luxury liner were expected to be social as well as navigational. Born in Stoke-on-Trent, he was now aged 62 and married with one daughter, Helen Melville Smith. Generally referred to as 'E.J.', the captain was a solidly built man with full white beard. In an interview with the New York press in 1907 he said:

> When anyone asks me how I can best describe my experience in nearly forty years at sea, I merely say, uneventful … I never saw a wreck and never have been wrecked, nor was I ever in any predicament that threatened to end in disaster of any sort. You see, I am not very good material for a story.[28]

Smith's career had not been entirely without incident, however. On 20 September 1911, some four months after its maiden voyage, the *Olympic*, under Smith's command, collided with the Royal Navy cruiser HMS *Hawke* in the Solent. The *Hawke*'s bows were shattered, and the *Olympic* sustained a 12×14 foot hole from the water-line to D deck. Both closed their emergency doors. The *Hawke* limped for repairs at Portsmouth, while the *Olympic* disembarked passengers at anchor before returning to Southampton on the next available tide. The *Olympic* was patched up with wood and steel in Southampton before returning, slowly, to Belfast for complete repairs. Needless to say, legal action ensued. The Admiralty exonerated the commander of the *Hawke* from blame,[29] claiming, amongst other things, that the 7,000 ton *Hawke* had been sucked along by the 45,000 ton *Olympic*'s displacement. The court ruled for the Admiralty, criticizing the faulty navigation of the *Olympic*. The White Star Line took the case to the Court of Appeal (where they lost again) and then all the way up to the House of Lords, where White Star lost the case for a third and final time, with costs. The owners, captain and crew of the *Olympic*, however, escaped personal blame as the liner had been under compulsory pilotage at the time.[30]

The effects on the White Star Line and the *Titanic* were more than wounded pride. White Star had to bear the cost both of repairs and legal action, together with the loss of revenue while the *Olympic* was being repaired. In addition to the hole in the hull, the *Olympic* had also suffered damage to its starboard propeller shaft. The *Titanic*, meanwhile, was still being completed in Belfast, and as its own propeller shaft was still awaiting fitment, this was taken from the younger 'sister' to repair the elder. The consequence for the *Titanic* was that its maiden voyage was delayed by three weeks from 20 March to 10 April 1912.

The *Titanic*'s fitting out continued, albeit on a delayed schedule. In photographs up to this period, the *Titanic* is practically indistinguishable from the *Olympic*. However, as a result of the *Olympic*'s early experiences at sea, it was decided to enclose the forward end of the open promenade on A deck, as passengers had been getting wet in the ocean spray. It is this enclosed section which, to the informed eye, provides the only obvious difference between photographs of the two liners. Sea trials took place on 2 April 1912, and lasted a total of twelve hours. The designer Thomas Andrews was on board, as was Harold Sanderson, a director of the White Star Line. The command was taken by Captain Smith, fresh from his experiences with the *Olympic*.[31] The *Titanic* was taken out from Belfast Lough and into the Irish Sea, where it was tested for speed, handling and manoeuvrability. A top speed of 21 knots was accomplished, and the ship performed an 'emergency stop' in half a mile at 20 knots. All was pronounced well. The ship duly proceeded to Southampton where it arrived shortly after midnight on 4 April. Victualling and other preparations proceeded over the Easter Bank Holiday, with the majority of the seamen being recruited, as was the usual practice, on the Saturday. As for the officers, the chief officer was Henry Wilde, the first officer was William Murdoch, the second Charles Lightoller, the third Herbert Pitman, fourth Joseph Boxhall, fifth Harold Lowe and sixth James Moody.

Early on Wednesday, 10 April, Captain Maurice Clarke, the Board of Trade's inspector and assistant emigration officer, came on board for final checks, including the statutory lowering and raising of two lifeboats, which was duly accomplished. Clarke signed the appropriate paperwork, including the Certificate of Clearance for an emigrant ship,[32] and went ashore. Passengers of all classes began to arrive in increasing numbers, nearly 1,000 in all. Travelling on a complimentary ticket was White Star Chairman J. Bruce Ismay, who took the prime suite B52, 54 and 56 with the private promenade deck on the port side.[33] Thomas Andrews took the unlisted cabin A36.

Shortly after noon on 10 April, the *Titanic* finally slipped away from Berth 44. Smith was on the bridge, as was Trinity House harbour pilot George Bowyer, the very pilot who had been involved with Smith in the collision of the *Olympic* with the *Hawke* the previous September. The departure of the *Titanic* was not without incident. As the *Titanic* moved away from the dock and towards the River Test, it passed the liners *New York* and *Oceanic* which were moored side by side at Berth 38 due to congestion in Southampton as the result of a recent coal strike. As the *Titanic* passed within 80 feet of the smaller *New York*, the vast bulk and resulting suction caused by the *Titanic* caused the moored ship's lines to pull tight and then snap completely. The *New York*'s freed stern consequently pulled out towards the passing *Titanic*, narrowly missing the larger ship, which took swift avoiding action and finally drew to a halt, delaying the *Titanic*'s final departure from Southampton for an hour.

The *Titanic* was due to take on further passengers at Cherbourg and Queenstown (now called Cobh) in Ireland before setting off across the Atlantic towards New York. As a result of the *New York* incident, however, the *Titanic* did not reach France until 6:30 pm, and the tenders ferried out 279 joining passengers in gathering darkness. The *Titanic* then sailed overnight to Queenstown, where a handful of passengers disembarked, but over 100 more emigrants joined the ship, ferried out by tenders along with over 1,000 sacks of mail. At 1:30 pm, the *Titanic* weighed anchor and slipped out of sight of land.

The remainder of Thursday, together with Friday, Saturday and the majority of Sunday were uneventful days at sea. The captain made his daily inspections of the ship; the weather was good and the ship steady. The *Titanic* followed the standard great circle route along the outward southern track of the accepted sea lane towards New York. The *Titanic*'s speed was comparing well enough with the *Olympic*'s, and everything seemed to be going according to plan.

In histories of the universe, a disproportionate amount of attention is given to the first few seconds of cosmic explosion. Histories of the *Titanic*, on the other hand, concentrate with increasing detail on the liner's last few hours. It is as though the history of the *Titanic* gears itself down seamlessly from condensed time and into slow motion. This brief history will be no exception. At 9 o'clock (*Titanic* time) on Sunday morning, the *Titanic* received by wireless an ice warning from the eastbound Cunard steamer *Caronia*: 'Captain, Titanic: West-bound

steamers report bergs, growlers, and field ice in 42° N., from 49° to
51° W., April 12. Compliments. Barr.' Smith acknowledged and posted
the message. At 10:30 am, the captain led a Protestant service in the
first-class dining room, while the assistant purser presided in the
second. A Roman Catholic mass was held in both the second-class and
later in the third-class areas. At 1:41 pm a second ice warning was
received, this time from the White Star liner *Baltic*. Smith showed the
message to Ismay, who put it in his pocket and showed it to several
passengers before it was returned to the captain and posted in the
chart room more than five hours later. Further ice warnings were
picked up or received from the German *Amerika* at 1:45 pm, the
Leyland liner *Californian* at 7:30 pm, and the SS *Mesaba* at 9:40 pm.
The *Amerika* and *Mesaba* warnings failed to reach the bridge. At 10:55
pm the freighter *Rappahannock* sent an ice warning to the *Titanic* by
Morse lamp, which the *Titanic* acknowledged. At 10:55 pm the
Californian attempted to radio another ice warning to the *Titanic* but
was told to 'shut up' by the *Titanic*'s harried radio operators. Again,
the message did not reach the bridge.

The *Titanic* was cruising at a speed of 22 knots, slightly below its
anticipated top speed, which had yet to be attempted. From 6:00 pm
the weather was clear and fine. 'There was no moon, the stars were
out, and there was not a cloud in the sky.'[34] The temperature,
however, dropped by 10° Fahrenheit in less than two hours, falling to
32°. At 6:00 pm, Second Officer Lightoller came on duty; at about
9:00 pm Captain Smith came onto the bridge, and their conversation
was recalled by Lightoller at the subsequent British inquiry:

> *Smith*: There is not much wind.
> *Lightoller*: No, it's a flat calm.
> *Smith*: A flat calm.

Lightoller remarked it was a pity that the breeze had dropped completely, as the water breaking at the base of any ice would have made
it easier to see.

> *Lightoller*: In any case, there will be a certain amount of reflected
> light from the bergs.
> *Smith*: Oh, yes, there will be a certain amount of reflected light.

The conversation, recalled Lightoller, concluded with Smith saying: 'If
it becomes at all doubtful let me know at once; I will just be inside.' At
9:30 pm, Captain Smith went to his room.[35]

Lightoller instructed the two men in the crow's nest to keep a sharp look out for ice. At 10.00 pm he relinquished his watch to First Officer Murdoch. By 11:00 pm most of the passengers and off-duty crew members were in bed.

At 11:40 pm Lookout Frederick Fleet suddenly spotted a dark object looming up directly in the ship's path. He gave three sharp rings on the crow's nest bell and immediately telephoned the bridge: 'Iceberg right ahead.' Murdoch attempted emergency action to avoid a collision, turning the ship hard to port and reversing the engines, but it was too late. Although he succeeded in avoiding colliding with the iceberg head-on, the *Titanic* struck the iceberg on the starboard side, the submerged section of the ice dragging along the bow section beneath the water-line. Murdoch closed the emergency doors.

As the *Titanic* had struck the iceberg only a glancing blow, many of the passengers did not even notice the collision. It was only when the engines (and thus the vibration) stopped that people began to wonder if something was amiss. Further, as the damage was below the water-line, the extent of the trouble was not at all apparent to the un-informed. As far as the majority of people were concerned, the *Titanic* had simply stopped. In fact, the *Titanic* had been holed beneath the water-line in the forepeak, holds one, two and three, and boiler rooms five and six. Rather than ripping an enormous gash, however, it seems that the iceberg had ruptured the plates and rivets with a series of narrow slits along the steel hull, a distance of over 200 feet in all.[36] It is in this way that the *Titanic* began to take on water below decks.

The *Olympic* and *Titanic* had been designed to float with any two of their 16 watertight compartments flooded. The British inquiry believed that in practice as many as four could have been flooded and the *Titanic* would still have remained afloat. Six, however, were now damaged, and although generally referred to as 'watertight' compart-ments, the watertight bulkheads extended only part way up the ship. Consequently, if water rose high enough, it was able to spill over from one bulkhead into the next. As the forward compartments filled, the *Titanic* began to go down at the head, and water rose and spilled into successive 'watertight' compartments rather like water spilling into adjacent compartments of a tilted refrigerator ice tray.[37] It was inevitable that the *Titanic* was going to sink.

Smith, Andrews and Ismay were soon on the bridge. While they became quickly and grimly aware of the *Titanic*'s true condition, news travelled only slowly and often inaccurately through the rest of the ship. Initially, many passengers were simply curious about why the ship had stopped. As news of an iceberg began to spread, the reaction was often one of novelty rather than of fear. There was, after all, no damage at all to be seen from the passenger accommodation. The lights continued shining brightly, and only gradually did some of the more observant passengers begin to notice the ship tilting slightly towards the bow. Shortly after midnight, Captain Smith gave the order to the crew to prepare the lifeboats.

It is at this stage that the history of the *Titanic* becomes increasingly conjectural. Events began to unfold with steady but increasing confusion and can only be reconstructed from the evidence and memories of those who survived. Of one thing there is no doubt, however: the *Titanic*'s lifeboats had the capacity to carry only 1,178 people. There were 2,201 people on board.

At 12:10 am Captain Smith gave the order for the ship's Marconi operators Jack Phillips and Harold Bride to send out a distress call. Phillips began sending out what was then the international distress signal – CQD – followed by the *Titanic*'s 'call' letters MGY and details of its estimated position. At 12:20 am, the order was given to swing out the lifeboats, and at 12:30 am the captain gave the further order to begin putting women and children into them. The first boat was lowered into the water at 12:45 am, and the others continued on an occasional basis, approximately every five or ten minutes. The loading and lowering of the boats took place in considerable confusion. There had been no lifeboat drill, and no formal, general instruction was given to abandon ship. Although crewmen had been assigned to responsibility for particular boats in advance, in practice many had not looked at the lists and so did not know what their responsibilities were. The *Titanic* had no public address system, and so orders to crew and instructions to passengers were conducted by word of mouth against the increasing noise of steam blowing off from the boilers. Lightoller subsequently claimed that the noise was so great that he could not be heard and he had to give directions with his hands.[38]

The disorganized way in which the boats were 'filled' and lowered exacerbated the lack of lifeboat accommodation. If every boat had been filled to capacity, there would have been room for approximately half those on board the *Titanic*. In the event, however, the majority of boats were sent away considerably less than full. Lifeboat number one, for example, was designed to carry 40 people, but went away with only 12 on board.[39] Of the 1,178 spaces available in the lifeboats, only 854 of them were taken up.

While the boats were being loaded (or not), the Marconi operators Phillips and Bride continued to send out distress signals. In addition to the CQD signal, the operators sent the newer SOS signal, which had officially superseded CQD in 1908, but had still to come into universal use. Fourth Officer Boxhall sent up regular distress rockets and attempted to contact what he took to be a ship some five or six miles away by Morse lamp. There was no reply. Of all the ships contacted, either direct or by radio messages relayed from one to another, only the Cunard liner *Carpathia* was close enough to respond. The *Carpathia* was a 13,600 ton ship of secondary financial importance, designed to run at 14 knots. On the night of 14–15 April, it was carrying just over 1,000 passengers and crew from New York eastbound to Gibraltar under the command of Captain Arthur Rostron. At 12:25 am, *Carpathia* Marconi operator Harold Cottam was whiling away his time at the radio and called the *Titanic* for a chat. He was astounded to hear the *Titanic* reply that it had struck an iceberg and was in urgent need of help. Captain Rostron calculated that he was 58 miles south-east of the *Titanic*'s reported position and immediately changed course to go to the rescue. Rostron and his chief engineer managed to get the *Carpathia*'s speed up to an unaccustomed 17.5 knots and prepared his ship in every detail. Even at 17.5 knots, however, it would take the *Carpathia* some three and a half hours to reach the sinking *Titanic*.

One of the *Titanic*'s two string ensembles, under the leadership of Lancashire-born violinist Wallace Hartley, had begun playing. The lights continued to shine as the last of the lifeboats left the *Titanic* at 02:05 am, loaded with between 40 and 50 passengers. Amid increasing confusion, the captain released the two Marconi operators from their posts. As the water closed over successive decks, the last of the collapsible boats was floated off from the roof of the officers' quarters, serving as a raft for those who could clamber onto its upturned hull. Many of those left behind made their way to the stern of the ship which, as the bow slipped steadily and further into the Atlantic, rose higher into the air. The ship's propellers were now out of the water; there was a loud crashing sound as gravity overcame the *Titanic*'s internal fixtures and fittings and cascaded towards the submerging bow. Only then did the lights go out. The *Titanic* split into two sections: the stern finally reached the perpendicular position and, at 2:20 am, the *Titanic*, with nearly 1,500 people still on board, slowly and inexorably disappeared from view.

The *Titanic*'s 20 lifeboats were now alone on an empty sea, surrounded by floating ice and in air temperatures around freezing point.

Collapsible boat B remained belly up, with some 28 men standing or clinging onto what they could. Collapsible A, although upright, was over a foot deep in water. There was a marked reluctance among those in any of the boats to return to pick up survivors in the water. Of the 20 boats, only two did so. A number of those who had found places in the boats died during the night, mostly of exposure.[40]

The *Carpathia* arrived at the scene shortly after 4:00 am. It was first light, an hour and 45 minutes after the *Titanic* had sunk and more than three hours since the first of the lifeboats had been lowered. The gathering dawn revealed an ocean strewn with icebergs. The lifeboats had been scattered over an area of several miles, and it took four hours for the *Carpathia* to steer its way among the ice and pick up all the survivors. Photographs taken from the *Carpathia* survive of several of the *Titanic*'s lifeboats approaching the rescue ship, with their passengers wrapped in heavy coats, hats and life preservers. Captain Rostron's planning had been meticulous, with hot drinks, medical attention and emergency accommodation awaiting all those taken on board. At 8:00 am the *Carpathia* turned about and headed for New York.

Of the 2,201 people aboard the *Titanic*, 1,490 died and 711 survived. Those in the first class had the greatest chance of surviving, with 62.46 per cent saved. Of the second class, 41.40 per cent survived, while among the third class, only 25.21 per cent were saved. The crew fared proportionally worst, among them only 23.5 per cent surviving. Among the total passengers and crew, 74.35 per cent of the women survived, 20.27 per cent of the men and 52.29 per cent of the children.[41] Among the better-known passengers, J.J. Astor, Benjamin Guggenheim, Archibald Butt, Mr and Mrs Isador Straus all died, along with *Titanic* designer Thomas Andrews, Marconi operator Jack Phillips, all the *Titanic* musicians and Captain Edward John Smith. Among the survivors were Marconi operator Harold Bride, Second Officer Lightoller and J. Bruce Ismay, chairman and managing director of the White Star Line.

The history of the *Titanic* now enters a transitional stage. The physical *Titanic* had sunk, but news of its demise had yet to reach the public. The mythical *Titanic* had yet to emerge.

News that the *Titanic* had struck an iceberg and was putting passengers into lifeboats was relayed from ship to ship, picked up on land and gradually began to reach the newsrooms of America. The papers also learned that a number of other ships were steaming to the *Titanic*'s aid. The extent of the damage, however, was still a matter for speculation, and so a number of highly conjectural stories began to appear in the press of Monday, 15 April. The *New York Times* was able soberly to report: 'New Liner Titanic Hits An Iceberg; Sinking By The Bow At Midnight; Women Put Off In Lifeboats; Last Wireless At 12:27 Am Blurred'.[42] Others were less restrained. 'All Saved from Titanic After Collision' reported the New York *Evening Sun*. 'Liner is being towed to Halifax after smashing into an iceberg.'[43] The fact that the *Titanic* had actually sunk was only officially confirmed some 16 hours after the event, news reaching the White Star Line's New York office at 6:16 pm (New York time) in a message from the captain of the *Olympic*. This was duly conveyed to a press conference shortly afterwards and the loss of the *Titanic* finally and fully became public knowledge.

News from the *Carpathia* itself, however, was considerably less forthcoming. Captain Rostron only confirmed the sinking of the *Titanic* some 18 hours after the event, dictating a Marconi message to the Associated Press at 8:20 pm (Carpathia time): 'Titanic struck iceberg sank Monday ... Carpathia picked up many passengers am proceeding New York.' At Rostron's prompting, J. Bruce Ismay also dictated a message to the White Star offices in New York: 'Deeply regret to advise you Titanic sank this morning ....' It was two days, however, before this message was finally sent. Incoming inquiries from the press were ignored as, indeed, was a message from the White House inquiring about the fate of President Taft's friend and aide Archibald Butt. *Carpathia* Marconi operator Harold Cottam, later joined by the recovering *Titanic* operator Harold Bride, limited their transmissions to lists of survivors and, later, those believed dead. Back on land, news organizations had to piece together information about the disaster as best they could from intercepted radio messages between other ships still at sea.

The virtual 'news blackout' surrounding the *Titanic* and the *Carpathia* resulted from a combination of innocence and shrewd practice. On the one hand, Captain Rostron of the *Carpathia* was an honest Edwardian seaman, unversed in the rudiments of modern-day media relations. His duty, as he saw it, was to his ship, his passengers and his crew. The demands of the world's press were of little importance to him, even had he known how to handle them. Captain Rostron, like the majority of his contemporaries, had yet to enter the 'information age'. The White Star office in New York was better versed in the finer points of business practice. Even they, however, did not have the benefit of a media relations team, 'spin doctors' or even a basic grasp of the increasing importance of media management in the modern world. They were, after all, a shipping company and did not expect suddenly to be responsible for one of the greatest news stories of the twentieth century.

There were, however, two – and possibly four – men who were perfectly well aware of the significance of the media in the breaking story of the sinking of the *Titanic*. They were Carr Van Anda, managing editor of the *New York Times*, and Guglielmo Marconi, inventor of wireless and founder of the Marconi Wireless Telegraphy Company, Ltd. As the *Carpathia* headed to New York, all news of the sinking of the *Titanic* was, quite literally, in the hands of just two men, Marconi operators Cottam and Bride, as they tapped away at their Morse keys. No news could pass in either direction without passing through them.

By the time the *Carpathia* docked at New York's Pier 54 on the night of Thursday, 18 April, the lack of information had only added to the excitement. It is estimated that 30,000 people crowded onto the dockside area. Newsmen were held back, despite their best efforts to get on board. Guglielmo Marconi, however, was allowed to pass through, taking with him a journalist, Jim Speers, of the *New York Times*. Bride was paid $1,000 for his exclusive story; Cottam $750.

Although the *New York Times* got the exclusive on Bride and Cottam, it could not buy up the exclusive stories of all on board. A journalistic frenzy ensued with teams of reporters waiting at the gangplanks. Stories were told, embellished and recirculated. The physical *Titanic* existed only in memory. The reanimation of history into myth had now begun in earnest.

There were two formal investigations into the loss of the *Titanic*. The first began in New York the morning after the *Carpathia* arrived. The American inquiry was both initiated and chaired in spirited style by Republican Senator William Alden Smith of Michigan. Smith was no expert in maritime matters, but maintained that 'Energy is often more desirable than learning' in the pursuit of uncomfortable information.[44] Certainly, he was darkly suspicious of business trusts and critical of what he perceived as outdated legislation. Smith and his colleagues interrogated J. Bruce Ismay, Second Officer Lightoller, Marconi Operator Harold Bride and Guglielmo Marconi himself, together with scores of additional witnesses in an investigation which reconvened in Washington before Smith delivered his findings in a somewhat grand two-hour address to Congress on 28 May. Smith criticized the lack of 'sufficient tests' on the *Titanic*'s mechanical and life-saving equipment, and the 'absolute unpreparedness' of the crew in the face of emergency.[45] As for the British Board of Trade, it was to that organization's 'laxity of regulation and hasty inspection the world is largely indebted for this awful fatality'.[46] He referred to Captain Smith's 'overconfidence' and 'indifference to danger' as one of the 'direct and contributing causes' of the disaster.[47] The Senator urged that ships' wireless equipment should in the future be staffed 24 hours a day, and called (successfully) for a $1,000 Congressional medal to be presented to Captain Rostron of the *Carpathia*. Senator Smith then introduced two bills extending marine legislation and setting up a maritime commission for the construction and equipment of ocean-going ships.

Senator Smith's inquiry was thought by many, particularly in Britain, to have been conducted in a rather cavalier manner. He was perceived as a political grand-stander rather than a dispassionate analyst. He had begun interrogating witnesses the very morning after the *Carpathia* had docked in New York, and demonstrably had no expertise in marine practice or law. Many in the British press construed his criticism of a British ship and of British legislation as an attack on Britain itself. The Senator was even satirized on the London musical stage: 'When I says that a thing has got ter be/ That thing's as good as done, d'yer see?' went the song.[48] Despite the reforms that followed his inquiry, criticism of Senator Smith has continued, with Gardiner and Van Der Vat, for example, referring to his 'butterfly mind'[49] and depicting him as 'an unsatiable, uncritical omnivore of information, swallowing up facts at random'[50] before delivering to Congress 'an oration to stretch the limits even of the florid standards of old-style American political rhetoric'.[51]

Where the American inquiry had been headed by a politician, the British inquiry was chaired by a bureaucrat. John Charles Bigham had worked in the shipping business before being called to the Bar, becoming a Queen's Counsel in 1883. In 1895 he became a Member of Parliament for Liverpool, at which he served for two years before being appointed a High Court Judge. Twelve years later he was made president of the Probate, Divorce and Admiralty Division, and in 1910 he became Baron Mersey of Toxteth. Ill health forced him to discontinue his regular work in the courts, but following his elevation to the Lords he became a frequent member of commissions and inquiries. The week after the *Titanic* sank he was appointed Wreck Commissioner, and when on 30 April the Board of Trade formally requested an investigation into the loss of the *Titanic*, Mersey got to work again. He appointed his son, the Honourable Charles Bigham, as secretary and together with five assessors appointed by the Home Secretary, began proceedings at the Scottish Hall, Buckingham Gate, London, on 2 May 1912.[52]

The brief of the British court of inquiry was both focused and comprehensive. The Board of Trade formulated 26 specific questions which the inquiry was instructed to address, covering the construction, operation and sinking of the *Titanic*, together with the rescue of its surviving passengers. Finally, the inquiry was asked to make recommendations on the law and upon procedures for the improvement of safety at sea. The inquiry sat for 38 days and called a total of 97 witnesses, many of whom had previously been questioned in the United States. The concluding report was duly presented to both Houses of Parliament on 30 July 1912.

The inquiry report began with a detailed technical description of the *Titanic*, including its structure, engines, decks, accommodation, life-saving appliances, pumping arrangements, electrical installation and machinery. Details were also given of the numbers of passengers (by class of accommodation) and crew (by rating). The second section examined the *Titanic*'s sailing orders and route followed, before detailing the ice warnings received during the voyage and then the collision with the iceberg. Section three described the damage and its effect on the ship, including the sinking, while the fourth accounted for the saving and rescue of the survivors. Section five was specifically concerned with the role of the steamship *Californian* in the events of 14 and 15 April, while section six concerned itself with the Board of Trade's administration of shipping regulations. The findings of the court were given in section seven, with the subsequent recommendations providing the eighth and final part of the inquiry.

The initial description of the ship, while of course necessary in context, contained little in the way of information which could not have been found elsewhere. The system of bulkheads and emergency doors was duly documented, and the whole vessel was found to have been 'constructed under survey of the British Board of Trade for a passenger certificate, and also to comply with the American immigration laws'.[53] The inquiry reported that no particular 'sailing orders' were given to masters of White Star vessels for specific voyages. However, it was understood that accepted 'sea lanes' should be adhered to, although masters were allowed to deviate from them in the interests of safety. There were no special instructions in regard to ice. When appointed to command of a ship, masters were issued with a letter from the company which included the passage:

> You are to dismiss all idea of competitive passages with other vessels and to concentrate your attention upon a cautious, prudent, and ever watchful system of navigation, which shall lose time or suffer any other temporary inconvenience rather than incur the slightest risk which can be avoided.[54]

The *Titanic*'s route from 10 April was along the accepted sea-lane for mail steamers at that time of year. It was a track which avoided predicted areas of field ice, but within an area in which icebergs might be seen.[55] The *Titanic* received five radio messages warning of ice in the vicinity on the day of the collision.[56] The inquiry found that: 'The entire passage had been made at high speed, though not at the ship's maximum, and this speed was never reduced until the collision was unavoidable.' At the time of the collision, the *Titanic*'s speed was 22 knots.[57] However, Lord Mersey did not believe that the captain had been under any pressure from White Star Line chairman J. Bruce Ismay (who as we know was on board) to make a fast crossing on the maiden voyage. 'He was not trying to please anybody,' stated the commissioner.[58]

Lord Mersey took time in his report to ponder upon what Captain Smith ought to have done. In light of the ice warnings received, the captain could either have reduced speed or taken a more southerly course, but did neither, relying instead on his look-outs. In doing so, however, Captain Smith was following a practice 'justified by experience'.[59] It was the experience of 'a quarter of a century or more' of ocean liners using this track, and no casualties had at that stage resulted from it. Only the event had 'proved the practice to be bad'.[60] Mersey was thus able to state:

> In these circumstances, I am not able to blame Captain Smith. He had not the experience which his own misfortune has afforded to those whom he has left behind, and he was doing only that which other skilled men would have done in the same position.[61]

Lord Mersey was thereby able to make a fine but germane distinction over the conduct of Captain Smith. Captain Smith, he declared, had been mistaken but not negligent. In the absence of negligence, it was 'impossible to fix Captain Smith with blame'.[62] However, what had been a mistake in the case of the *Titanic* would without doubt be negligence in any similar case in the future.[63]

In the fourth section of his report, Lord Mersey noted that there had been no proper boat drill or muster on the *Titanic*, and he both noted and lamented that the law had not required any. Discipline among passengers and crew had been good when the lifeboats did need to become loaded, but 'the organization should have been better, and if it had been it is possible that more lives would have been saved.'[64] He found difficulty in explaining why so many of the boats went away comparatively empty; perhaps the drop of 65 feet from the boat deck to the water had intimidated many. 'I have no doubt that many people, particularly women, refused to leave the deck for the boats,' he said, and continued: 'Another explanation is that some women refused to leave their husbands.'[65] Once the *Titanic* finally sank, Lord Mersey regretted that some of the lifeboats failed to save the lives of those struggling in the water, even though they had the opportunity to do so. There was praise, however, for Captain Rostron of the rescue ship *Carpathia*. The court recorded its great admiration for the captain. 'He did the very best that could be done.'[66]

Section five of the report dealt exclusively with 'The Circumstances in Connection with the S.S. "Californian"'. The role (or otherwise) of the *Californian* provides one of the abiding controversies surrounding the *Titanic*, inspiring books such as Peter Padfield's *The Titanic and the Californian*[67] of 1965 and Leslie Reade's *The Ship That Stood Still*[68] of 1993. The question of the *Californian* continues to provide heated debate among *Titanic* enthusiasts, but as this has only tangential bearing on the current study I do not intend to examine it in any detail here. I shall confine my discussion to what Lord Mersey had to say in his report. According to the inquiry, the Leyland liner *Californian* was in the area on the night that the *Titanic* sank. It was a ship of 6,223 tons on its way from London to Boston, Massachusetts, under the captaincy of Stanley Lord. The *Californian*, which was not carrying any passengers at the time, was stopped and surrounded by ice on the night of 14 April. Despite the 'contradictions and inconsistencies' in the accounts of the various witnesses at the inquiry, Mersey concluded that the *Californian* was between 5 and 10 miles away from the *Titanic* at the time of the disaster. The *Californian* had seen what must have been the *Titanic*'s distress rockets (the *Californian*'s radio operator was asleep) but the ship had failed to act. 'Had she done so she might have saved many if not all of the lives that were lost.'[69]

Section six of the report concerned itself with two allegations which had been made during the course of the inquiry: first, that the Board of Trade had failed to keep up to date with their rules and regulations regarding life-saving at sea, and second, that the Board's officials had failed properly to supervise the *Titanic*'s plans and construction.[70] Lord Mersey found that Board of Trade regulations fixed the number of required lifeboats at 16 for all vessels over 10,000 tons. The *Titanic* carried 20 with accommodation for 1,178 people, 'a number far in excess' of the rules.[71] He thought that the rules should be revised so that liners, regardless of size, should carry lifeboat accommodation for everyone on board. The *Titanic* as a whole was efficiently designed and constructed, and the bulkheads more than met the requirements of the existing regulations. Subdivision by bulkheads could, however be improved. As regards any complaints against the Board of Trade's supervision and inspection of the *Titanic*, Lord Mersey found 'no evidence' to support these. The Board's officials, he declared, had discharged their duties 'carefully and well'.[72]

The seventh section of the report provided the 'Finding of the Court'. Here, Mersey formally set about answering the list of 26 questions submitted by the Board of Trade. The majority of these had, however, effectively been answered in the body of the report. The eighth and final section provided 24 recommendations for adoption by foreign-going passenger and emigrant steamships. These were of varying degrees of importance, but the most significant were as follows. Recommendation one suggested that a 'bulkhead committee' should examine whether ships should subsequently be provided with a double skin extending above the water-line and/or longitudinal watertight bulkheads in addition to the transverse bulkheads as provided on the *Titanic*. Recommendation six called for the provision of lifeboat and raft accommodation based on the number of people that could be carried on a ship rather than upon its tonnage. Recommendation 12 called for the Board of Trade's inspection of lifeboats to be 'of a more searching character than hitherto',[73] while the 16th recommendation was that all ships should be required to hold regular boat, fire and watertight door drills. According to recommendation 20, all foreign-going passenger and emigrant ships should be required to carry wireless telegraphy equipment, and this should provide a 24-hour, continuous service. The 21st recommendation was that when ice was reported, ships should either moderate their speed or alter their courses during the hours of darkness.

The overall finding of the court of inquiry, printed on the opening page of the report, was a single-sentence statement that the loss of the *Titanic* 'was due to collision with an iceberg, brought about by the excessive speed at which the ship was being navigated'.[74] This examination of the whole document, however, has revealed that the findings were actually more complex. That is, of course, to be expected. What remains at issue, however, is whether the British court of inquiry provided a full, fair and sufficiently rigorous appraisal of the events. Reaction to the inquiry at the time was moderate; it did, after all, seem to be an entirely diligent, methodical and decorous affair after the perceived grand-standing of its American predecessor. From a late twentieth century perspective, however, it is possible to undertake a less sympathetic reading of Lord Mersey's report. His inquiry was, after all, conducted under the auspices of the British Board of Trade, a body theoretically under examination at its own inquiry. If (and unlike Senator Smith of Michigan) Lord Mersey was an 'establishment man', then it might be argued that his and the establishment's underlying interest was the continued welfare of the British shipping industry, and not a swingeing indictment of the *Titanic* and the system that had allowed it to sail, and to sink, as it did. It is for reasons such as these that the verdicts of recent commentators on the British inquiry have ranged from suspicion to outright condemnation. According to Michael Davie, Lord Mersey's inquiry was not 'a deliberate, conscious, calculated whitewash, but it was a whitewash nevertheless'.[75] According to Lynch and Marschall, the aim of Lord Mersey's inquiry was to 'sanitize' the disaster and 'remove its sting'. It was, after all, 'a creature of the vested interests who had most to lose from a full investigation.'[76] In this way, the unfortunate Captain Lord of the *Californian* made the 'perfect scapegoat'.[77] Geoffrey Marcus concluded that the whitewash had been 'liberally applied',[78] while Gardiner and Van Der Vat went further:

> To discern no negligence amid this morass of shortcomings was no mere whitewash: it was a mockery of those lost in the worst peacetime transport disaster then on record.[79]

It is not the purpose of this brief history to embark upon an analysis of the shortcomings (or otherwise) of the British inquiry report. Whatever one may think of its conclusions, Lord Mersey's inquiry still represents the most sober and detailed documentary account available of the loss of the *Titanic*. For the historian, it remains an invaluable resource. It is perhaps worth noting, simply, that Lord Mersey's inquiry was conducted at the beginning and not at the end of the twentieth century. His aim, unlike more recent inquiries, was to discover what took place rather than to attribute blame. If his inquiry was a creature of the culture in which it was held, then that is exactly the thinking that underlies the whole of the current study.

The publication of the British inquiry report provides an appropriate closure to the history of the actual *Titanic*. There remain two post-scripts, however: one physical and one official. The physical postscript is provided by the discovery and photography of the wreck of the *Titanic* on 1 September 1985. The rusting ship was located in two main pieces 12,460 feet down on the ocean floor by a Franco-American expedition led by Dr Robert Ballard of the Woods Hole Oceanographic Institution, Massachusetts, and Jean-Louis Michel of the French oceanographical institute IFREMER. The team produced photographs of the wreck using a remote camera submersible called *Argo*, returning to Woods Hole amidst international media attention eight days later. The following year, Ballard returned to the wreck site, this time without the French as a result of political differences between the two institutions. As before, however, the expedition was primarily funded by the US Navy, who were keen to investigate the potential of deep-sea exploration and submarine technology. On this expedition, Ballard explored the wreck not by remote camera but by descending all the way in a manned submersible called *Alvin*. In this way, he was able fully to explore and to bring back the first high quality still and video photographs of the wreck of the *Titanic*.[80]

Ballard's aim in 1986 was simply to explore and to photograph the *Titanic*. As a scientist, he said it was his wish that the site should remain undisturbed. Inevitably, perhaps, his wish was not granted, for the following year the French IFREMER, funded by a consortium of American investors called RMS Titanic Inc., arrived and retrieved some 900 artifacts from the site. These were duly displayed on television and in exhibitions around the world. Subsequent expeditions have continued in similar vein, creating a marked 'schism' in *Titanic* circles. On the one hand, the group around Ballard and the Titanic Historical Society argue that the *Titanic* is a gravesite and should remain undisturbed. Ballard even accuses the 1987 expedition of seriously damaging the hull 'in their eagerness to bring back booty'.[81] In 1996, a further RMS Titanic expedition attempted (unsuccessfully) to raise a section of the hull itself as 'enthusiasts' watched from a specially chartered cruise ship above. Salvagers, exhibitors and others, however, argue that the removal and preservation of artifacts from historic and archaeological sites have a long and respectable history. 'We are guarding the memory and telling the tale of the ship, the survivors and the victims,' said the organizer of a

1997 exhibition at the Memphis Pyramid in Tennessee.[82] The debate continues.

The official postscript to the history of the physical *Titanic* came in the form of a reassessment of the case of Captain Stanley Lord, the master of the *Californian*, who had been criticized by Lord Mersey for not going to the aid of the sinking *Titanic*. Lord's case had been taken up over the years, by his trade union, his family and by a growing number of supporters (known as 'Lordites'), who considered he had been unfairly treated by the British inquiry and sought to redeem his reputation. Eventually, in July 1990, then Transport Secretary Cecil Parkinson ordered a re-examination of the case, partly because of new evidence provided by the 1985 expedition to the *Titanic* wreck site and partly, it was reported, because the controversy was taking up so much staff time that it was thought more cost-effective to try to resolve it.[83] The report, published on 2 April 1992, failed fully to resolve the issue, however. Although the *Titanic* wreck site, accurately charted by the 1985 expedition, suggested that Lord was in fact between 17 and 20 miles away from the sinking liner (as opposed to the 5–10 suggested by Lord Mersey), the 1992 report failed to conclude that the ship seen by the *Californian* was indeed the *Titanic*. 'I do not think any reasonable probable action by Capt Lord would have led to a different outcome of the tragedy,' reported Captain James de Coverly, Deputy Chief Inspector of Marine Accidents. 'This, of course, does not alter the fact that the attempt should have been made.'[84] The inconclusive nature of the reassessment was further compounded by disagreements among the three people responsible for the investigation and the report.[85] Needless to say, the debate continues.

These two postscripts conclude this brief history of the physical *Titanic*. The rest of this study concerns itself with the mythical *Titanic*, a *Titanic* that existed (and still exists) in representation. It would be a mistake to surmise, however, that the end of this chapter marks a hermetic break between the factual and the mythical *Titanic*, for as I hope to demonstrate in my argument, representations, too, are facts.

2 Myth and the *Titanic*

A myth is not a falsehood. Rather, a myth is a sophisticated social representation; a complex relationship between history, reality, culture, imagination and identity. Nowadays, it is popular culture which is both the repository and the purveyor of myth, a role that was once held by the soothsayers and story-tellers of 'primitive' societies. The story of the *Titanic* is a modern myth *par excellence*. To describe it as a myth is not, however, to attempt to reduce it (or ourselves) to a 'primitive' level. On the contrary, our examination is to take myth and the *Titanic* extremely seriously; to make universal and non-hierarchical claims for cultures ancient and modern, distant and familiar. By examining the *Titanic* as modern myth, we shall reveal something not only of the late Edwardians, but also of ourselves.

This chapter seeks to examine both what a myth is and how the *Titanic* might be one. What is a myth? Typically, and in the vernacular, 'myth' is a pejorative term. It is used frequently to describe a 'popular misconception'; a bubble waiting to be burst. Bogart never did, for example, say: 'Play it again, Sam' in *Casablanca*. As the anthropologist Percy S. Cohen has observed, in everyday use the term 'myth' is 'synonymous with fallacy'.[1] The pejorative use of 'myth' is not, however, limited to the uninformed. Even Claude Lévi-Strauss, in *The Savage Mind*, complained of the way in which his fellow countrymen believed in the 'myth' of the French Revolution, despite the fact that 'the French Revolution as currently conceived never took place.'[2] Lévi-Strauss, as one should expect, was perfectly correct in his use of the term 'myth' when dealing with distant and 'primitive' societies, but lapsed into the popular and pejorative when dealing with the culture of our time. As Cohen indignantly pointed out:

> it is all very strange to see Lévi-Strauss resort to the pejorative use of the term myth when confronted with his fellow countrymen, but not when confronted with the inhabitants of the forest regions of southern America ...[3]

It is not surprising, therefore, to see that 'myth' is frequently used to mean 'falsehood' when discussing the myth of the *Titanic*. A classic example was provided by journalist Alan Hamilton's article 'Sunk at Last: Some Myths About the Titanic' in *The Times* in 1982. Writing to mark the 70th anniversary of the sinking, Hamilton claimed that the story of the *Titanic* had gathered such a 'patina' of unreliable information that it was time now 'to take a tin of Brasso to scrub off some of the more persistent myths'.[4] Hamilton then proceeded to apply his proprietary metal polish to a number of the better-known *Titanic* stories: the *Titanic* was supposed to be unsinkable; the *Titanic* was attempting a trans-Atlantic speed record; so many people drowned because there were insufficient lifeboats; the band played 'Nearer, My God, to Thee' as the ship went down; most, if not all, of the lives would have been saved if the *Californian* had come to the rescue; the captain should have reduced speed in the ice-field; chairman Bruce Ismay was ushered into a lifeboat ahead of women and children; and a provincial Scottish newspaper reported the disaster under the headline: 'Aberdeenshire Man Drowns at Sea; He Was a Butcher in Union Street'.

Such (mis)use of the term 'myth' is not limited to journalism. Geoffrey Marcus in his full-length *Titanic* study, *The Maiden Voyage*, refers disparagingly to the 'luxuriant growth' of myth which threatened 'to submerge the true facts of the affair altogether'.[5] A rigorous study of myth, however, is not simply a matter of sifting out the 'true facts'. This is so for two reasons. First, facts – and certainly those concerning the *Titanic* – are rarely conveniently either totally true or false. Truth is not a binary concept. Of Hamilton's eight *Titanic* 'myths' for example, only two are palpably false (the speed record and the Aberdeenshire butcher). The rest are partial (un)truths or matters of degree. Second, and most importantly, the question of 'true facts' isn't really the point. It is a question which applies only to the first of my two *Titanics*, the physical ship at the bottom of the ocean. What really happened, if we could ever fully find out, is not the concern of the mythographer. What is much more important is what people chose to *believe* took place. Myths are about beliefs and not facts. Indeed, beliefs, erroneous or not, are facts in themselves. For example, whether or not the band played 'Nearer, My God to Thee' as the ship went down, it is a fact that this was widely believed to have happened. As I said at the end of the previous chapter, representations are facts in themselves. This is relevant not only to the story of the *Titanic*, for social memory influences social action as a whole. If, for example, I believe that you shot my dog, and I respond by poisoning your cat, the death of your cat was caused by my belief about the demise of my dog, whatever subsequent historians may establish about the 'true facts' of the matter.

Terence Turner reaches a similar conclusion in his studies of South American Indians. In many cases, he argues, 'myth can be seen to provide the foundation for historical awareness and action'.[6] If, then, myth influences the way in which actual people behave, we have a responsibility to take even popular misconceptions seriously.

If a myth is not simply a falsehood, and the opposite of myth is not simply a 'true fact', we must return in greater depth to our question: 'What is a myth?' Myth, like popular culture, is a messy concept. As Peter Burke put it in 'Social Memory', myth is 'a slippery term'.[7] Just like popular culture, it may appear simple, but in reality it defies reductionist definition and analysis. This is particularly true when we examine myth not in its vernacular sense, but in the anthropological context necessitated by this study of the myth of the *Titanic*. Even this, however, creates complications, because there is no one theory of myth. Rather, there has been a series of anthropological theories of myth, and these have varied considerably. They began with the folkloric studies of the nineteenth century, and have run the whole gamut of functionalism, structuralism and semiotics. Recent concerns have included concentration on myth in oral performance, on explaining myth 'from the native point of view', and upon the relationship between myth, history and 'social memory'. Within this intellectual history, such theories have oscillated between empirical fieldwork and cross-cultural approaches. Empirical fieldwork is concerned with the collection, description and explanation of the particular myths of particular peoples, and is heavily context-based. Comparative studies, on the other hand, are more concerned with the ontology of myth, and seek to find and to explain common properties among myths and their usage. Comparative theories, therefore, hold that myths, although widely separated, have strikingly similar features.[8] Both traditions, then, are relevant to the current study, which seeks both to investigate the particular myth of a particular people (the *Titanic* myth of the late Edwardian British) and also to explain that myth within a general theory of myth and its usage.

Percy Cohen, delivering the Malinowski Memorial Lecture to the London School of Economics, traced seven types of myth theory starting with 'nineteenth century intellectualism' and ending with the structuralism of the 1960s.[9] Important though this lecture was, it was given in 1969, and so was not able to describe some of the more recent movements in the study of myth. These have included fieldwork concentrations on the performance and reception of myths in their specific geographic contexts, and work by scholars such as Nick Thomas, Joanne Rappaport and Peter Burke, who have sought to reconsider the relationship between myth and history.

Social theories are, however, rarely completely 'right' or 'wrong'. It is reasonable, then, to argue that three supposedly different theories of

myth may actually all be particularly relevant to our understanding of
the myth of the *Titanic*: the 'functionalism' of Malinowski, the myth-
history of the later theorists, and the 'structuralism' of Lévi-Strauss.

For Bronislaw Malinowski, myth was not a matter of idle, abstract
speculation, but had a solid, practical, hard-working use. Thus: 'The
reality of myth lies in its social function.'[10] That function was socially
and politically to validate and justify existing institutions, conventions
and practices. These might range from territorial rights, property
claims, the dominance of one sub-clan over another, or even the
authentication of magical practices.[11] In this way, Malinowski was able
to assert: 'myth serves principally to establish a social charter.'[12] The
way in which myth supported the status quo was by appealing to
history – not to a documented history, but to a mythical or even
invented history beyond fact, reason, memory and ordinary time.[13] In
this way, the status quo, which might not be (at best) explainable or
(at worst) defensible through everyday logic or concepts of social
justice, could be legitimized by the 'higher' authority of myth, especially when the myths were held to be sacred. As Malinowski
explained:

> The function of myth, briefly, is to strengthen tradition and endow it
> with a greater value and prestige by tracing it back to a higher,
> better, more superior natural reality of initial events.[14]

This 'reality', these 'initial events', of course, may have been invented
or partially invented.[15] Either way, Malinowski's functionalist theory
of myth embraces the relation between history and myth. He demonstrates how myth can be used, for example, to bolster dubious claims
and rights among the Melanesian clans:

> Whatever the hidden reality of their unrecorded past may be, myths
> serve to cover certain inconsistencies created by historical events,
> rather than to record those events exactly.[16]

He continues: 'the incidents by which this inconsistency is obliterated,
if not hidden, are most likely fictitious',[17] therefore:

> Myth, taken as a whole, cannot be sober, dispassionate history,
> since it is always made ad hoc to fulfil a certain sociological func-
> tion, to glorify a certain group, or to justify an anomalous status.[18]

Malinowski was, as we can see, speaking of myth as it drew upon
distant and unrecorded history, and certainly as it affected what he
described as 'primitive' peoples.[19] History, however, need not be con-

cerned only with a distant and unrecorded past. Certainly, it is concerned not only with 'primitive' peoples. Might we not, therefore, be
able to make 'functionalist' claims for the myth of the *Titanic*? If so,
we shall be able, just as Malinowski did of the Melanesians, to suggest
that the story of the *Titanic* was used to transpose recent and debat-
able history into a modern myth which served sociologically 'to glorify
a certain group' and to justify the present. The next three chapters of
this study will examine what the myth of the *Titanic* had to 'say' about
gender relations, national and racial superiority, and class distinction
in late Edwardian British society. If Malinowski is correct, we shall
see that the glorification of certain gender, national, racial and class
groups, and the consequent and implicit justification of their status,
power and authority, is a central feature of the myth of the *Titanic*.

Malinowski's functionalist theory of myth does seem to suggest that
myth is something of a dishonest form of history. He was not alone in
his thinking. To M.I. Finley, myth was 'the antithesis of history',[20]
while to the anthropologist Jack Goody, history and myth were distinct categories, the difference between them being literacy. Literacy,
he believed, was linked to accuracy, and so helped check up on myth.
In this way, myth was for primitive people, but history was for the likes
of us.[21] Is the *Titanic*, then, myth or history?

Recent theorists have found the relationship between history and
myth to be considerably more complex than Malinowski and Finley
supposed. Indeed, even by the time of Edmund Leach, such distinctions were becoming considerably less clear. In his *Political Systems of
Highland Burma*,[22] Leach argued that it was wrong to view myths as
correct or incorrect versions of history. To discriminate between myth
and history was an anthropological 'prejudice', and so the ordinary
anthropological definition of myth had to be revised.[23] Myths, he said,
'had no special characteristics which make them any different from
tales about local happenings 20 years ago.'[24]

According to Joanne Rappaport, historians are now starting to view
history much as anthropologists see myth. Distinctions between the two
are becoming clouded, and it is therefore important to beware what she
describes as the 'myth-history snare'.[25] For the efficacy of myth lies in
'the very merging of myth and history, not in any separation of the
two'.[26] Jonathan Hill, similarly, has noticed a recent 'rapprochement'
between anthropologists and historians. In *Rethinking History and
Myth*, Hill uses a study of Andean and Amazonian Indians to conclude that both history and myth are 'modes of social consciousness'
through which people construct 'shared interpretive frameworks'.[27] In

this way, history and myth 'complement rather than oppose one another'.[28]

This may all seem to have come a long way from the *Titanic*. Hill, was after all, discussing the Waurá, an Arawak-speaking society of the Upper Xingu region in Brazil, and not British people from 1912–14. What is important, though, is to realize that if we have rethought the relationship between history and myth, then it is inappropriate to think of societies 'progressing' from myth to history. Terence Turner, another anthropologist specializing in South America, agrees:

> it seems clear to me that myth and history cannot be conceived as mutually incompatible modes of consciousness or as consecutive stages of cultural evolution. Rather, they must be considered in some sense complementary, and mutually informing. Not 'from myth to history,' then, but 'myth and history together,' in parallel, as two sides of the same coin.[29]

Turner was not speaking only of 'primitive' South American tribes. For him, history and myth were also intricately related in 'complex societies with secular historical traditions (including our own)'.[30] This, then, is a crucial argument in support of the myth of the *Titanic*: myth and history combine in contemporary culture just as they always have done, be they in Upper Xingu or Lower Boddington.

My argument has now taken an important universalist turn. It is time, therefore, to introduce the structural anthropology of Claude Lévi-Strauss. Lévi-Strauss developed a theory of 'structural anthropology' based on the linguistic structuralism of Ferdinand de Saussure. The intricacies of Lévi-Strauss's linguistic model do not concern us here. What does concern us is his conclusion that the purpose of myth was intellectually to mediate and if possible overcome the inevitable paradoxes and contradictions of lived experience.[31] Myths served, in other words, to try to make the world make sense.[32] So, where Malinowski had stressed the practical, functional, hard-working nature of myth, Lévi-Strauss saw it as much more cerebral: myths were intellectual tools; abstract ideas embedded in concrete form. Indeed – and this is a crucial point for us – Lévi-Strauss argued that this 'logic of the concrete'[33] as evidenced in pre-literate myth was a mode of thinking just as sophisticated as any thinking we have today. So, where previous work had supposed there to be a difference between the 'primitive' mind and contemporary 'scientific' thought, Lévi-Strauss concluded:

> If our interpretation is correct, we are led toward a completely dif-
> ferent view – namely, that the kind of logic in mythical thought is as
> rigorous as that of modern science.[34]

In this way, the difference between mythic and scientific thought lay
not in the quality of intellectual process, but simply in the nature of
the things to which it was applied.[35] Myths could no longer be
described as 'pre-logical'.[36] Man, therefore, 'has always been thinking
equally well',[37] and so 'societies observed by ethnographers are no
more "primitive" than others'.[38] For Lévi-Strauss, therefore, the study
of myth 'shows us to be closer – rather than farther from – forms of
thought very foreign to ours in appearance.'[39]

Let us now take Lévi-Strauss's 'universalism' one step further than
he did himself, and in so doing make a point crucial to our examination of the *Titanic* as myth. If 'primitive' man, who thought in myth,
was in fact just as logical and intellectually sophisticated as we are
today, then people today are just as likely as 'primitive' man to think
in terms of myth. Consequently we should no longer speak of the myth
of the *Titanic* pejoratively, but rather as an important intellectual step
to taking it very seriously indeed. If Lévi-Strauss is correct, then the
late Edwardian British were just as likely to think in terms of myth as
their pre-literate forebears. And according to Lévi-Strauss's theory of
the purpose of myth, the late-Edwardians will have consequently used
the myth of the *Titanic* to try to 'make sense' of the sinking of the
Titanic and its relationship to their conceptual world. It is in just this
way that in Chapter 7 I shall investigate the myth of the *Titanic* as the
'unsinkable ship'. This will lead us to concur with Malinowski when he
claimed: 'Myth ... is an essential ingredient of all culture'[40] and not
just those traditionally studied by anthropologists. Here, we shall see
the late twentieth-century British reanimating the historical data surrounding the *Titanic* to try to make sense of an arbitrary event.

We can now follow our discussion of theories of myth with the
identification and discussion of six characteristics which we shall see
shared between 'primitive' or pre-literate myth and the myth of the
Titanic. The first of these concerns the relationship between history
and myth. I have already spent some time arguing that history and
myth are not distinct categories, and that this is equally true of pre-
literate and contemporary cultures. This is not to contend, however,
that history and myth, just like the factual and the fantastic, are one
and the same. Again, they coexist within a very complex relationship.
Myths, whether handed down by tribal storytellers or disseminated

through contemporary popular culture, do not provide us with a direct, mirror or 'documentary' image of the societies from which they arise. If we were to believe that they did, we would be in grave danger of being misled.

The dangers of interpreting myth literally were well understood, for example, by Lévi-Strauss in his study of the Asdiwal myths of British Columbia. The Port Simpson version of this myth tells the story of a young man named Asdiwal who, armed with a magic bow and arrow, together with the ability to make himself invisible, follows a great white she-bear up a ladder into heaven. The bear turns out to be a beautiful young woman, whom he marries. Various trials and adventures follow, including Asdiwal's resurrection from death, his descent into hell and his transformation into a bird. Finally, he and his dog are turned to stone and can still be seen at the top of the mountain by the lake of Ginadâos.[41]

Not surprisingly, Lévi-Strauss stressed that the Asdiwal myths were not be read as an 'accurate picture of ethnographic reality'.[42] This did not mean, however, that the myth of Asdiwal told us nothing about Tsimshian life. In order to explain this, Lévi-Strauss distinguished four constituent aspects of the myth: the geographic, the techno-economic, the sociological and the cosmological. Geographically, he showed, the populations and places described in the myth really did exist. Economically, the seasonal migrations around fish harvests were equally realistically portrayed. Cosmologically, Asdiwal's ascent into heaven and descent into hell made no sense at all. On the sociological level, however, fact and fiction energetically combined.[43] He was therefore able to conclude:

> The first two are exact transcriptions of reality; the fourth has nothing to do with it, and in the third, real and imaginary institutions are interwoven.[44]

It is this third, sociological, area which proves most interesting to us. Here, as Lévi-Strauss observes:

> It is not a question of an accurate documentary picture of native life, but a sort of counterpoint which seems sometimes to be in harmony with this reality, and sometimes to part from it in order to rejoin it.[45]

Myth, then, is what Roland Barthes, speaking now of Western twentieth-century culture, described as 'a story at once true and unreal'.[46] This fusion of fact and fiction within myths might at first appear problematic. In terms of pure 'documentary' evidence it certainly is. But it seems to me that this combination of the actual and the imaginary serves to increase the potency of the myth, and that the inclusion of credible, 'authentic' detail serves to increase the illusion of credibility, and thus the power, of the myth as a whole.

Authentic-seeming touchstones to reality have long been employed in myth. Homer's *Iliad*, for example, is an epic in which the gods appear at every turn, personally interceding on the field of battle when circumstances require. The supernatural content, however, is made to appear credible by the inclusion of passages of vivid and authentic description. In book ten, for example, Odysseus and his comrades are depicted arming themselves for a foray against the Trojans:

> and Thrasymedes the stubborn in battle gave the son of Tydeus
> a two-edged sword (his own had been left behind by his vessel)
> and a shield; and he put over his head a helmet
> of bull's hide, with neither horn nor crest, which is known as
> the skull cap ...'[47]

It reads as though it were a 'documentary': we are told the names and relationships of the protagonists, the type of sword used and why a new one was required. We are shown that a shield was also carried into battle, that a helmet was worn, what the helmet was made of, how it was decorated and what it was called. History and archaeology support this vivid and detailed description of Hellenic armoury, together with the existence of the Trojan War. Yet within 20 lines of this 'documentary' description of preparation for battle, the goddess Pallas Athene sends down a heron as an omen to the Greeks. They recognize the sign, pray to the goddess and their prayers are heard. As Peter Burke reminded us, therefore: a myth is not to be despised, but reading it literally is not to be recommended.[48]

As a modern myth, the myth of the *Titanic* similarly combines fertile imagination with authentic detail. Accounts of the sinking in British popular culture from 1912 to 1914 are replete with factual information: there are passenger lists, plans and descriptions of the ship, intricate narratives of personal valour and 'verbatim' transcriptions of conversations on board. There is, perhaps, slightly less room for the imaginary element of myth in twentieth-century, Western culture than there is in pre-literate myth. Ours is, after all, a widely literate society with a voracious appetite for documentation. The *Titanic* was photographed and even filmed. Yet despite this wealth of 'documentary' evidence, many – or even most – of the best known stories about the ship are disputable or even demonstrably false. We are left, therefore, in that heady realm which Nathaniel Hawthorne described in *The Scarlet Letter* as 'somewhere between the real world and fairy-land, where the Actual and the Imaginary may meet, and each imbue itself with the nature of the other'.[49]

In the process of mixing and imagining, myths frequently rewrite the past in order to create preferred versions of history. Jonathan Hill, for example, noticed how South American tribes, whom we have already seen have an interrelatedly complex concept of history and myth, are able mythically to rewrite history to their own advantage. In this way:

> South American mythic histories attempt to reconcile a view of 'what really happened' with an understanding of 'what ought to have happened'.[50]

This process is equally observable in post-literate, Western culture. Ernst Bloch, for example, believed that cultural texts (in which category he included both 'high' and 'popular' culture) provided 'wishful landscapes'[51] rather than literal or documentary images. Take, for example, Pieter Brueghel's painting 'Land of Cockaigne', which was painted:

> exactly as the poor folk always dreamed it would be. As an eternal Sunday, which is one because there is no sign of any treadmill, and nothing beyond what can be drunk, eaten, boiled or roasted is to be found.[52]

The wishful landscape need not be merely physical, however; it can be historical, too. Just as Hill noted with his South American tribes, Bloch observed 'the wishful rewriting of history, where the wrong turn is righted and the missed opportunity achieved',[53] while the cultural historian Roger Chartier has found similarly that popular cultural texts serve to describe society as people 'thought it was or wished it to be'.[54] This is exactly what happened with the myth of the *Titanic*, and so the social theorist Slavoj Žižek was perfectly able see the *Titanic* as 'an image of society not as it really was but seen as society wanted to be seen in order to appear likeable'.[55] As we shall explore in greater depth in later chapters, the myth of the *Titanic* is frequently a wish-fully rewritten history of 'what ought to have happened', rather than what actually (or at the very least demonstrably) did.

Myth does not only rewrite the past, however. It is also capable of presenting preferred views of the present. Lévi-Strauss perceived such wishful speculation at work in his case-study of the Asdiwal myths of British Columbia. He noticed that the myths did not (as we have seen) exclusively portray life as the natives knew it, but also how it might otherwise have been. Thus:

> Mythical speculation about types of residence which are exclusively patrilocal or matrilocal do not therefore have anything to do with the reality of the structure of Tsimshian society, but rather with its inherent possibilities and its latent potentialities.[56]

The crucial phrase here is: 'inherent possibilities and latent potentialities'. For that is what so much of myth explores. In our fantasies (what Lévi-Strauss called 'untamed thinking'[57]) we can dare to imagine, and dare to wonder what would happen if our wishes came true. In interpreting myth, then, we should always be alert to the encodement of those possibilities and potentialities, whether they are articulated overtly or expressed latently. It is often in these unguarded dreams that societies find themselves, as Geoghegan put it, 'thinking the unthinkable'.[58]

To an extent, such thinking is indeed Utopian. The Utopian content of myth need not be entirely optimistic, however, for as Geoghegan says, the classic Utopia criticizes as well as anticipates. Indeed:

> Its alternative fundamentally interrogates the present, piercing though existing societies' defensive mechanisms – common sense, realism, positivism and scientism. Its flagrant otherness gives it a power which is lacking in any other analytical devices.[59]

Anthropologists have similarly noticed speculation of the fearful sort in a variety of cultural texts. Clifford Geertz, for example, argued that the violence of the Balinese cockfight was 'a powerful rendering of life as the Balinese most deeply do not want it'. It was a form of open conflict which they avoided in everyday life, but which revealed itself in the imaginative text.[60] Similarly, in his study of the Asdiwal stories, Lévi-Strauss stressed that while the myths do indeed explore societal possibilities and potentialities, these scenarios are not always, in the final analysis, preferred to the status quo. Often, indeed, these 'extreme positions are only imagined in order to show that they are untenable'.[61]

Fenella Cannell made a similar observation in her ethnographic study of public reaction in Britain to the Warnock Report and the 'Gillick debates' on surrogacy, human fertilization and contraception in the 1980s.[62] She noticed that a discussion ran in the media in parallel to official legal and parliamentary debate. While the official discussion

was designed to produce actual legislation and public policy, newspaper stories

> seem to have been designed to test the extremes. In the stories
> relating to the Gillick debate, visions of various 'possible worlds' of
> social sterility or social fertility were presented ... A world shriv-
> elled up by promiscuity was one such vision; a world in which all
> distinctions collapsed into incest was another.[63]

We note how, in this way, anthropologists studying the pre-literate
myths of the Tsimshian Indians and the popular press in twentieth-
century Britain are able to arrive at very similar conclusions. They
serve further to remind us that myth encodes not only preferred worlds
but also 'nightmare' scenarios. Consequently, the myth of the *Titanic* is
able to serve both as a deftly rewritten 'ideal' history in which human
(and especially Anglo-Saxon) virtue prevails, and also (as we shall see
in Chapter 7) a wrathful warning of the consequences of human pride.

If myth is a potent but intricate combination of the actual and the
imaginary, what value can it be to us as evidence in our investigation
of late Edwardian culture? I have already hinted at the answer to this:
the value of myth lies in its values. The myth of the *Titanic* may not
provide literal evidence of what actually took place on the physical
ship (the first of my 'two' *Titanic*s), but it does provide vital and reliable evidence of other, more important, sorts of truth.

Lévi-Strauss, we remember, argued in *The Savage Mind* that myths
were abstract ideas made concrete. What is likely to interest us as
non-literalist interpreters of myth, then, are the notions rather than
the tools. This is why Lévi-Strauss was concerned not so much with
the 'obvious narrative' and the 'apparent content' of a myth, but much
more with the 'schemata' which contained the 'latent content'.[64]

Such a terminology would have come as no surprise to Walter
Benjamin, who investigated not distant but his own culture. We recall
from the introduction how in *The Origin of German Tragic Drama*,
Benjamin sought to strip away what he described as the 'material
content' of the Baroque *Trauerspiel* to arrive at its greater, inner 'truth
content'. It was the allegory, and not the storyline, that carried the
actual meaning. Benjamin, therefore, did not take the dramatic
excesses of the *Trauerspiel* to be a literal reflection or description of
German daily life at the time. Rather, he used the allegorical content
of the *Trauerspiel* to gain an 'invaluable insight into the fecundity of a
spiritual age that had been hitherto either neglected or abused'.[65] It
follows, then, that the story of the *Titanic* can be a deeply revealing

myth just like the German *Trauerspiel* or the Tsimshianian story of Asdiwal and his great white she-bear.

The importance of looking beyond the overt, cosmetic content of cultural forms is emphasized by the way it does not matter very much whether the narratives are literally 'true' or not. It is in just such a way that Graham McCann is able to show in his study of Marilyn Monroe that while her biographies may not tell us much about the actual Marilyn, they nevertheless reveal the cultural praxis alive in each interpretation. 'One might not find out "All About Marilyn",' says McCann, 'but the meta-biography can provide (at least) a proper appreciation of her fictions.'[66]

The importance of understanding 'fictions' lies in an understanding that 'fictions' are often told in the pursuit of what we might dangerously describe as 'truth'. Indeed, Joanne Rappaport believes that written fiction can contain greater truth than written history. This is particularly so, she says, in the writings of Gabriel García Marquéz, who in his novels, 'rewrites Colombian history, interweaving legendary and mythic images with historical fact, thus sharpening the truth he wishes to convey.'[67] Her use of the word 'truth' is both deliberate and revealing, and she expands upon its consequences:

> Perhaps for this very reason, many Colombian intellectuals see García Marquéz as one of the few who is able to convey the true meaning of Colombianness, and to do it in a form more gripping and natural than those 'real and natural' histories. This is why he rushes to tell his stories before the historians have time to arrive.[68]

Such a concept need not be limited to Colombian society. The myth of the *Titanic* is a similarly gripping tale, told in late Edwardian popular culture. This narrative of what we might call 'the true meaning of Britishness' was told in newspapers, magazines, songs, postcards and all manner of commemorative ephemera long before the inquiry reports were published and long before British historians arrived to work on those.

To say that fiction is – simply – a more truthful form than history is clearly a dangerous, reductionist claim. Fiction, in that it is invented, might equally be described as 'misinformation'. However, as the social psychologist Thomas Gilovich has pointed out, sometimes people 'knowingly provide misinformation in the service of what they believe to be "the greater truth"'.[69]

This has certainly been the case in propaganda. During the First World War, for example, it was alleged in *The Times* that the Germans had a factory in which they boiled human corpses to make soap. The British Government explored the possibility of exploiting the propaganda potential of this story overseas. The Foreign Secretary Arthur Balfour knew that the documentary evidence for the claim was inconclusive, but added: 'there does not, in view of the many atrocious actions of which the Germans have been guilty, appear to be any reason why it should not be true.' The story was later exposed as a fabrication.[70] We shall not be surprised, therefore, in Chapter 5 to find Captain Smith of the *Titanic* being roundly praised in 1914 for saying 'what we would have expected and wanted' him to have said as the ship went down.[71]

The realignment of what may be true into what 'ought' to be true may apply equally to stories of a more spiritual nature. In *The Last Temptation of Christ*, Nikos Kazantzakis speculated what might have happened had Christ not been crucified and resurrected as in the New Testament story. In Kazantzakis's novel, St Paul finds the worldly Christ living a quiet and anonymous family life in an obscure village. Christ angrily tells Paul that he is not the Son of God, and that Paul should not go round telling 'lies'. Christ himself would now proclaim 'the truth'.[72] Paul explodes: 'True or false – what do I care! It's enough that the world is saved!' Christ continues vociferously to protest, but Paul storms that it really doesn't matter whether the actual Christ was crucified or not:

> I create the truth, create it out of obstinacy and longing and faith ... If the world is to be saved it is necessary – do you hear? – necessary for you to be crucified, and I shall crucify you, like it or not; it is necessary for you to be resurrected, and I shall resurrect you, like it or not.[73]

There is a double allegory at work here. Kazantzakis is using the cover of narrative to make a profound point. He is using a work of fiction to tell what he believes to be the 'truth' about the relationship between history and myth. In this case, he is calling for a non-literal interpretation of the New Testament. But even if everything contained therein is not literally true, the Bible is still, according to Kazantzakis, capable of deep and profound truths. 'I create the truth,' rages Paul. Truth, in the theology of *The Last Temptation of Christ*, is a product of human need, and not of documented reality.

Much of the myth of the *Titanic*, let us remind ourselves, is not literally true. Certainly, much of it is at best non-provable. In the myth of the *Titanic*, the *Titanic* is clearly depicted as 'the unsinkable ship'. In Chapter 7 I shall show that it was necessary for the *Titanic* to be represented as unsinkable just as, according to Kazantzakis's St Paul, it was necessary for Christ to rise again. It would seem, then, that in myth, fiction can indeed be just as 'true', and sometimes even 'truer', than fact. Or, as Thomas Keneally put it in *Schindler's Ark*: 'the thing about a myth is not whether it is true or not, nor whether it *should* be true, but that it is sometimes truer than truth itself.'[74]

In psychoanalysis, the analyst will frequently ask the patient to speak about his or her dreams. In the interpretation of popular culture as modern myth, on the other hand, we ask the dreams what they can tell us about the patient. It is what Leo Lowenthal thought of as a kind of 'psycho-analysis in reverse'.[75] The idea that myths are like dreams is not new to anthropologists. A number of psychoanalytical theories of myth developed under the influence of both Carl Jung and Sigmund Freud.[76] Common to them all is the idea that the symbols and underlying themes of myth well up from the unconscious and that this unconscious can be shared by the cultural group.[77] The result is a potent combination of fact and fiction, and of the overt and the latent. This again reminds us of the dangers of taking myth as documentary evidence, but at the same time shows us that an analysis of myth can bear richer fruit in terms of its unguarded, unconscious content. As Lévi-Strauss noted in his study of the Asdiwal myth:

> This conception of the relation of the myth to reality no doubt limits the use of the former as a documentary source. But it opens the way for other possibilities; for in abandoning the search for a consistently accurate picture of ethnographic reality in the myth, we gain, on occasions, a means of reaching the unconscious categories.[78]

Unconscious thinking is no more superfluous in myth than it is in psychoanalysis. The value of the unconscious content of myth to us lies precisely in its vibrant, unselfconscious nature. It is in this way that Lévi-Strauss was able to speak of the 'untamed thinking'[79] which was manifest in myth and therefore able to provide great insight into the unrestrained human mind.[80] This is of enormous value to us. In the same way that psychoanalysts seek to probe beneath the self-conscious, learned or mannered projections and defences of their patients, we are seeking to probe beneath the self-conscious, learned or mannered projections and defences of society. This is as true in 'primitive' as it is in contemporary popular culture. Roland Barthes, for example, believed that advertisements:

> now belong to a region of French daily life which the various types of psycho-analysis would do well to pay some attention if they wish to keep up to date.[81]

The importance of the unconscious has been similarly noted by cultural historians and philosophers. Roger Chartier, for example, stressed the 'unconscious expression' which popular culture gives to individual and group interests in cultural history:[82] what a text *aimed* to say was not its only meaning.[83] Similarly, Bloch believed that the encodement of utopian content in popular texts was done by way of an *überschuss* (overshot) in which the creator of a work unknowingly went beyond his or her original intentions.[84] Thus, the work could have significant content of which even its creator was unaware.[85] This concept is crucial to our understanding of the myth of the *Titanic*. When we discover the cultural values and assumptions contained within the *Titanic* myth, we are therefore able to accept them as evidence without having at the same time to believe that they were deliberately 'put there' by the people responsible. As T.S. Eliot noted, culture can never be 'wholly conscious', for 'there is always more to it than we are conscious of'.[86]

It is important to remember that the body under 'analysis' here is collective and not individual, for myth, and specifically the myth of the *Titanic*, is a collective rather than an individually authored 'work'. As Lévi-Strauss showed in *The Raw and the Cooked*: 'Myths have no author ... they exist only embodied in a tradition.'[87] In this way, we quite rightly attribute the authorship of myths to societies and not individuals. Thus, for example, we are entitled to think of the Asdiwal stories as a Tsimshian myth, and not just as the product of an individual Tsimshian, for myth is collective in its conception, its telling and its retelling. Accordingly, analysis of a myth is revealing of the collective culture and not of an individual author.

This is a concept which we can apply equally to modern myth. It is impossible, for example, to say who is the individual author of the myths of John F. Kennedy or Che Guevara. We may, in post-literate society, be able to pinpoint individual contributions to those myths (specific books, films, newspaper articles, and so forth), but the myths remain essentially both collective and amorphous; mosaics comprising innumerable component parts.[88] And even those component parts, whatever their individual origin, tend to display a remarkable homogeneity. This can be explained by the symbiotic relationship between the individual and the culture within which he or she lives, for although contemporary Western society seems to subscribe very much to the 'cult of the individual', cultural texts are not produced in any sort of cultural vacuum. In *Patterns of Culture*, anthropologist Ruth Benedict studied the Zuni of New Mexico, the Dobuans of Melanesia and the Kwakiutl of Vancouver Island to conclude that: 'no man ever looks at the world with pristine eyes'.[89] Everything he sees is 'edited by a definite set of customs and institutions and ways of thinking'. Even the extent of his philosophical probings are limited by his culture because his very concepts of true or false are culturally conditioned.[90] In this way, individuals assume 'the behaviour dictated by that society',[91] and individuals are therefore 'plastic to the moulding force of the society into which they are born'.[92]

The power of this 'moulding force' is not limited to pre-literate peoples: it is equally true of contemporary Western culture. The ethnographer Fenella Cannell's study of the Warnock and Gillick debates in Britain revealed considerable common ground among apparently disparate publications ranging from the archly tabloid *Sun* to the solidly academic *British Medical Journal*. She found that despite the apparent disparity of individual sources and opinions: 'the various voices are ultimately bounded by a common limit', in this case an argument about the nature of naturalness.[93] Even though conflicting positions were examined, they were all ultimately found to inhabit 'a single ideological terrain, one in which the naturalness of the family is pre-supposed'.[94] So, just as Ruth Benedict claimed that in Zuni, Dobuan and Kwakiutl society thinking took place only within the established cultural limits of those societies, Cannell found discussion of a moral issue in the contemporary British press to be equally bound by pre-existing notions of naturalness and the family.

The myth of the *Titanic*, for all the disparity of its component sources and media, shows an even greater unity of opinion. The 'ideological terrain' inhabited by its constituents is practically identical.[95] In this way, we are especially entitled to view the myth of the *Titanic* as a collective text. It is a stance that would certainly gain methodological support from Clifford Geertz, who, we remember, interpreted collective Balinese cultural texts to reveal 'the Balinese sense of self'.[96] In this way, the cockfight was 'a Balinese reading of Balinese experience, a story they tell themselves about themselves'.[97] We can say exactly the same thing about the myth of the *Titanic*: it is a late Edwardian reading of late Edwardian experience, a story they told themselves about themselves.

As a product of the collective unconscious, myth can be greatly revealing of collective need, the articulation of which may be either consciously or unconsciously withheld in everyday discourse. This relationship between myth and need was of particular interest to Malinowski, especially in the cases of magic and religion. Myth, he claimed, is often 'told in satisfaction of deep religious wants' and 'moral cravings'; it expresses and codifies belief.[98] The Trobriand islanders, for example, had myths of life after death, a belief 'born from the innermost instinctive and emotional reaction to the most formidable and haunting idea'.[99] It is a myth, therefore, reflective of a deep psychological need, a need to believe in something beyond the cold, empty finality of human mortality. Indeed, Malinowski demonstrated how myth helped the Melanesians better to face death: on the one hand, they were depressed by the reality of it, on the other:

> the same people would clutch at the hope given to them by their beliefs. They would screen, with the vivid texture of their myths, stories and beliefs about the spirit world, the vast emotional void gaping beyond them.[100]

Indeed, for Malinowski, belief, whether in magic or religion, 'is deeply associated with the deepest desires of man, with his fears and hopes, with his passions and sentiments'[101] The Trobriand life-cycle myths, then, both reflect and (if believed) fulfil a need for a belief in life after death.

The theologian Don Cupitt has shown that contemporary stories similarly satisfy 'by meeting a need',[102] but myth – and the myth of the *Titanic* is no exception – is concerned not only with the need to believe in life after death. Myth is also concerned with a larger and more widely embracing need: the need to find meaning in the world in which we actually exist.

While myth does indeed both reanimate the past and explore the future, one of its most important functions is to try to make sense of the present. This one of the most vital features of Lévi-Strauss's theory of myth, and is at the same time one of the most significant features of the late Edwardian myth of the *Titanic*: it served to find meaning in a random event.

As Cupitt has said, 'everything is the product of time and chance',[103] and so 'nothing says it must all add up ... Life is not obliged to make sense.'[104] This may seem a very gloomy prospect. Therefore, people have consistently devised ways to find order among the arbitrary and to make meaning out of the meaningless.[105] Culture is what we use to structure this incoherent universe, and culture, as Geertz so memorably put it, consists of webs of significance which we ourselves have spun.[106]

The idea of culture being used to make 'sense' of the world is a theme which runs throughout Geertz's work, and although his ethnographic case studies have focused on the specific rather than the general, he has described his work as a whole as an effort to write about 'particular attempts by particular peoples to place these things in some sort of comprehensive, meaningful frame'.[107] His celebrated example of the Balinese cockfight, therefore, both demonstrates the spinning of a particular 'web of significance' in Bali, and also suggests that similar webs are spun with different texts among different peoples: 'Like any art form ... the cockfight renders ordinary, everyday experience comprehensible.'[108] His use of the term 'art form' is particularly useful, because it helps us to understand that exactly the same human process is at work in the seemingly anthropologically distant cockpits of Bali as it is in the salons of Western Europe:

> What [the cockfight] does is what, for other peoples with other temperaments and conventions, Lear and Crime and Punishment do; it catches up these themes ... ordering them into an encompassing structure.[109]

This ordering of a disordered universe is something that fellow anthropologists have found particularly prevalent in myth. In his studies of American Indians, Lévi-Strauss showed that myths were used to try both to articulate and overcome the contradictions of their worldly lives.[110] Asdiwal, for example, was faced in his story by 'unresolved oppositions' which he then struggled to overcome through a series of 'mediations'.[111] Lévi-Strauss was therefore able to conclude that: 'the purpose of a myth is to provide a logical model capable of overcoming a contradiction.'[112] Malinowski had found similar patterns amongst the Melanesians, and so, functional as ever, believed that myth was 'a powerful means of assisting primitive man, of allowing him to make the two ends of his cultural patrimony meet'.[113] Terence Turner found the same of the myths of South America, and argued that history worked in much the same way: 'Both history and myth are primarily narrative forms. They consist of sequences of actions and events arranged so as to constitute an intelligible pattern.'[114]

The finding – or the imposition – of intelligible patterns among random events is, of course, not limited to 'primitive' or pre-literate culture. Marcus Raskin reached much the same conclusion as Turner did of mythical South America in his discussion of conspiracy theories and the assassination of John F. Kennedy:

> To fatalists, the world may be nothing more than a series of random events and accidents, but most people crave a coherent explanation

of why the events which shape their destiny occur. Indeed, this is a psychological function of history. Without this grounding, a person feels uneasy and unable to shape at least part of his or her destiny.[115]

According to Gilovich, the need to find order in disorder runs throughout human nature. He explains:

> We are predisposed to see order, pattern and meaning in the world, and we find randomness, chaos and meaningless unsatisfying. Human nature abhors a lack of predictability and the absence of meaning. As a consequence, we tend to 'see' order where there is none, and we spot meaningless patterns when only the vagaries of chance are operating.[116]

The tendency to impute order into ambiguous stimuli, he states, is built into the cognitive machinery we use to apprehend the world.[117] It is little wonder, then, that in the 'untamed thinking' of myth, our cognitive machinery imputes order with un-tamed abandon.

Gilovich notes three further developments of the human tendency to find patterns where none exist. First, when people suspect that a phenomenon exists, they 'generally have little trouble in explaining *why* it exists or what it means'.[118] Indeed, it goes even further:

> once a person has (mis)identified a random pattern as a 'real' phenomenon, it will not exist as a puzzling, isolated fact about the world. Rather, it is quickly explained and readily integrated into the person's pre-existing theories and beliefs.[119]

Applied to a group rather than just an individual, this cognitive tendency becomes a veritable mythographer's charter. Second, Gilovich notes the (erroneous) belief that 'big events have big causes, complex events should have complex causes and so on.'[120] This might help, for example, to explain the integration of grand conspiracy theories into the story of the assassination of President Kennedy. A single gunman, acting alone, just doesn't seem a big enough cause for the death of a president, any more than a random iceberg seems sufficient to sink the *Titanic*.[121] A.J.P. Taylor said much the same thing about the causes of the First World War.[122] Third, Gilovich notes the human tendency towards what we might call 'rationalization' and what he calls 'the wish to believe'.[12] This is another human trait in which 'we are inclined to adopt self-serving beliefs about ourselves, and comforting beliefs about the world.'[124] It is just the sort of societal behaviour Ruth Benedict observed in *Patterns of Culture*, speaking this time not of distant tribes but about the First World War, with its alleged 'foster-ings of courage, of altruism, of spiritual values'.[125] This was an act of societal 'rationalization'[126] of our own society's less flattering and more war-like traits, argued Benedict, and it took place 'because all peoples always justify the traits of which they find themselves pos-sessed'.[127] It is, we might say, a continuation of every society's need to make sense of the world.

Making sense of the world, and adopting Gilovich's 'comforting beliefs' about it, is a function which Cupitt believes is performed by stories. Stories, he says, are interpretive resources 'through which we make sense of what is happening to us'.[128] Indeed, every story is actu-ally theological because 'every story just by being a story constitutes a promise that life can be meaningful. That is the job of stories, they make life make sense.'[129] Indeed, Cupitt argues that this is a function performed by both stories and religious myths, a process in which 'barren chaos is made into a friendly habitable cosmos'.[130] The more anomalous the real-life circumstance, the more (as Lévi-Strauss would have surely agreed) it attracts the creation of myths.[131] In this way:

> Once that great primal mythopeic faculty in us has been activated, life becomes bearable. Stories, remember, have the power to order chaos, reconcile conflict, solve problems, compensate for loss and inadequacy, beguile the night and defer death. So long as we can keep our stories going, life can continue.[132]

Both anthropology and theology, then, have noted the role of culture in this 'struggle against meaninglessness'. There is agreement within literary and social theory, too. Pierre Maranda, in 'The Dialectic Metaphor', argued that 'the mythic process is a learning device in which the unintelligible – randomness – is reduced to intelli-gibility – a pattern.'[133] Žižek similarly felt that a dread and impossible 'Thing' in the Lacanian sense could be domesticated by giving it a metaphorical meaning, thus reducing it to a symbolic status 'by pro-viding it with a meaning'.[134]

This is exactly what happened with the myth of the *Titanic*. The sinking of the *Titanic* was a random event which took place entirely within the realms of probability. It both was and is extremely rare for a ship to hit an iceberg in the middle of an ocean. Insurance companies had for years accepted the chance of a liner striking an iceberg as one in a million.[135] However, with enough ships, enough crossings and enough ice, it is entirely within the realms of probability that over a sufficient number of years, a ship and an iceberg will collide. It is, after all, an insurable risk. The *Titanic* was not alone in hitting ice. The Anchor liner *City of Rome* rammed an iceberg in 1899; earlier, in 1879, the Guion liner *Arizona* crashed into another at 14 knots, 'mounted a submerged ledge and slid off with nothing worse than the telescoping of 20 feet of her bow'.[136] That the *Titanic* could collide with an iceberg, then, was statistically possible, and as we saw in the previous chapter, the chances of it doing so were increased by the particular circumstances of 14 April 1912. As we shall see in Chapter 7, however, statistical circumstance plays little part in the myth of the *Titanic*. According to the myth, the *Titanic*'s collision with the iceberg was direct and consequential retribution for the human temerity of daring to defy the elements by building an 'unsinkable ship'. In this way, what was, quite literally, an accident was transformed into an epic myth of hubris and nemesis in order to make meaning out of an arbitrary event.

What we have, then, with the story of the *Titanic* is a modern myth, communicated, encoded and preserved in popular culture. In this chapter, I have shown that a myth is not a simple falsehood, and that as the basis for both social memory and social action, even seeming falsehoods deserve to be taken seriously. I have, then, examined functional, historical and structural theories not only to aim towards an understanding of myth, but also to identify six features shared between the myth of the *Titanic* and the myths of pre-literate or 'primitive' peoples. First, both comprise a complex blend of fact and fiction, in which realistic detail is used the better to anchor the fantastical elements in apparent credibility. Second, myth frequently incorporates the wishful rewriting of history to create preferred worlds. In this way, although myths still have a complex relationship with the past, that past is partly idealized, invented, selectively remembered or reanimated in the interests of the present. Third, although they may be distinctly unreliable as documentary evidence, both ancient and modern myths still contain societal as opposed to historical truths. As such, they express the values of the societies that made and encoded them in concrete form. Fourth, both pre-literate and contemporary myths can be thought of psychoanalytically in that they are the unconscious results of 'untamed thinking' in which societal needs are expressed and fulfilled. Fifth, both may be understood, in the final analysis, as the work not of individual authors but as collective representations of the cultures and societies from which they arise and whose condition they articulate. Sixth, both are the result of social need, and are used to spin 'webs of significance' out of the raw materials of lived experience. In this way they reanimate the actual to construct order and meaning from an arbitrary world.

Why, though, do we need modern myths such as the myth of the *Titanic*? What is wrong with the old ones? The answer brings us back to Geertz's definition of the Balinese cockfight as 'a story they tell themselves about themselves'.[137] Different societies may have common concerns, but the ways in which they portray those concerns need to be specific to them. They need to be stories about *themselves*.[138] Lévi-Strauss likened this mental operation to that of the French *bricoleur*, or handyman, who constructs objects from the odds and ends he happens to find around him.[139] In this way, the ancient Greeks made myths about ancient Greece, chivalric knights about chivalric knights, and late Edwardians about late Edwardians. With this in mind, we can now combine theory with a practical, detailed examination of the myth of the *Titanic* in British popular culture from 1912 to 1914.

3 'Women and Children First!'

According to a poem by Harold Begbie, those who went down with the *Titanic* died 'like men'.[1] According to Philip Gibbs, on the other hand, some of the female survivors of the disaster were 'mad with grief'.[2] All the popular texts agree that the celebrated edict 'Women and children first!' was universally obeyed. What, then, does the myth of the *Titanic* reveal to us about late Edwardian attitudes to men, manliness, women and gender difference? British popular culture from 1912 to 1914 is sharply revealing.

Before we delve into a detailed analysis of the contemporary texts, however, it is worth spending a few moments describing the range, type and number of late Edwardian sources available on the *Titanic*.

For reasons which will become increasingly clear as this study proceeds, there was very little material on the *Titanic* published before it sank. Essentially, the 'pre-maiden' *Titanic* appears only in the limited amount of publicity material produced by its builders, Harland and Wolff of Belfast, and its owners, the White Star Line of Liverpool. Additionally, there were a number of specialist articles in trade and technical journals, notably *The Shipbuilder*, *The Engineer* and *Engineering*. Typically, the *Titanic* here is featured not in its own right, but in tandem with its 'sister' ship, the RMS *Olympic*, which pre-dated the *Titanic* in construction, launch and service (the importance of the *Olympic* will provide a major theme in Chapter 7). Of the 'pre-maiden' literature produced, the most detailed and informative is *The Shipbuilder* magazine's special issue: 'The White Star Liners "Olympic" and "Titanic"',[3] published in 1911. This comprises a full technical description of both ships, from engines to decor and passenger accommodations, and includes detailed fold-out plans depicting both vessels. It provides an invaluable resource for students of the physical *Titanic*.

Once the *Titanic* sank, however, there was an absolute outpouring of material on the ship, its passengers and the circumstances of its demise. This began to flow from the moment the news of the disaster broke in April 1912 and only dried up with the unveiling of a statue to Edward John Smith, the captain of the *Titanic*, in July 1914. The outbreak of the First World War marked the end of late Edwardian interest in the *Titanic*.

There was, of course, a vast amount of day-to-day news coverage of the *Titanic* disaster and its aftermath, but this study deliberately focuses on more considered and deliberate texts; those that sought to provide an overview of events; those, therefore, of popular culture rather than pyrrhic journalism; those that actively sought to enshrine the *Titanic* in the social memory. We can conveniently break down the popular cultural material on the *Titanic* into seven component groups. The first group comprises the special *Titanic* 'In Memoriam' issues of popular newspaper publications. Among these two stand out: the mass circulation *Lloyd's Weekly News*' 'The Deathless Story of the Titanic', and the 'Titanic In Memoriam Number' of the *Daily Graphic*.[4] The first of these (plate I) was written by the prolific author and journalist Philip Gibbs (1877–1962),[5] and boasted a 'Complete Narrative With Many Illustrations'. At a cover price of two pence, it told the story of the *Titanic* in narrative and highly rhetorical form. It was published within two weeks of the disaster, and featured special 'inset' features on topics of special interest, such as 'The Titanic's Millionaires' and 'Death the Divider', together with what purported to be a full list of the passengers and crew who were saved.

'The Deathless Story of the Titanic' proved so commercially successful that it ran to three editions. Records do not show how many were printed in total, but the need for three editions, together with the large circulation figures of *Lloyd's Weekly News* itself, suggest that it was immensely popular. *Lloyd's Weekly News* was a slightly scandalous Sunday newspaper with a particular penchant for crime, 'human interest', Royalty and sport. In 1912, its masthead boasted a circulation of 'over 1,450,000'. As such, its only real competitor in terms of sales was the equally popular *News of the World*.[6] 'The Deathless Story of the Titanic' was first advertised in the 28 April edition of *Lloyd's Weekly News* through a large, illustrated display advertisement which announced that the 40-page booklet was 'now ready'. It was the 'Thrilling narrative of the great tragedy of the sea which has startled the world' and was available through newsagents or by post, direct from the publishers.[7] A revised edition was advertised two weeks later, headed by a testimonial from 'a Cheltenham correspondent' who declared: '"The Deathless Story of the Titanic" is one of the finest bits of writing I have ever read.' The publishers went on to claim that the 'insistent demand' for the booklet had made it 'imperative' to produce a further supply. This revised edition formed 'one complete, vivid and haunting narrative'. Indeed, it formed 'a memento which should be treasured by all who recognise that the pride of race has been amply justified by the bravery of the lost heroes.'[8] Further advertisements were published in each of the two following weeks.[9] Even when taking the publisher's hyperbole into account, the publication of three editions, its advertisement over a five-week period, and the large base sales of *Lloyd's Weekly News* itself suggests that a huge number of 'The Deathless Story of the Titanic' were indeed produced and sold. This in turn suggests that the tone and content of the publication met with public approval and reflected the views of a large numbers of ordinary people in late Edwardian Britain.

The *Daily Graphic* special (plate II) was published on Saturday, 20 April 1912, at a cover price of a penny. It comprised 20 pages and 90 illustrations.[10] Although more modular and typically newspaper-like in its format, it was similar in both tone and content to 'The Deathless Story of the Titanic'. The *Titanic* alone appeared on the front cover, an artist's impression of the liner steaming through an ice-field at night, the image surrounded by a black double-border as a sign of mourning. There were photo features on 'Some of the Titanic's Notable Passengers' and rhetorical prose on 'The Ocean Grave of the Titanic'. A cutaway drawing showed the *Titanic* in technical detail, while a photo montage compared a typical north Atlantic iceberg to the size of St Paul's Cathedral. Both special editions dwelled not on the possible blame and recriminations for the disaster, but chose, rather, to celebrate the deeds of heroism which they reported to have accompanied it. As a daily newspaper, the *Graphic* was more sober in tone than *Lloyd's Weekly News*, but its focus on illustration nevertheless reveals it as a deliberately popular publication. Circulation was in the region of 40,000 copies a day.[11] The first advertisement for the *Titanic* 'In Memoriam Number' appeared in the main paper on 20 April 1912. It had been prepared, claimed the publishers, 'to meet the wishes of the large number of persons who wish to retain a permanent memorial of the tragedy'. It was available through booksellers and newsagents.[12] A similar advertisement was published the following Monday.[13]

The second group among the popular cultural materials comprises the books which were specially (and hurriedly) published in the wake of the disaster. These can be broken down into two further subgroups. First among these are the survivors' accounts, notably Lawrence Beesley's *The Loss of the RMS Titanic: Its Story and Its Lessons*,[14] and Colonel Archibald Gracie's *The Truth About the Titanic*.[15] Beesley, a second-class passenger, was a Cambridge

University graduate who had become a science master at Dulwich College before selecting the *Titanic* for his first trans-Atlantic voyage at the age of 36. He proved an acute and reliable witness to the disaster, sending carefully prepared – and much quoted – statements to the press immediately after his rescue, and then compiling and expanding upon his thoughts in his book, published in both London and Boston, the same year. Despite Beesley's determined attempts at objectivity, his book nevertheless remains, of course, very much rooted in the attitudes and assumptions common to the vast majority of other commentators on the disaster. Archibald Gracie, travelling first-class, was an American amateur military historian with an appetite for research and an eye for detail. Similarly, Colonel Gracie, despite his assiduous detective work, remains very much a figure of the late Edwardian era.[16] Both these volumes, therefore, are valuable to the cultural historian in ways, perhaps, unintended by their authors.

The second sub-group of books hastily published in 1912 were those by third parties not involved in the disaster but happy to benefit commercially from the enormous public interest in it. These were more numerous in the United States than in England,[17] and frequently contained glaring inaccuracies in both the text and in the graphic 'artist's impressions' of the sinking. More reliable was Filson Young's British publication *Titanic* (plate III).[18] Young (1876–1938)[19] was a prolific writer of books on topics as varied as Christopher Columbus, Wagnerian opera and Irish independence. His darkly rhetorical *Titanic* was completed in May 1912 and published so quickly that a copy was received at the Cambridge University Library (for example) by 14 June. Young's book tells the story of the lost liner from ominous beginning to dramatic end. It is so heavily laden with cultural pronouncement that it remains an invaluable source for the scholar in search of attitudes not only to the *Titanic* but also to much else in Britain at the time.

The importance of picture postcards in late Edwardian popular culture may strike the contemporary reader as somewhat surprising. However, this third category provides a broad and useful insight into perceptions and representations of the *Titanic* at the time. In the days before widespread domestic use of the telephone, postcards provided a cheap and easy way for people to communicate with short notes. Manufacturers eagerly responded to the demand, and the cards themselves became collectable (even in their own day) thanks to the wide variety of designs and topics covered.[20] Many of the cards thus bought, sent and collected are still extant, providing valuable source material for the researcher. *Titanic* postcards can themselves be sub-divided into two categories. First there are the postcards published before the *Titanic* sank. These are few in number and tend to be hugely sought after by collectors today. These, in turn tend to be of two types: those showing the *Titanic* under construction (many of them published by Hurst & Co. or Walton of Belfast), and those pub-licizing the ship once complete. Postcards depicting all the major liners of the day were widely available, both on board and on shore, no matter how seemingly distant from the sea. By far the greater number of *Titanic* postcards, however, were published after the disaster. Again, it may strike the contemporary reader as strange that so many people would buy and send postcards depicting an accident in which nearly 1,500 people died, but it certainly was the case in 1912–14. Some of these cards carried images of the ship, overprinted with details of the disaster (plate IV). Others celebrated the bravery of the captain, crew or the musicians on board. A widely published series of six postcards by Bamforth & Co. Ltd, of Holmfirth, West Yorkshire, depicted angels weeping over a sinking *Titanic*, accompa-nied by verses from the hymn supposed to have been played as the ship went down. Cards such as these were produced in such numbers that they are relatively easily available (at a price) from collectors' fairs today.

Just as postcards pre-dated the general use of the telephone, sheet music pre-dated the home stereo system and the radio request show. This provides our fourth category of popular cultural *Titanic* texts. The Lawrence Wright Music Company of London, for example, pro-duced both 'Be British!' (a 'descriptive song and recitation', dedicated to the 'gallant ill fated crew of the "Titanic"')[21] and 'The Wreck of the Titanic' (plate V), a 'descriptive musical sketch for the piano'. E. Marks and & Son published 'The Ship that Will Never Return',[22] while Rossi and Spinelli produced 'The Band Was Playing as the Ship Went Down',[23] as part of their 'favourite edition of song successes sung by all the best artistes with enormous success'.

Statues and memorials to the *Titanic* provide our fifth category of popular cultural texts. The two largest and most impressive of these are to be found in Southampton and at Lichfield, in Staffordshire. The Southampton memorial is to the engineers of the *Titanic*, all of whom died in the disaster and are believed to have remained at their posts, below decks, keeping the steam vented and the lights burning as the ship went down. The memorial, sited at East Park, is dominated by an angel with arms and wings outstretched. Two engineers are depicted at work, and the names of all those who died are engraved into the stone. One hundred thousand people are estimated to have attended the unveiling ceremony on 22 April 1914. As the port from which the *Titanic* set sail, and which provided so many of its crew, it is not surprising that Southampton is also home to six additional (and smaller) *Titanic* memorials.[24]

The choice of Lichfield for the location of the statue to Captain Smith of the *Titanic* is rather more difficult to explain. Following the disaster, a group of the captain's more influential friends and acquaintances subscribed to a large work, commissioned from the sculptress Lady Kathleen Scott, widow of the late Polar explorer. The bronze statue (plate VI) is 7 feet, 8 inches high, stands on a base of Cornish granite, and is sited at Beacon Park, just across from the city's cathedral. Officially, Lichfield was chosen as 'being about half-way between Liverpool and London'[25] (Liverpool was the *Titanic's* official port of registry). Lichfield was also (somewhat bafflingly) argued to be 'convenient alike to British and American subscribers'[26] and was certainly a city within the county of the captain's birth. Captain Smith was actually born at Hanley, Stoke-on-Trent. Hanley was not chosen, the memorial appeal secretary F.S. Stevenson explained, because it already had a memorial tablet in the Town Hall, and because in addition to its allegedly greater accessibility, Lichfield was further considered: 'in other respects also more suitable'.[27] Exactly what these 'other respects' were was never disclosed. It is possible that the committee considered the ancient cathedral city to be a more decorous location than industrial Hanley. Certainly, the decision smacks of being arrived at as a compromise by a committee. It remains possible, however, that public enthusiasm for the *Titanic* was wearing thin by July 1914, when the statue was officially unveiled. Tellingly, the tablet affixed to the granite plinth, while extolling the personal virtues of Smith himself, mentioned nothing whatsoever about his connection with the *Titanic*.

The sixth category, that of *Titanic* ephemera, includes a 78 rpm record and a memorial paper handkerchief. The record, released in 1912, features two specially written songs: 'Be British' and 'Stand to Your Post' 'In remembrance of the "Titanic"'.[28] Both songs praised the heroism of captain and crew, and urged listeners to donate money to their surviving relatives. 'Be British' concludes with the exhortation: 'Show that you are willing/ with a penny or a shilling/ for those they've left behind!'[29] 'Stand to Your Post', includes the line: 'They died like heroes true/ Now something we must do/ For the wives and little ones

they left behind them.'[30] It is not stated whether or not any of the proceeds from either the printed or recorded versions of these songs were
intended to be donated to the causes for which they encouraged
others to give support. The release of any kind of 'charity' record as
early as 1912 does serve to put the much publicized charity records of
the 1980s and 1990s into an interesting historical perspective,
however.

The memorial paper handkerchief was produced by the Palatine
Printing Company of Wigan, Lancashire, but distributed further
afield. It was block-printed with dogwood blossoms in pink and gold,
and issued 'In Memory of the Captain, Crew and Passengers who lost
their lives by the Wreck of the Titanic.'[31] An image of the ship is
flanked by sorrowful verses, and a prose description of the disaster
follows. Messages of sympathy from the King and Queen are concluded with a 'local list of crew' and a quotation from the hymn: 'God
Moves in a Mysterious Way'. Again, it is not stated whether any proceeds were intended for charity, but the telephone number of the
printing company is clearly given.

The seventh and final group among the 1912–14 *Titanic* popular
cultural texts comprises souvenir literature designed to accompany
commemorative and memorial events. The most important among
these are the Royal Opera House, Covent Garden souvenir programme for the Titanic Disaster Fund Matinée of 14 May 1912,[32] the
Royal Albert Hall Titanic Band Memorial Concert programme for
24 May 1912,[33] and the pamphlet: '"Be British" Captain E.J. Smith
Memorial: A Souvenir of July 29th, 1914'.[34] The Royal Opera programme contained poetry including Thomas Hardy's specially-written
poem 'The Convergence of the Twain', while the 'Be British' souvenir
booklet, published to mark the statue unveiling at Lichfield, contained
tributes from many prominent public figures and the full texts of stir-
ring addresses given by Admiral Lord Charles Beresford and
Millicent, Duchess of Sutherland. The ceremony took place under the
foreboding shadow of the First World War, and provides a natural
break at which to conclude a study of the popular material. Practically
nothing was then published on the *Titanic* for the next 41 years.[35]

We can now return to our examination of attitudes towards men,
manliness, women and gender issues as encoded in the late Edwardian
popular cultural texts on the *Titanic* disaster. We recall from Harold
Begbie's poem (which introduced Gibbs's 'The Deathless Story of the
Titanic'), that those who went down with the *Titanic* died 'like men'.[36]
It is an attitude echoed by a memorial postcard, published by Joe

Dixon of Hull.[37] According to the 'Be British' record, the 'men behaved like men should do'.[38] Gibbs himself reported that they did their 'manly duty'[39] and responded to the old traditions of 'manhood',[40] as did James Adamson in a memorial booklet to the *Titanic*'s engineers.[41] What exactly did it mean, though, to have behaved and died 'like men'? What precisely is implied by 'manhood' and 'manly duty'? The popular cultural texts are deeply revealing.

'As long as the sons of men read the history of heroism,' wrote Philip Gibbs, 'so will this story be remembered.'[42] The men of the *Titanic* were hailed as heroes across the entire spectrum of the popular cultural texts, from memorial editions to songs, postcards and statues. Indeed, the words 'hero' and 'heroism' were bandied about so freely that it is only possible here to give selected examples. Gibbs described the whole *Titanic* saga as 'the drama of heroism' in 'The Deathless Story of the Titanic',[43] while B. Scott's recorded composition 'Stand to Your Post' included the lines: 'They died like heroes true/ Now something we must do/ For the wives and little ones they left behind them.'[44] The souvenir booklet to the unveiling of the statue to Captain Smith included a testimonial from one Ernest Thompson to 'the men who left an undying record of peace time heroism',[45] while the inscription on the Southampton memorial to the *Titanic* engineers also commends the 'heroism' of these men.[46] The honour of being called a 'hero' was not reserved for any particular group of men aboard. 'Heroes All' boasted one 'In Memoriam' postcard to 'Capt. Smith Officers Crew and Passengers' of the *Titanic*.[47] And as one surviving passenger was quoted in the *Daily Graphic* 'In Memoriam' special issue: 'Every man of them was a hero.'[48] 'All heroes, every one,' intoned the baritone Ernest Gray.[49] Indeed, it seemed as though one had only to be present on the *Titanic* to be dubbed a hero.[50]

Was it necessary, therefore, to have actually *done* something during the sinking to be hailed as a hero? No. Simply being there was usually enough. When one examines the texts to find specific examples of heroism, one finds that most of these involved what we might describe as passive, rather than active, heroism.

One notable exception, however, must be noted: the death of Captain Smith. There are five versions of the death of Captain Smith[51] in the myth of the *Titanic*, but only one of them involves active heroism. This is the version which has him saving a small child before refusing to save his own life. According to 'The Deathless Story of the Titanic', the captain remained on his bridge until the last possible moment, before being removed from it by the icy and encroaching seas. A strong swimmer, he remained alive, spotted a lifeboat and

> swam up to it, supporting a baby on his left arm and swimming with his right.
>
> 'Take the child!' he gasped.
>
> A dozen hands reached forth to grasp the baby which was taken into the boat. They tried to pull the captain into the boat, but he refused. 'What became of Murdoch?' he asked.
>
> When someone answered that he was dead, 'the captain', said Mr. Williams, 'released his grasp of the gunwale and slowly sank before our eyes'.[52]

The death of Captain Smith, concluded Gibbs, was 'sublime in its heroism'.[53] But what did the others do to earn the same accolade? For the most part, their heroism was passive rather than active. They were hailed as heroes not because of what they actively did to help others at the time of the sinking, but because of the way in which they faced their own fate.

At one end of the spectrum, this passive heroism could nevertheless be described as constructive in that it involved self-sacrifice, and this particularly revolved around the now celebrated lack of lifeboats on board the *Titanic*. The *Titanic* carried only 16 lifeboats, and even if they had been sent away full (which they weren't), they would have contained space for only a little over half the people on board. As the *Titanic* began to sink, it became increasingly clear that many would have to remain behind. And as celebrated in the myth, it was the edict 'women and children first' which decided who was to be saved.

That such an order was both given and obeyed is undisputed and indeed celebrated in the late Edwardian texts. It was, they all agreed, not only the noble but, indeed, the natural thing to do. 'Women and children first!'[54] reported Gibbs in 'The Deathless Story of the Titanic'. It was, he continued, an order given 'according to the old law of the sea in time of shipwreck, according to what Second Officer Lightoller called "the law of human nature"'.[55] Filson Young, in his hastily published book *Titanic*, was in full agreement: 'At last a boat was cleared and the order given, "Women and children first."' The officers, he said, had revolvers in their hands ready to prevent a rush, but there was none.[56] It was, nevertheless, a rule 'rigidly enforced by the officers'.[57] The publishers of the memorial paper handkerchief confidently stated that 'The lifeboats were occupied almost exclusively by women and children',[58] while, according to Gibbs, the 'heroic' merchant Mr Isidor Straus, when urged to save himself, responded: 'Not as long as a single women remains on board.'[59] The popular music of the time was particularly impressed by such behaviour, which again was both celebrated and yet expected. Scott's recorded song proclaimed: 'The order came to lower the boats/ And one thing had to be:/ The women and the children first,/ For that's the way at sea'.[60] F.V. St Clair's song 'The Ship That Will Never Return' boasted 'The women and children the first for the boats –/And sailors knew how to obey',[61] while Pelham and Wright (on both record and sheet-music) included the couplet: 'Captain and crew when they knew the worst/ Saving the women and children first'.[62] Haydon Augarde's descriptive piano sketch 'The Wreck of the Titanic' had a section titled: '"Lower the Boats!" The Captain Cried! "Women and Children First!"'[63] Indeed, the captain, according to the *Daily Graphic* 'In Memoriam' number, was as good as his word. A fireman who claimed to have been on the bridge towards the end was quoted as saying: 'How did he act on the bridge while I was there? Always directing the lowering of the boats himself, and he was always shouting, "Women and children first."'[64]

The self-sacrifice of the men in favour of the women was duly praised. 'The Brave Dead', announced a headline in the *Daily Graphic* special edition: 'Women Saved by Men's Sacrifice'.[65] Gibbs was (predictably) more colourful in his praise: 'every little act which was revealed momentarily on those decks shines with the bright light of self-sacrifice'.[66] Scott dedicated his *Titanic* record 'in proud remembrance of those who sacrificed their lives for others',[67] while the Dean of Lichfield Cathedral, quoted in the souvenir to the captain's statue unveiling, praised the 'self-abnegation and heroism' of everyone concerned.[68] An 'In Memoriam' postcard and the Southampton memorial to the engineers both used the same biblical quotation: 'Greater Love Hath No Man Than This, That a Man Lay Down His Life For His Friends' (John 15: 13).[69]

Yet as we observe the praise for the men and their heroic self-sacrifice, we cannot help but notice that there are no obvious dividing lines between praise for what they did and praise for the way in which they did it. There is often an imperceptibly smooth transition between praise for action, praise for behaviour and praise for manner. One could often display manly heroism simply by 'taking it well' and dying with dignity.

Examples of the manly, late Edwardian 'stiff upper lip' abound in the popular cultural texts. Again, it is not of prime concern to us

whether or not these incidents actually took place, for in interpreting the *Titanic* as modern myth, it is enough that these stories
were solemnly related and the behaviour of the *dramatis personae*
commended.

It is with the filling and lowering of the lifeboats that the majority of
the 'stiff upper lip' behaviour is described as having taken place. 'All
this time there was no trace of any disorder,' reported the *Daily
Graphic* 'In Memoriam' edition:

> When the boats had cleared from the doomed vessel's towering
> sides there was nothing the passengers who remained could do but
> await death bravely and unflinchingly, which they did.[70]

The captain, according to the memorial handkerchief, 'was seen by
those in the boats to remain on the bridge of the ship calmly awaiting
death',[71] while Second Officer Lightoller, quoted in 'The Deathless
Story of the Titanic', reported that 'the men stood as quietly as if they
were in church'.[72] Filson Young encapsulates the mood:

> There was no theatrical heroism, no striking of attitudes ... they
> simply stood about the decks, smoking cigarettes, talking to one
> another, and waiting for the hour to strike. There is nothing so
> hard, nothing so entirely dignified, as to be silent and quiet in the
> face of an approaching horror.[73]

A much related story in this vein is the death of the millionaire
J.J. Astor. According to a steward quoted by Gibbs, Colonel Astor
helped load the women into the lifeboats, including his new wife,
Madeleine. Astor promised her that he would meet her later in New
York, and they exchanged an 'affectionate farewell, but no more
affectionate than that of a couple separating just for a week instead
of eternity'. Madeleine, we recall, was five months pregnant. Gibbs
continues:

> As the boats with the women went away from the side of the ship
> Colonel Astor stood for a moment at the salute. He called out a
> last farewell to his wife: 'Good-bye, dearie. I will join you later.'
> Then he turned calmly and lit a cigarette, and leaned over the rails,
> staring though the darkness.[74]

Such conduct was, of course, celebrated in song. 'What a glorious
thing it is to know', sang Ernest Gray in Pelham and Wright's
recorded song, 'When danger's hour was nigh/ When the mighty liner
sank to her rest/ Our men knew how to die'.[75] Knowing 'how to die'

was clearly an important part of manly heroism, whether that heroism was active or passive, and even if it involved no more then lighting a cigarette. Our grief, reported the *Daily Graphic*, was tempered by the thought that 'the men died as we would have them die, as we would like to have died ourselves'.[76]

In facing death in such an ideal manner, it was imperative that no man should cry. Tears and manliness were totally incompatible, no matter how great the temptation. The lip of Captain Smith, according to a crewman quoted in the *Daily Graphic* 'In Memoriam' number, remained particularly stiff even in the face of enormous adversity. As the rising water reached the captain's knees, reported a crewman:

> He gave one look around, his face firm, and his lips hard set. He looked as if he might be trying to hold back the tears, as he thought of the doomed ship. I felt mightily like crying myself as I looked at him.[77]

But of course, neither of them did. Tears, sobbing and hysterics were expected of women, not men. For example, Lawrence Beesley, the graduate and schoolmaster quoted in the *Daily Graphic* special edition, said that one generally pictured 'women sobbing hysterically' at such times,[78] while the same paper did indeed report the subsequent 'sobbing of the women at the street corners of Southampton'.[79] According to St Clair's song: 'Mothers sobbed in pray'r/ As they parted from their loved ones there',[80] but that was mild compared with the women described by Gibbs and Young. According to Gibbs, some of the female survivors of the disaster were 'mad with grief',[81] while Young not only had some of them 'limp with fright' at the loading of the lifeboats,[82] but when they were taken aboard the rescue ship, 'Bedlam broke loose'. Some of the women were in 'shrieking hysterics', while others 'went clean out of their minds; one or two died in the very moment of rescue'.[83] Clearly, women were not expected to behave like 'men': quite different standards were both expected and described.

'Women and children first' is a very potent ingredient of the *Titanic* myth. The fact that it is a part of the myth, however (as we recall from Chapter 2) is not to say that it is also a falsehood. On the contrary, the statistics do indeed show that a considerably greater number of women and children got into the lifeboats than did men. The evidence presented to Lord Mersey's inquiry suggested that a total of 704 women and children entered the lifeboats, compared with only 43 male passengers.[84] The order to place women and children in the boats was given at approximately 12:30 am,[85] and Mersey remained satisfied that 'the officers did their work very well and without any thought for themselves.'[86]

Those men who did obtain places in the boats, and thus survived the sinking, found themselves in many places having publicly to defend their action – even though a large number of the boats went away with empty places. Most prominent among these was J. Bruce Ismay, managing director of the White Star Line. His case is a particularly interesting one. Ismay was the chief witness on the first day of the American inquiry into the disaster, which began in New York at the Waldorf Astoria hotel on 19 April. He came in for sharp and hostile questioning from the inquiry chairman Senator William Alden Smith. Smith was not alone in his criticism of Ismay, however. The American press took an equally unsympathetic stance, and he earned the soubriquet 'J. Brute Ismay'.[87] According to Wade, he promptly became 'the Ahab of the captains of industry'.[88] Colonel Archibald Gracie even went so far as to declare in his own survivor's account that 'so long as there was a soul that could be saved, the obligation lay upon Mr. Ismay that one person and not he should have been in the boat.'[89] It was common knowledge that the captain and the designer of the *Titanic* had both gone down with their ship, having made no apparent attempt to save themselves. If anyone had a moral obligation to go down with the ship, American public opinion had it, it was the chairman. Ismay, however, found a place on the last lifeboat to leave the starboard side. The hostility towards Ismay surfaced again at the British inquiry, prompting Lord Mersey to go so far as to comment upon it in his official inquiry report 'for fear that my silence might be misunderstood'. Ismay, he concluded, had helped many other passengers, and on finding room in collapsible boat 'C' with no others waiting, jumped in. Mersey did not agree that Ismay was under any 'moral obligation' to remain on board until the ship foundered. 'Had he not jumped in he would merely have added one more life, namely, his own, to the number of those lost.'[90] Yet while both the American press and certain elements at the British inquiry were openly hostile to Ismay, the British popular cultural texts were much more sympathetic. The *Daily Graphic* 'In Memoriam' number ignored the issue altogether.[91] Gibbs' 'The Deathless Story of the Titanic', however, leapt to his defence. As the ship began to sink, it reported, Ismay was to be seen 'hiding his despair by helping the women to the boats'. He was 'a tragic figure' who had seen his dream ripped apart by an iceberg on the liner's maiden voyage. As the last boat was being lowered, 'the officers called out to see if there were any more women to go. No woman answered, and there were no passengers on the deck.' Ismay climbed into the final boat.[92] Filson Young, too, hurried to the defence of Ismay. 'Mr Ismay', he reported, 'was among the foremost in helping to sort out the women and children and get them expeditiously packed into the boats', despite the fact that he had 'a burden of misery and responsibility on his heart that we cannot measure'.[93] It was not, however, a burden which he bore with shame 'for he had no cause for shame'.[94] Rather, he bore it 'with a dignity which was proof against even the bitter injustice of which he was the victim in the days that followed'. There had been pity for all, said Young, except for this man who, 'of all the ragged remnant that walked back to life down the *Carpathia*'s gangway, had perhaps the most need of pity'.[95]

The contrast between the treatment of Ismay in the United States and in Britain serves further to underline the crucial point we have already begun to note concerning the *Titanic* in late Edwardian popular culture. While the Americans were keen to attribute blame for what was, after all, a dreadful loss of life under appalling circumstances, the British were grimly determined to play up the heroism of all concerned. It had, after all, to be a triumph, and not a tragedy. The awkward behaviour of Ismay (whom some claimed even to have had some sort of a breakdown after the disaster)[96] had to be explained away in order to save spoiling the preferred story.

The behaviour of J. Bruce Ismay is not the only issue to have been almost studiously avoided in the British popular texts. Reading them, one would be not in the least bit aware that the drama of 'women and children first' took place against the background of increasingly militant suffragist claims for equal rights for women. The suffrage movement in Britain had taken formal political shape with the formation of the Women's Franchise League in 1889 and particularly the Women's Social and Political Union in 1903. Its founder Emmeline Pankhurst was arrested and imprisoned several times between 1908 and 1913. Among the tactics advocated by the movement were arson and hunger strikes. Agitation reached a visible peak when one suffragette, Emily Wilding Davison, threw herself to her death beneath the hooves of the King's horse at the Epsom Derby in 1913. Against such a background, it would be reasonable to expect that the concept of 'women and children first' would have provoked animated discussion among both supporters and opponents of the women's suffrage movement. In a fair and equal world, would not both men and women have taken their chances getting into the lifeboats? How should a suffragette – or at least a female suffragist – have reacted if offered a place in a boat simply on account of her gender? Did priority in the lifeboats amount to the preferred status of women, or was it, rather, a complex articulation of their presumed inability to fend for themselves? How could women continue to take violent action in search of the vote when men had responded at a time of crisis by giving them their lives? Questions such as these were never asked, let alone answered, in the British, late Edwardian *Titanic* texts. It is as though the suffragettes – to say nothing of the issues they so visibly raised – had never existed.[97]

Once again, it was the Americans who were prepared to raise the awkward issues. For example, the Reverend Dr Leighton Parks of St Bartholomew's Church, New York City was moved publicly to observe: 'Those women who go about shrieking for their "rights" want something very different.'[98] The *St Louis Post-Dispatch* printed a poem comparing the cries of 'Votes for Women!' with those of 'Boats for Women!' and finding the latter considerably more natural and commendable.[99] On the other side of the debate, Harriot Stanton Blatch, President of the American Women's Political Union, declared that since it was men who had drafted the maritime regulations, it was quite right that men should have gone down with the ship. Asked if her position would change should women be given the vote, she riposted: 'Then we would have laws requiring plenty of lifeboats.'[100] The British, by comparison, were silent. It is as though, just as with the case of J. Bruce Ismay, an uncomfortable comparison of 'Votes for Women' with 'Boats for Women' would have spoiled the story.

There is a final angle to the gender analysis of the *Titanic* in popular culture which is in danger of being overlooked because, as Roland Barthes might have put it, it seemingly 'goes without saying'.[101] As Barthes would agree, however, 'what goes without saying' is often just as eloquent as that which is most deliberately stated. In this study, I have deliberately referred to the *Titanic* is 'it' rather than the conventional 'she'. If the reader has found this somewhat jarring, then my point has already been made: while it might seem to 'go without saying' that all ships are feminine and should be referred to as 'she', this is in fact neither natural nor inevitable. Rather, it is a cultural construct which in the current context is particularly revealing. The English language, unlike many others, does not normally attribute gender to objects. The case of ships, therefore, is a notable exception. In English usage – and certainly in late Edwardian British popular culture – however, this gendering does not merely limit itself to the grammatical use of the feminine pronoun 'she'. Rather, the idea of the ship itself is endowed with 'female' or even 'feminine' attributes. It follows, then, that in all the *Titanic* popular texts of the period, ships are without exception referred to as 'she' and that the *Titanic* itself is not merely gendered but also personified in keeping with the assumptions of the day. According to the *Daily Graphic* special number, for example, people took 'joy in her strength and beauty' as the ship set sail from Southampton.[102] Both Gibbs and the *Graphic* refer to the *Titanic*'s 'sister' the *Olympic*.[103] It is telling that in both instances neither uses the term 'sister ship' but merely the word 'sister', indicating that the *Titanic* has become a person rather than just a mechanical object. It is in this same way that the popular texts proceed, in keeping with the common practice of the day, to endow the *Titanic* with body parts rather than mechanical features. Thus, the *Titanic* has a head, side, bottom and even bowels.[104] It follows, then, that when the *Titanic* is damaged in collision with the iceberg, it feels physical pain. After the initial shock, it can be found 'lying so quietly',[105] but in its 'last agony' one 'saw her stagger and reel above the waters'.[106] Finally, the ship descends not simply to the bottom of the sea, but, rather, to its 'grave'.[107]

We can see from examples such as these that the *Titanic* is very much represented as natural rather than mechanical. Its gender is definitely female and in some places almost animal with all its lying, staggering and reeling. In the imagery of the 'maiden voyage', however, the *Titanic* is human, nubile – and vulnerable. Again, there are many who may take it as read that ships are female and have 'maiden' voyages, but just as with the gendering of objects, this is by no means inevitable. The image of a mechanical object as a young woman about to undergo her first sexual experience is worthy of particular note. Young described the beginning of the *Titanic*'s 'maiden' voyage as it set from Southampton. There was no shortage of eager assistance when it came to cajoling the hesitant young vessel in its first steps towards womanhood:

> Small enough was her experience of the sea that day. Many hands had handled her; many tugs had fussed about her, pulling and pushing her this way and that as she was manoeuvred into the waters ...[108]

One is put in mind of Marcel Duchamp's 'The Bride Stripped Bare by her Bachelors, Even'[109] or indeed the 'seduction' scene from Bertolucci's 'The Last Emperor' in which the hands of numerous and previously unseen courtiers emerge to help the emperor undress a beautiful and inexperienced young woman.[110] The *Titanic*'s 'right of passage' quickly becomes more of a rape than a seduction, however. The *Titanic*, reported the *Graphic* 'In Memoriam' number, 'met at her maiden issue with the sea a challenge that broke her utterly'.[111] It is not simply that the *Titanic*'s metaphorical hymen had been 'broken' as part of her maiden experience, it had been an act of extreme sexual violence: 'She had been struck by an iceberg; she had been rent.'[112]

The *Titanic* here, then, is a strong, beautiful and appropriately inexperienced virgin, eagerly (perhaps too eagerly) assisted on her passage into womanhood and ultimately raped and utterly broken as a result. In this way, an analysis of the popular texts produces a collection of images which are revealing not only of late Edwardian representations of the *Titanic*, but also of late Edwardian notions of women. It is not sufficient simply to understand the *Titanic* as pretty, passive and ill-used, however. The popular texts also reveal something of a dichotomy in their representation of the *Titanic* as a woman, for rather like the character of 'Maria' in Fritz Lang's early expressionist film 'Metropolis' of 1927, she has something of a dual personality. On the one hand she is virginal, natural and pure, but on the other, she is a man-made 'monster', an unnatural being, an affront against nature.

Much of the darker *Titanic* imagery in the popular texts casts the ship as a kind of golem[113] or female version of Frankenstein's 'monster.' Just as the eponymous hero of Mary Shelley's nineteenth-century novel[114] had the audacity to create life through scientific experiment, Bruce Ismay, according to Young, was the figurehead of 'that pride and power which had given being to the Titanic'.[115] In both cases the monster, of course, was ultimately to destroy its creator. In the case of the *Titanic*, therefore, the phrase 'given being' is particularly important. It implies not only that the mechanical *Titanic* has (again) been personified – it is a 'being' rather than an object – but it suggests also that this gift of life has been given by a man and not by God. It is, in the late Edwardian mindset, an affront against nature indeed. Just as with the golem or the monster of Dr Frankenstein, no good can be expected to result.

Young's *Titanic* begins with a vivid description of the 'unnatural birth' of the ship. It is a description which is almost gothic in its power and intensity. 'It was the shape of a ship,' he declares, but

> a ship so monstrous and unthinkable that it towered high over the buildings and dwarfed the very mountains beside the water. It seemed like some impious blasphemy that man should fashion this

most monstrous and ponderable of all his creations into the likeness of a thing that could float upon the waters.[116]

Just like Frankenstein's unnatural creation, then, Young's *Titanic* is
'monstrous and unthinkable'. It is so vast that it dwarfs mountains
and, worst of all, man had committed some 'impious blasphemy' in
creating this monster in the likeness of something else. It is in the likeness of something that could 'float upon the waters', but ultimately it
is only a likeness and inevitably doomed to sink to the very bottom.
Young leaves us in no doubt what he thinks of this, for the night-
marish *Titanic*, which while it took both the shape and properties of a
ship 'in hideous exaggeration', was in fact 'like an evil dream'.[117]

The launching of the *Titanic* gives Young further scope for his
'monster' imagery. The slipway was constructed in such a way as 'to
support the bulk of a monster when she was moved',[118] and the whole
apparatus was designed to 'set this monster afloat'.[119] Tellingly, Young
frequently refers to the emerging ship as 'it' in his first, dark, chapter.
This is, as we have come to understand, deliberately jarring against the
convention of referring to ships as 'she'. By the time the 'monster ship'
begins to move, it is even referred to as a 'thing': 'And then, while men
held their breath, the whole thing moved, moved bodily ...'[120] Men,
then, had given being not simply to a ship but to a 'thing' which moved
'bodily'. Finally, Young stresses that the *Titanic* was not christened at
its launch. Although it was never in fact White Star Line practice to
christen ships, Young portrays the *Titanic*'s case as remarkable and
significant. As an unchristened ship, the *Titanic* is conceived, delivered
and remains in darkness. It is not received into the family of Christ;
it is a ship – a 'thing', even – without God. Young reveals its name:
Titanic only in the chapter's final sentence.[121]

On the one hand, then, the *Titanic* is a beautiful and virginal young
woman; on the other, it is an unnatural she-monster; in the worst
extreme, even a godless 'thing'. How can a ship so seamlessly move
along a sliding scale from virgin to 'thing'? The answer can be found
to lie in late Edwardian notions of gender and the natural. At one end
of the scale, ships are automatically presumed to be female and thus
beautiful. Young and 'inexperienced' ships are consequently presumed to be vulnerable and virginal. As a 'she' she can be controlled
by men; if she performs spiritedly or unpredictably, she is simply
behaving like a capricious woman. With a firm combination of coer-
cion, strength and control, however, she can be brought back under
the domination of men.[122] Yet if the *Titanic* is thought in any way to

deviate from such feminine stereotypes (by being huge or powerful) this is a threat to its feminine status. Consequently, 'she' is depicted as behaving unnaturally or even perversely. Again, a cultural comparison can be made with the dual characters of Maria in Lang's 'Metropolis'. The 'good' Maria is seen in the company of children against a background of nature. She dresses in white, is sexually innocent and obedient to men. The 'bad' Maria, on the other hand, is vampish and aggressive. She lives in the world of darkness and machinery. She aims to lead man and their world astray and is, inevitably, exposed as a robot, the unnatural construction of a 'mad' male engineer. In this way it is possible to see the *Titanic* as both the 'bad' and the 'good' Maria, representing either (or both) of the late Edwardian constructs of 'natural', 'unnatural', 'good' or 'bad' women. The gendering of the *Titanic* in late-Edwardian popular culture, then, is by no means culturally neutral.

In its 'worst' manifestation, though, the *Titanic* is not permitted even to be a 'bad' woman; the *Titanic* is an 'it', a 'monster', a 'thing'. In order to be at its most terrible, then, the *Titanic* must be stripped of its 'feminine' characteristics altogether. Again, the cultural resonance for this is strong. Lady Macbeth in Shakespeare's tragedy is represented as needing to be more of a 'man' than her husband in order to commit murder. She calls upon the spirits to 'unsex me here'. Only when the 'female' part of her is stripped away can her blood be thickened and she be filled with cruelty. There may be no compunctious visitings of female 'nature'.[123] She must, indeed, be 'unsexed' to the extent of killing her own smiling, suckling baby before she can perform the equally 'unnatural' act of a woman committing foul and ambitious murder. She needs to be unsexed, in other words, in order to behave unspeakably. It is exactly the same with the *Titanic*; she can be a 'good' woman or a 'bad' woman, but in her most dreadful manifestation, she must not even be a woman at all.

In its representation of men and women aboard the *Titanic*, and even in its representation of the *Titanic* as a woman itself, the myth of the *Titanic* reveals unspoken assumptions about gender roles and attitudes in late Edwardian culture. In its articulation of the 'natural' behaviour expected of women, a comparison with Jewish folklore, Shakespearean tragedy, Gothic literature and expressionist film suggests that the late Edwardians were not alone.

4 'We Shall Die Like Gentlemen'

If the males aboard the *Titanic* died like 'men', the most celebrated stories revolve around those who also died like 'gentlemen'. The ideal late Edwardian *Titanic* death, therefore, carries with it assumptions not only of gender but also of social class. According to the myth, it was among the upper and upper-middle classes that the virtues of 'manliness' were best exhibited.

Perhaps the finest example of 'gentlemanly' death on the *Titanic* is provided by the story of the American multi-millionaire Benjamin Guggenheim.[1] Guggenheim was a man whose family had made a fortune in mining and smelting. He boarded the *Titanic* at Cherbourg, and was travelling with his valet, Victor Giglio, and chauffeur, René Pernot. Guggenheim and the valet shared a first class suite, while the chauffeur travelled second class. Mrs Guggenheim remained in New York. Gibbs describes Guggenheim as 'a member of a family of capitalists',[2] and it is interesting to note that he does not use the term in any sort of derogatory sense. Indeed, describing one group among the first-class passengers, he speaks of wealth only with awe and admiration. These were 'Great merchants, the princes of trade, the controllers of the world's markets'.[3] He estimated the total wealth of one group of 'rich Americans' as at least £120 million.[4] Such people were what Leo Lowenthal was later to describe as 'idols of production', a group much admired by the general public in the years before the war.[5] These people were not merely immensely wealthy, however, for according to Gibbs' 'The Deathless Story of the Titanic': 'Not only wealth was represented here but intellectual ability and great qualities of character.'[6] Wealth, intellect and character, it seemed, went hand-in-hand. The Guggenheims, like the Astors, the Strauses, the Wideners and other passengers of that class, represented a great deal of both earned and inherited income. From a contemporary, left-leaning perspective, they were capitalists in the strongest sense of the word. Nowadays, those of huge and recent wealth (the *nouveaux riches*) are not necessarily thought of as being among the intellectual elite, nor necessarily being endowed with the most virtuous of characters. In the late Edwardian popular texts, however, wealth, intellect and character were deemed inseparable.

It is against such a background of social assumptions, therefore, that Gibbs narrates the story of Guggenheim himself. The lifeboats were being loaded with women and children and gradually sent away, according to 'the old rule of the sea'.[7] The ship's band was still playing (as will be discussed more fully in Chapter 6) and Guggenheim himself was offered a place in one of the boats. He refused, however, saying: 'No woman shall remain unsaved because I was a coward.' He gave Steward Etches a message for his wife, which was afterwards delivered: 'If I don't turn up, tell my wife I have done the best I could.'[8] Gibbs continues:

> He and a friend found time to return to their cabins and put on evening dress. When the steward expressed his amazement Mr. Guggenheim smiled and said, 'If we have to die, we will die like gentlemen.'[9]

And die he did, a 'gentleman' resplendent in the uniform of his class.[10]

Yet Guggenheim was not the only wealthy man reported to have died 'like a gentleman'. Robert Donnelly's *Titanic* song 'The Band Was Playing as the Ship Went Down' praises not one but all the 'men of great wealth who boldly faced death/ To help others reach home sweet home'.[11] To some extent, of course, it was easy for men such as Guggenheim to die 'like a gentleman'. He was a multi-millionaire from a privileged family; he was travelling first class, and so (naturally) had the necessary evening dress to hand in his stateroom. Gibbs, however, extends the mantle of 'gentlemanly' death to *everyone* who had faced death bravely. Their names would be 'written in gold'; they were those who, 'whatever their condition, died like noble gentlemen and ladies of quality'.[12] To some extent, this may all seem very democratic: to die like a gentleman wasn't simply a case of *looking* the part, like Guggenheim, it was also a matter of *acting* the part, like the men of various condition described by Gibbs. The telling word in Gibbs' phrase, 'died like noble gentlemen', therefore, might be 'like' as much as 'gentlemen'. Even if one wasn't actually a gentleman, that is to say a man of 'breeding', wealth and leisure, one could at least aspire to die as though one were.

An informative case is that of Captain Edward John Smith himself. Smith was born in a small terraced house, 51 Well Street in Hanley, Stoke-on-Trent, in 1850. His father was a manual worker in the pottery industry, while his mother kept a shop. He was educated at local schools, which he left at the age of 12[13] to become a steam hammer operator at a local forge. At 17 he left the Potteries district to join the Mercantile Marine, signing on to a sailing ship with the rank of 'boy'.[14] Smith, therefore, for all that he accomplished professionally, was not a 'gentleman' by birth. Nevertheless, at the ceremony to unveil his statue at Lichfield two years after his death, Admiral Lord Beresford described Captain Smith as a 'British gentleman'.[15] Again, this may seem surprisingly democratic for a late Edwardian England in which it was still possible officially to describe one's occupation as 'gentleman' if one had no need to work for a living. That any man could have acted 'like a gentleman' in the myth of the *Titanic* may seem to suggest that gentlemanliness was a status that could be achieved by action instead of merely by birth or (possibly) by wealth. Yet it would be misleading to take this literally, for two reasons. First, as we recall from Gibbs, some aboard the *Titanic* had died like gentleman 'whatever their condition', suggesting that although they had behaved *like* gentlemen, they still definitely were not. In this way, many of those who died 'like gentlemen' were in fact only 'honorary' gentlemen for this brief episode of high rhetorical drama. In reality, class mobility was finite.

The expression 'like a gentleman' is also revealing in a second way. Used approvingly as it is in the *Titanic* texts, it strongly implies that, in the eyes of people using the term, to be a gentleman was a very good thing. It is simile of comparison which holds the gentleman as the benchmark against which ideal behaviour should be measured. In this way, it reveals not only what people thought about those who died on the *Titanic*, but also – and on a broader cultural level – what they thought about gentlemen as a whole. To describe someone in this context as a 'gentleman', then, is to reveal cultural values beyond the *Titanic*. It is, further, a phrase whose use suggests that such standards of exemplary behaviour were culturally taken as given (or at the very least expected) among members of the gentlemanly class. Others had to work at it (perhaps even to die on the *Titanic* in the process), but gentlemen were born to it: it came naturally to them.

This equation of manly and heroic behaviour with social class did not end with mere gentlemanliness, however. The popular cultural texts on the sinking of the *Titanic* go even further; indeed, they proceed so far up the class scale as to equate heroic behaviour with gallantry, chivalry and indeed nobility. Admiral Beresford, quoted in Gibbs' 'The Deathless Story of the Titanic', praised the 'gallantry' of Captain Smith, together with his officers, seaman and passengers, all of whom did their 'manly duty'.[16] Speaking two years later at the statue unveiling and recorded in the 'Be British' souvenir, Beresford asserted that Smith's 'gallantry descended to the men under his command'.[17] Scott's recorded song, meanwhile, tells how the 'gallant crew soon realized/ The sea must be their tomb'.[18] And a black-edged postcard published in verse was produced: 'In sorrowful Memory of her gallant Crew'.[19]

Gibbs was particularly impressed with the 'chivalry' shown by the men of the *Titanic*. Indeed, 'every little act which was revealed momentarily on those decks shines with the bright light of self-sacrifice, of chivalry ...'[20] The memorial service subsequently held at St Paul's Cathedral, according to Gibbs, commemorated 'how brave men died, and how love and chivalry shone above the black terror of it all'.[21] Admiral Lord Beresford, reliably perhaps by now, described everyone's behaviour as 'chivalrous' in a letter to *The Times* (it was also reproduced by Gibbs),[22] and at the statue unveiling he particularly praised the 'chivalrous conduct' of Captain Smith.[23]

Equally of note is the way in which the 'noble' conduct or indeed even the 'nobility' of those on board is commended. The *Daily Graphic* praised those who had suffered a 'death so noble',[24] and even ran a sub-headline: 'The Noble Element in the Ocean Tragedy'.[25] Indeed, those who behaved so commendably had 'presented us with the most inspiring of spectacles – the inherent nobility of mankind'.[26] Gibbs, too, was struck by the nobility of it all in 'The Deathless Story of the Titanic'. Every act on board, he wrote, was one of 'noble dignity',[27] and those who died had done so 'like noble gentlemen'.[28] An 'In Memoriam' postcard recorded in verse that: 'The brave ship's noble captain/ To save every life vainly tried'.[29] The ceremonial unveiling of the statue to Captain Smith, as recorded in Stevenson's 'Be British' souvenir, was littered with similar references. Mr and Mrs John Thallon declared that Smith was 'so noble a man',[30] while John Sinclair Armstrong wrote of 'that noble man, whom we loved'.[31] Millicent, Duchess of Sutherland, told the gathering that Smith had 'died nobly at his post of duty',[32] While J.E. Hodder Williams wrote that all concerned had 'died well and nobly'.[33] Ernest Thompson Seton even went so far as to declare that those who died had left 'a standard of nobility that must forever have helpful results among all those who go by the waters'.[34]

Gentlemanliness, gallantry, chivalry and nobility are all associated with social class. This is not simply a matter of each word referring to class in itself. The terms are also connected through shared, common or overlapping assumptions (even to the degree of synonymity) with each other, and are even united through frequent juxtaposition in the *Titanic* texts. Finally, they also share a common, cultural connection in the idea of the medieval knight. A gentleman is someone who, even today, is entitled to bear arms. He is also a man of good breeding (a telling phrase, suggesting that class is inherited), of wealth, leisure and of chivalrous instincts; one who is gallant is chivalrous, brave, courteous and attentive to women. A gentleman, as Guggenheim showed, is frequently well-dressed. Gallantry itself involves both courtliness and dash. A chivalrous man is the ideal knight, courteous and gallant. He is devoted to the service of women. A noble man is illustrious by rank, title or birth, and usually belongs to the nobility itself. His character and ideals are equally lofty. We note, therefore, that not only does each word relate directly to high social class, but that each is repeatedly cross-referenced to the other: gallants are chivalrous and vice versa, for example. There is a chain of connected meanings, with class as the common link, especially by birth, rank, title, breeding and, occasionally, simple wealth. We note the connections demonstrated through juxtaposition in speeches such as Admiral Lord Beresford's:

> Captain Smith was an example of the very best type of British seaman and *British gentleman*. His bravery, his resolution, his *chivalrous* conduct, and his *gallantry* descended to the men under his command ... he was one of the examples of the best *class* of man you meet so frequently in the mercantile marine.[35] (my emphasis)

He was chivalrous, gallant and a gentleman of class. And of course, as we shall see in the next chapter, he was British.

These qualities, shared by the best of the men on the *Titanic*, can also be found in the traditional, mythical figure of the medieval knight.[36] The ideal knight, according to Arthurian romance, was chivalrous, gallant, courteous and attentive to women. To be courteous, of course, was to behave as though one was a courtier: a member of the king's court. They were elevated by the king and had the right to bear arms. They were, therefore, a social élite. In other words, the ideal medieval knight combined class with character. The two were inseparable. By comparison, to act 'churlishly' was to act like an ill-bred person the exact opposite of the knight in both breeding and behaviour. This is exactly the sort of cultural value we see revealed in the myth of the *Titanic*. Commenting on the first-class passenger list, we recall Gibbs reporting: 'Not only wealth was represented here, but intellectual ability and great qualities of character.'[37] It is as though they were synonymous. And again, by comparing those who died 'well' to those of (increasingly) high social class, the *Titanic* texts reveal temporal cultural values beyond those of the story of the *Titanic* itself.

Let us return, then, to Benjamin Guggenheim's celebrated gesture of changing into evening dress so that he could die like a gentleman. It can now be seen as a semiotic gesture *par excellence*. It was entirely symbolic, being of no intrinsic value or practical purpose whatsoever. Indeed, it was remarkably impractical, white tie and tails being entirely unsuitable for swimming and surviving in icy sea-water at dead of night. What it was, though, was an extremely theatrical and eloquent gesture which publicly and symbolically stated his dying allegiance to and membership of the upper class. He wore their clothes; he represented their values. He was like an Arthurian knight, resplendent in his (chivalric) arms as he died. By helping the women and refusing to get into a boat himself, he had already shown himself to be a (courtly) man. By changing into evening dress, he was now signifying himself to be a special kind of man: a *gentle*man. By pledging this class allegiance at the time of his death, he expressed his conviction that being a gentleman was an excellent thing to be. By telling the story in such a panegyric tone, the myth reveals that, in late Edwardian Britain, to be a gentleman was indeed an excellent thing to which to aspire.

Class consciousness was built not only into the social but also into the physical structure of the actual *Titanic*. From the outset the *Titanic* was conceived, as was the common practice of the day, with three distinct levels of accommodation, facilities and service on board: first, second and third class. This was neatly translated into upper-, middle- and lower-class passengers. And although the White Star Line claimed, not without some justification, that their second-class accommodation was equivalent to some of their competitors' first-class accommodation, the deliberate and significant distinctions between the different classes remained.

First-class passengers on the *Titanic* were accommodated in the choicest positions, on five levels from the upper to the promenade decks. These decks were at the top of the ship, provided plenty of open space for walking and recreation, and were close to facilities, including lifeboats (the significance of which will be discussed later). The first-class cabins (White Star preferred to call them 'staterooms') were located in the upper and most central portions of the ship. There was a special saloon for maids and valets on the shelter deck so that they could easily and quickly be summoned to service. The second-class accommodation was on the middle, upper and saloon decks of the *Titanic*: The second-class promenade was a whole deck lower than that for the first-class passengers, and the cabins were towards the rear

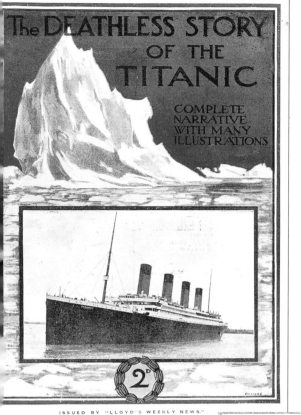

The DEATHLESS STORY
OF THE
TITANIC

COMPLETE
NARRATIVE
WITH MANY
ILLUSTRATIONS

2ᴰ

ISSUED BY "LLOYD'S WEEKLY NEWS."

I Front cover of 'The Deathless Story of the Titanic', published by *Lloyds Weekly News*, April 1912, third edition, price 2d. The text is by Philip Gibbs.

II Front page of the *Daily Graphic* 'Titanic in Memoriam Number', 20 April 1912, price 1d.

THE·DAILY·GRAPHIC

TITANIC
·IN·MEMORIAM·NUMBER·

ONE PENNY

41° 16′ N; 50° 14′ W.

III Frontispiece of *Titanic* by Filson Young, published in hardcover by Grant Richards Ltd, London, May 1912. The artist is not credited.

WHITE STAR LINER TITANIC.

LENGTH 882 ft. 6 ins. BREADTH 92 ft. 6 ins. 45,000 TONNAGE.

SAILED FROM SOUTHAMPTON ON HER ILL-FATED MAIDEN VOYAGE ON APRIL 10TH, 1912 CARRYING 2,350 PASSENGERS AND CREW. STRUCK AN ICEBERG OFF THE COAST OF NEWFOUNDLAND PERISHED ON MONDAY, APRIL 15TH, 1912.

ROTARY PHOTO. E.C.

IV Postcard commemorating the loss of the *Titanic*, published by the Rotary Photographic Company in 1912. This example was used postally on 9 May 1912. The ship is pictured leaving Southampton on 10 April 1912.

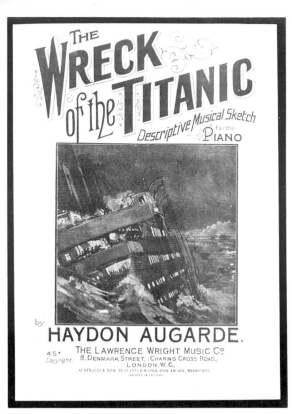

V Front cover of 'The Wreck of the Titanic', a 'descriptive musical sketch for the piano' by Haydon Augarde, published by The Lawrence Wright Music Co., London, 1912.

VI Statue of Captain E.J. Smith of the *Titanic*, sculpted by Lady Kathleen Scott, Beacon Park, Lichfield, Staffordshire, and formally unveiled on 29 July 1914.

VII Record label, 'Be British', composed by Lawrence Wright, performed by Ernest Gray, 'The Winner' label, UK, 1912.

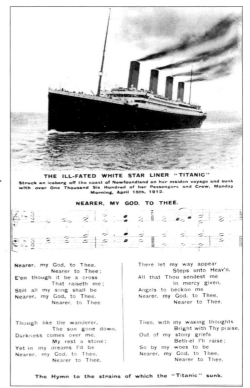

VIII Postcard commemorating 'Nearer, My God, to Thee', the hymn widely believed to have been played as the *Titanic* sank. The opening of the setting by J.B. Dykes is reproduced. This card was published by the Rotary Photographic Company, in 1912, and used the same photograph as in plate IV, superimposed on a different background. Additionally, an artist has fancifully added smoke coming from all four of the *Titanic*'s funnels: the fourth was, in fact, a dummy.

IX Grave of Wallace Hartley, the bandleader of the *Titanic*, who was buried at Colne, Lancashire, on 18 May 1912.

X Detail of the grave of Wallace Hartley, *Titanic* bandleader, Colne, Lancashire, 1912.

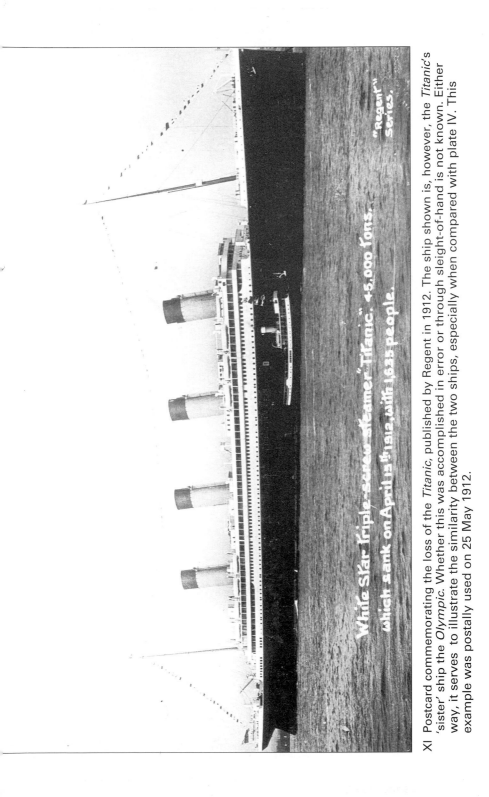

White Star Triple-Screw Steamer "Titanic." 45,000 Tons. which sank on April 15th 1912 with 1,635 people.

"Regent" Series.

XI Postcard commemorating the loss of the *Titanic*, published by Regent in 1912. The ship shown is, however, the *Titanic's* 'sister' ship the *Olympic*. Whether this was accomplished in error or through sleight-of-hand is not known. Either way, it serves to illustrate the similarity between the two ships, especially when compared with plate IV. This example was postally used on 25 May 1912.

WHITE STAR LINE

TRIPLE-SCREW R.M.S. "OLYMPIC."

XII Postcard of the *Titanic's* 'sister' ship the *Olympic*. The publisher and date are not given, but it is certainly post 1913,

of the ship. Second class passengers were provided with their own dining room, library and smoke room, similarly located. The third-class accommodation on the *Titanic* was situated on the lower, middle, upper, saloon and shelter decks. In this way, the third-class promenade was (again) a whole deck below its second-class equivalent, while at the lowest level, third-class cabins shared the lower deck with the engine casings, coal bunkers and baggage stores. Third-class passengers had their own dining saloon, smoke room, general room and promenade. The third-class cabins were to be found at the lowest, fore and aft extremes of the ship.

Each class had its own entrances and staircases on the decks, and it would be entirely possible for passengers of one class to have no contact whatsoever with those of another during the whole voyage. And as the upper classes inhabited the upper – and the lower classes the lower – parts of the ship, the physical structure of the *Titanic*, in common with other ships of the day, precisely represented the hierarchical gradations of late Edwardian social life on shore. To describe the physical structure of the *Titanic* as a metaphor for the social structure of the era is not, perhaps, the most original of observations[38] – but that does not make it any the less true. It is and it was. These class divisions were observed in death as in life. After the ship went down, the floating *Titanic* corpses were gathered and transported back to Halifax, Nova Scotia, by the cable-laying ship the *Mackay-Bennett*. The bodies of the first-class passengers were put into coffins on deck, while those of the second and third class were sewn into canvas bags and stored on ice in the hold.[39] Many unidentified or badly disfigured bodies were buried at sea, but it was later revealed that all those identified as first-class bodies, whatever their condition, were brought to the mainland.[40] The survivors similarly disembarked from the rescue ship *Carpathia* in New York in order of class.[41]

While academics today show little reticence in discussing social class, the same cannot be said of the general population. Class is not – overtly at least – considered to constitute polite conversation, no matter how significant it may be in daily experience. The late Edwardians showed no such qualms, and their understanding of the *Titanic* is no exception. Unlike people today, they may have felt unable openly to discuss sex (no matter how significant it may have been in daily experience), but class could be considered without any kind of blushing or embarrassed silence. Gibbs, for example, noted that the *Titanic* disaster brought out the charitable instinct 'among all classes, from the richest to the poorest'.[42] Young went further, presenting his readers with a class-based, potted 'sociology' of the *Titanic*'s passenger population. The majority of the first class, he said, were Americans 'rich and prosperous people', while the majority of the second class were English, 'many of them of the minor professional classes'. As for the 'thousand odd steerage passengers',[43] they

> represented a kind of Babel of nationalities, all the world in little, united by nothing but poverty ... leaving behind them a life of failure and hopelessness.[44]

It was a Babel comprising:

> Jews, Christians, and Mohammedans, missionaries and heathen, Russians, Poles, Greeks, Roumanians, Germans, Italians, Chinese, Finns, Spaniards, English, and French – with a strong contingent of Irish, the inevitable link in that melancholy chain of emigration that has united Ireland and America since the Famine.[45]

Young, however, realized that class was not a matter of mere geography; it was also a matter of experience. For the first class, 'the world was a very small place'. These were people who would take an Atlantic liner 'as the humbler would take a tramcar'. They were going to America this week; they would probably come back next or the week after.[46] As for the 'steerage' passengers, this was no hasty holiday, but 'part of the drift of their lives', a road to be travelled 'once only, a road they would never retrace'.[47]

Young, for all his unabashed class consciousness, is unusual among the *Titanic* writers of the period for he does, at least, pay some attention to the third-class passengers. In the majority of the late Edwardian texts, however, the *Titanic* is the story of the rich and famous. The third class – who after all constituted the majority of those who both travelled and died – are mere supporting players if indeed, they are allowed to appear at all.

In 'The Deathless Story of the Titanic', for example, there are two photomontages depicting both those who died and those who survived, respectively. The first, 'Some well-known passengers who went down with the "Titanic"' comprises Senator Carter, W.T. Stead, Mr and Mrs Isador Straus, Major Archibald Butt, Colonel J.J. Astor, Senator Allison, T.W. Cavendish and Benjamin Guggenheim.[48] The second, 'Some of the well known people who were picked up by the "Carpathia"' is made up of Lady Duff Gordon, Mrs T.W. Cavendish, The Countess of Rothes, A.H. Barkworth, JP, Mrs J.J. Astor and Mr Bruce Ismay.[49] The *Daily Graphic* special edition contains two full broadsheet pages of over 30 posed portraits of 'Some of the Titanic's Notable Passengers'. In addition to the customary industrialists and financiers are socialites such as Mrs F.J. Swift, 'a New York society hostess', and Miss E.M. Eustis, 'well known in New York Society'.[50] These, clearly, were the celebrities of the day, as evidenced by the ready availability of file photographs to editors immediately following the sinking. All of those featured in 'The Deathless Story ...' are first-class passengers, as are all but one (racquets champion Charles Williams) of those pictured in the *Daily Graphic* 'In Memoriam' number. There is none from the third class. Similarly, all the well-known stories of passengers' exploits during the sinking (Guggenheim, Astor, Mr and Mrs Straus) concern only the first class passengers. All the popular interest, therefore, focused on a group who accounted for only a quarter of the *Titanic*'s passenger list.[51]

This is not to say that the complete stories of the first-class passengers were told. Indelicate details were omitted so as not to tarnish the images of these 'idols of production'. We have already noted, for example, the celebrated case of Benjamin Guggenheim who elected, theatrically, to die 'like a gentleman' in full evening dress. According to Gibbs, he also gave a final message: 'If I don't turn up, tell my wife I did the best I could.' What was *not* reported was the fact that Guggenheim was travelling not only with his valet but also with his mistress, Madame Aubert of Paris.[52] Mrs Guggenheim was later photographed visiting the White Star offices in New York in search of news. Her husband was among the dead; Madame Aubert (and her maid) survived.

John Jacob Astor is another of those of whom the whole tale was not revealed. According to 'The Deathless Story of the Titanic', Astor, returning from his honeymoon, helped with the boats and generally boosted the morale of all around him. He stood for a moment at the side of 'his beautiful bride' and told her that he would meet her in New York:

> As the boats with the women went away from the side of the ship Colonel Astor stood for a moment at the salute. He called out a last farewell to his wife: 'Good-bye, dearie, I will join you later.' He then turned calmly and lit a cigarette, and leaned over the rails, staring through the darkness.[53]

Young, on the other hand, hints – discreetly – that there was more to the story than this. According to his account, Astor's 'young wife was in a delicate state of health'. Astor, indeed, had got into a boat to look after her 'and no wonder'. He was ordered out, however, and saw her off with Gibbs' 'cheery wave'.[54] What Young was hinting at was that 19-year-old Madeleine was the second Mrs Astor and in fact was younger than Astor's own son. Having divorced Mrs Astor the first, the famous millionaire had remarried amid some public scandal. The newlyweds had gone on a tour of Europe and Egypt, partly to avoid the publicity and Madeleine was now five months pregnant.[55] As a human interest story, therefore, there was considerably more to the life and death of J.J. Astor than even Young dared intimate. Whether it was through genuine respect for the individuals concerned, through an overriding sense of public decorum, or even through an entirely practical fear of reprisals against insubordinate journalists, the public images of these 'idols of production' remained untarnished.

If the wealthy were celebrated and their 'misdeeds' forgotten, the names of their servants were usually not considered worth remembering. While the second and even the third class were listed by name, the majority of the servants, even though they accompanied their masters and mistresses in the first-class accommodation, were listed merely as 'manservant' or 'maid'. The first page of the maiden voyage first-class passenger list, distributed on board, for example, lists: 'Astor, Colonel J.J. and Manservant', 'Aubert, Mrs. N. and Maid', 'Allison, Master and Nurse'.[56] Such distinctions remained after the sinking. 'The Deathless Story of the Titanic', for example, reproduced a list of the surviving passengers as cabled to the White Star London offices. Madame Aubert's companion remained as 'Maid', just as Master Allison's carer continued as 'Nurse'. The fate of Colonel Astor's 'Manservant' was not recorded at all.[57]

Servants may not have been allowed the luxury of personal names, but they were certainly a part of both the economy and the life of the *Titanic*. The first-class passenger rate list, for example, listed suites such as B52 (occupied on the maiden voyage by the Cardeza party) for a price inclusive of 'one or two passengers and servant'.[58] Servants could also be 'berthed in rooms set apart for them'.[59] A White Star Line brochure drew prospective passengers' attention to the 'important innovation' to the aft of the upper deck in the form of the 'special Maids' and Valets' saloon, where servants may congregate and their meals be served'.[60] Young, atypically, took rather a dim view of both the segregation and the lifestyle inherent in the keeping of servants aboard the *Titanic*. Servants, he believed, made sure that the rich in first class enjoyed 'the best of everything' and ministered 'not so much to their necessities as to their luxuries'.[61] Young, as the author of a hardback book, probably felt better able to be critical of the class system in that he was addressing a more predominantly middle-class audience than the readers of *Lloyd's Weekly News* and the *Daily Graphic*.[62] He did not, however, deny that such a system was both extant and manifest. As for the authors of the penny and twopenny publications, there is no mention of any servants at all. Gibbs, for example, narrated the story of Guggenheim and the man we now know to have been his secretary-cum-valet, Victor Giglio. In Gibbs' version, however, Giglio is simply referred to as 'a friend'.[63] It would be wrong to assume that this implied any perceived social equality of the two; it reveals, rather, that the name of the man accompanying Guggenheim was not worth recording. Guggenheim, as a multi-millionaire and socialite had his name for ever linked with a gesture 'in the same spirit with which Lord Nelson put on his medals and stars before the Battle of Trafalgar'.[64] His servant, who made exactly the same gesture, died anonymously.

Unlike the servants of the first-class passengers, the crew of the *Titanic* were widely recognized in the popular texts. It is difficult to add too accurate a class dimension to this, however, as the crew ranged from Captain Smith, a friend of the famous who lived in some style in Southampton, to the firemen and stokers who toiled below and were hired on a casual basis. Whatever their social class, the relatively high profile of the crew in the popular texts can be explained not only by the roles which they were inevitably called upon to play after the ship struck ice, but also because so many were – understandably – called to testify before both the American and British inquiries into the disaster. Prominent among these were Second Officer Lightoller, the senior sur-viving crewman, radio operator Harold Bride, and fireman Harry Senior. Among the dead, Captain Smith, of course, received a great deal of attention both as commander and as a 'British gentleman',[65] but he was almost eclipsed by band-leader Wallace Hartley, who was fêted in print, song, postcards and memorials for, it was widely believed, keeping the musicians playing on deck until the end and con-cluding with the hymn 'Nearer, My God, to Thee'. The role of Hartley and the musicians will be fully considered in Chapter 6.

Of the rank-and-file crew, it was the engineers who received special popular acclaim. These were, according to Gibbs, '"the black squad" who stood to their posts in the bowels of the ship, to the last'.[66] In a tribute to the engineers and boilerroom staff of the *Titanic*, Lord Charles Beresford commended those who had kept the ship's lights burning until a few minutes before the *Titanic* made its final plunge.

'This proves that officers and men below remained at their posts when they knew that death – the most terrible and painful that it is possible to conceive – awaited them at any minute.'[67] Not one of the engineers survived. A memorial was raised at Southampton to 'the memory of the engineer officers of the RMS "Titanic" who showed their high conception of duty and heroism by remaining at their posts'.[68] The names of the 35 who died are listed without indication of rank, while the name of Thomas Andrews, the designer of the *Titanic* who also died, is added at the end. Some may be tempted to take this as an indication of equality in class before death. It would be wrong to take this too far, however: the inscription makes it clear that the statue is to the '*engineer officers*' (my emphasis) of the *Titanic*, while Beresford in his tribute betrayed a marked distinction between 'officers and men',[69] even though he praised them both. The majority of the firemen, stokers and other manual engine and boilerroom workers below decks also died on the *Titanic*, but they are not commemorated on the officers' grand memorial.

If the crew occupied an anomalous position in the representation of social class on the *Titanic*, the second-class passengers joined the servants in being, essentially, anonymous. In the myth of the *Titanic*, the protagonists are the extremes of rich and poor, with the crew as mediators. The second class, who in fact numbered almost as many as the first class on board,[70] are almost completely ignored. It is true that the names of the second class, unlike the third, did appear on the circulated passenger list, and that their accommodation on board was, by the standards of the day, extremely comfortable. But in the late Edwardian representations of the *Titanic*, they occupy an unconsidered hinterland between the upper and lower decks. The second class, after all, lacked both the glamour of the *Titanic*'s millionaires and the romance of its penniless emigrants. They represented what we recall Young describing merely as 'the minor professional classes'.[71] When we read of the *Titanic*'s lavish accommodations, these were occupied by the first class, and designed to attract the ostentatiously wealthy. As we recall from Chapter 1, it was the steerage class that provided the high-volume economy of trans-Atlantic travel. So the second lies in between the classes economically as well as socially and geographically. As a consequence, there is practically no mention of the second class either *en masse* or individually in the popular texts surrounding the *Titanic*. In Gibbs' description of 'Luxury on the Liner', there are 150 words on the first class facilities, followed by 30 on the third.[72] There is no mention of the second at all. Davie claimed in his study of the *Titanic* that like the poor on land, 'drowned steerage passengers have no history'.[73] Unexpectedly, perhaps, the second class on the *Titanic* have even less.

This is not to say, of course, that no second-class passengers are ever mentioned, but if they are, they are only very rarely identified as belonging to that most nonentitous of groups. Young, for example, identifies 'Mr. Caldwell, a second class passenger'[74] in an anecdote about the lifeboats, but it is informative that we are surprised by the reference. Perhaps the best-known of all the second-class passengers is Lawrence Beesley, a science teacher who was widely quoted in the newspapers, and whose book was published shortly after the sinking. Beesley was assiduous in his observation, articulate in his description and unflinching in his criticism, but reading the popular texts of 1912, one would be hard-pressed to identify him as emerging from the 'second cabin'. The *Daily Graphic* 'In Memoriam' number, for example, makes great use of his testimony, and introduces him simply as 'Mr Beesley of London'.[75] Gibbs' 'The Deathless Story of the Titanic' praises Beesley's account as 'the most clear and coherent description of the great tragedy from first to last' and describes him as 'Mr. Beesley, formerly a master at Dulwich College'.[76] Only from Young is it possible to discern that Beesley was in fact a second-class passenger, and then one needs to 'decode' the reference: Young describes the muted reaction in first class to the fact that the ship has made an unscheduled stop in the middle of the night. Then he then proceeds to describe the reaction 'lower down in the ship'.[77] This is his veiled reference to the second-class accommodation. He continues:

> So little excitement was there in this part of the ship that the man in his dressing gown (his name was Mr. Beezley [*sic*], an English schoolmaster, one of the few who emerges from the crowd with an in-tact individuality) went back to his cabin and lay down on his bed with his book, waiting for the ship to start again.[78]

This passage is particularly informative: it reveals the second class as an area of the ship in which little of excitement was to be expected, and that Beesley (who had written the best and most lucid account from which Young had drawn extensively) was one of the few to emerge from the anonymous second class crowd with 'an in-tact individuality'. Young then proceeds to misspell Beesley's name throughout the book. Presumably, as a second-class passenger, his individuality was only partly maintained.

The third class received little of the popular attention given to the first, but both their numbers and the drama of their predicament ensured that they were not ignored, even though they appeared as multitudinous 'extras' rather than 'featured players' with starring roles. They provided a human background against which the memorable deeds of the rich and famous were played out, but unlike the second-class passengers, their presence was at least acknowledged. Within the steel walls of the *Titanic*, reported Gibbs, the rich men of the world lay only a few decks away from 'Irish emigrants and from the people of poverty'.[79] Nevertheless, noted Young, the third-class accommodation was so dispersed among the less desirable parts of the ship that while a first-class passenger could easily stroll from his bedroom to his parlour, the steerage passenger had to walk to a spot 'a quarter of a mile away where he was to meet his friends'.[80] When the iceberg struck, the first-class passengers, continued Young, were initially unmoved, but 'The steerage people knew better and feared more.' Life had, after all, taught them that 'destiny is a thing to fear'.[81] It was these who comprised Young's 'Babel of nationalities, all the world in little, united by nothing except poverty'.[82] Young is unusual in giving a figure for the total of 'steerage' passengers on board ('a thousand odd')[83] and for creating a visual image of their number when 'a rush of people began from the steerage quarters, swarming up stairways and ladders …'[84]

Although the third-class passengers do exist in the *Titanic* narratives, two further points need to be noted. First, none of the third-class passengers is ever referred to by name; they are only referred to *en masse*. Second, when they are mentioned, it is frequently to suggest that the *Titanic* disaster broke down the divisions of social class. This is a crucial ingredient in the myth of the *Titanic*. The *Daily Graphic* 'In Memoriam' edition, for example, boasts that: 'Millionaire and steerage emigrant alike were called upon: alike they presented us with that most inspiring of spectacles – the inherent nobility of mankind.'[85] St Clair's commemorative song 'The Ship That Will Never Return' celebrated the belief that 'rich man and poor man went down side by side/ Where Rank made no difference and Death levelled all'.[86] Gibbs claimed that the class unity witnessed on the *Titanic* was reflected in the mourners at the commemorative service at St Paul's Cathedral, London, on 19 April. It was a tragedy which had, briefly, 'made our brotherhood close its ranks like little children who cling together in fear and grief'.[87] Indeed, 'people of rank and wealth' had joined with 'clerks', 'shopkeepers' and 'slum-dwellers' and 'come together' in a 'comradeship of grief, greater than the small conventions of life. Their hearts were unclothed'.[88] The popular texts even went so far as to celebrate the classlessness involved in filling the precious places on the *Titanic*'s lifeboats. All agree that while women were given priority, social class had made no difference. Young asserts that there was 'no discrimination between classes in putting the women into the boats'.[89]

> The woman with a tattered shawl over her head, the woman with a sable coat over her nightdress, the woman clasping a baby, and the woman clutching a basket of trinkets had all an equal chance; side by side they were handed on to the harsh and uncomfortable thwarts of the lifeboats; the wife of the millionaire sat cheek by jowl with a dusty stoker and a Russian emigrant, and the spoiled woman of the world found some poor foreigner's baby thrown into her lap as the boat was lowered.[90]

According to Gibbs, quoting Fifth Officer Lowe at the American inquiry, the same principle extended to the 'few men' who got away. They did so 'irrespective of rank or class'.[91]

These glowing egalitarian pronouncements were made, however, in the face of evidence which, certainly when taken at face value, suggested quite the contrary. It should have been clear to everyone at the time that there had been, in fact, an irrefutable correlation between social class and survival aboard the *Titanic*. The evidence was there for all to see, but in the popular culture of 1912–14, there were few who chose to notice it.[92]

We saw how Gibbs, for example, quoted Lowe telling the American inquiry that the men who got away did so 'irrespective of rank or class'.[93] Gibbs' recollection of the inquiry is both selective and partial, however, for the inquiry also concluded that 'the proportion of lost is larger among third-class passengers then either of the other classes'.[94] A table showing survival by both class and gender was reproduced on page 5 of the report, and the inquiry formally 'noted' the differing percentages among the three classes of passengers saved.[95]

While Gibbs overlooked the evidence linking class with survival, Young, at first glance, was much more publicly aware of the issue. He even went so far as to conclude *Titanic* with a table showing the loss of life on the ship, dividing the passengers into the three component classes.[96] The table plainly showed that 63 per cent of the first-class survived, compared with 42 per cent of the second-class and just 25 per cent of the third. In other words, there was a direct, obvious and descending correlation between social class and survival on the

Titanic. While Young's own figures do support the celebration of 'women and children first' (among the passengers and crew 76 per cent of the women and 49 per cent of the children survived), his figures do not, on the face of it, support his assertion that there was 'no discrimination between classes in putting the women into the boats'.[97] His figures show that 97 per cent of first-class women survived, compared with 84 per cent of second and only 55 per cent of third. In other words, despite the concept of 'women and children first', first-class women were almost twice as likely to survive the sinking as those in third. The discrepancies are even more pronounced with the survival rate for children. According to Young's figures, 100 per cent of both first- and second-class children survived, compared with only 30 per cent of those in third. Women and children may indeed have gone 'first', but their chances of survival were by no means 'equal' when social class was taken into account. So, while Young did indeed present figures in his book showing a clear connection between class and survival, he seems not to have taken his own evidence into account when concluding, boldly, in the body of his text that there was 'no discrimination between classes in putting the women into the boats'.[98]

The British inquiry into the disaster was more overtly interested in the connection between class and survival than were the popular texts. Indeed, question 20 of the 26 formulated by the Board of Trade specifically called upon Lord Mersey and his colleagues to investigate the numbers of those who got away in boats according to sex, class and rating.[99] Question 21 inquired of the total number of passengers who survived (by any means), distinguishing between 'the first, second and third-classes respectively'. It wanted, further, to know if there was any 'disproportion' among these who survived.[100] The resulting figures correspond with those used by Young and thus reveal the same discrepancies.[101] Yet while Young was summarily satisfied that all was well, Lord Mersey felt prompted, at least, to look further. Mersey concluded that there was indeed a discrepancy, but explained that: 'The disproportion was certainly not due to any discrimination by the officers or crew in assisting the passengers to the boats.'[102] Rather, the differences in the survival rates were due both to the locations of the various classes of accommodation and to the fact that so many of the third-class passengers were 'foreigners'.[103]

In the body of his report, Lord Mersey gives two further paragraphs to the question of the third-class passengers. Again noting the smaller proportion saved, he further explains this by describing their 'greater reluctance' to leave the ship, by their 'unwillingness to part with their baggage', by the difficulty in getting them up from their quarters at extreme ends of the ship, and by 'other similar causes'.[104] There is, in fact, some substance in Lord Mersey's apologia. The lifeboats on *Titanic* were on the top deck (the 'boat deck') and so were nearest the first-class cabins and facilities (decks A, B, C and, to a lesser extent, D and E). The second-class accommodation was, as we have seen, both slightly lower down (decks B, C, D, E and F) and further fore and aft of the ship. Finally, the third-class accommodation was to be found at the extreme ends of the lowest 'inhabited' decks (decks C, D, E, F and G). Simply put, the further away one started from the lifeboats, the less one's chances of survival. In this way, the discrepancies in survival rates could have been geographical rather than simply social. Even though the two were, of course, connected as were the physical and social structure of the ship, it would still be possible to agree that there was no discrimination in the loading of the boats *providing one had managed to find one's way up to the boat deck in the first place.*

Finding one's way to the boat deck depended on communication as well as topology, and this is where the significance of Lord Mersey's 'foreigners' comes in. The crew of the *Titanic* were almost exclusively British, while the third-class passengers were, in Young's phrase, a 'Babel of nationalities',[105] comprising Armenians, Italians, Syrians, Chinese, Russians, Scandinavian and Dutch in addition to those from the British Isles.[106] If we examine the available data, we can extrapolate that for every three third-class passengers who could speak English, there were four who could not.[107] The crew would, therefore, have been unable to communicate with the majority of third-class passengers at the best of times, let alone in time of crisis. The problem was further exaggerated by the fact that the *Titanic* had no public address system and had also had (as we recall) no lifeboat drill. It was a recipe, therefore, for chaos in which language (or lack of it) was a significant ingredient. The credibility of the language hypothesis is underlined by the fact, reported by Mersey, that 'Of the Irish emigrants in the third-class a large proportion was saved.'[108]

The question of class and survival also raises one of the most controversial issues surrounding the *Titanic*: the question of whether or not the third-class passengers were locked or even forcibly held below decks as the ship began to sink. According to Lynch and Marschall, this has become 'an enduring legend' of the *Titanic*.[109] It went on to provide, for example, one of the most powerful scenes in James Cameron's film 'Titanic' of 1997, and in view of the millions who have seen this film, is increasingly likely to have entered the recent social memory as fact. Yet while the mistreatment of the third-class is – revealingly – a potent ingredient of the myth of the *Titanic* in the late 1990s, it was not a part of the myth in Britain from 1912–14. It is an issue which is mentioned in none of the popular texts. One has to go to the formal British Inquiry Report to find reference to suggestions that the third-class passengers had been 'unfairly treated' and that 'their access to the Boat deck had been impeded'.[110] The use of the terms 'impeded' and 'unfairly treated' is non-specific and possibly deliberately euphemistic. Both terms are a long way, however, from overtly suggesting that the third-class passengers as a whole had been locked or deliberately held below decks. And even if Lord Mersey's reference to these suggestions is discreetly 'coded', his refutation of them is not: 'There appears to have been no truth in these allegations.'[111]

A further and under-appreciated point about class division on the *Titanic* is this: if any of the doors between third-class and other areas of the ship had been locked, this was not in anticipation of shipwreck, but in compliance with US immigration laws. These made class segregation mandatory on immigrant ships in the interests of immigration control and the feared spread of infectious diseases.[112] As passenger steamers such as the *Titanic* approached New York's inner harbour, they were required first to stop near Staten Island. Special immigration service ferries arrived alongside, and all third-class passengers would be taken to Ellis Island for health checks and, if they were immigrants, for immigration processing before being allowed to continue their journeys to the city or beyond by public transport. First- and second-class passengers, meanwhile, remained on board in order to disembark (if they were White Star passengers) at Pier 59 on the west side of Manhattan. Here, considerably less stringent entry procedures would apply.[113] We can see, therefore, that the physical segregation of third-class passengers on board the *Titanic* was necessary if US health and immigration procedures were to be enforced rather than circumvented. The *Titanic* had, after all, been built with American immigration laws in mind.[114]

Perhaps the case of the third-class passengers would have received more public attention had they enjoyed more representation at both the British and American inquiries. At both of these, they lacked a significant voice. At the American inquiry, which preceded the British and was quickly drawn upon in the popular texts, only three of the witnesses were from third-class. Two of these said they were prevented from going to the boat decks but the committee failed to follow this up.[115] Interestingly, the same witnesses also said they did not believe they had been the victims of discrimination.[116] At the British inquiry, not one third-class passenger testified.[117] They were formally represented, however, by a barrister, W.D. Harbinson, who was able to conclude:

> I wish to say distinctly that no evidence has been given in the course of this case that would substantiate a charge that any attempt was made to keep back the third class passengers. There is not an atom or a title of evidence upon which any such allegation could be based.[118]

If the third-class passengers' own barrister was able to make such a statement, then the inquiry was unlikely to investigate further.

The lack of determined interest on the part of the inquiries reflected the lack of popular interest beyond. We have already noted how little attention was given to the third class in the British popular texts, and the same must be said of the American press upon which the British, for reasons of chronology, drew. The *New York Times* issue which covered the arrival of the rescue ship *Carpathia* contained only two interviews with third-class survivors, while of the 43 accounts published in the New York *Herald*, again only two were third-class stories.[119]

So where does all this leave us? With strangely contradictory view of class relations. On the one hand, it reveals a popular vision of a distinctly stratified society in which the upper class were idealized, the middle class were ignored, and the lower class were understood as an anonymous but omnipresent horde. On the other hand, the late Edwardian myth of the *Titanic* boldly celebrates equality among the classes in the face of death. In fact, the popular texts pay only lip-service to notions of equality, and it is a temporary notion at that. For underlying the celebration of 'Millionaire and steerage emigrant alike'[120] remains a prevailing expectation of difference; a fundamental assumption that the two are not alike at all. We notice, for example, that the levelling of millionaires and emigrants provided us with the spectacle of 'the inherent nobility of mankind'[121] and not its inherent humility. The lower classes remained, in Gibbs' phrase, 'humble in rank',[122] with upper-class 'nobility' still providing the benchmark for ideal behaviour, to which the 'humble' ranks temporarily rose. The basic concept of this is never questioned. Gibbs, for example, spoke proudly of the 'comradeship of grief' at the London memorial service, but in the same breath explained that it was a grief shared by both 'people of rank and wealth' and 'slum-dwellers'.[123] They may have been equal in grief, but were clearly not so in rank. Similarly, we recall St Clair's commemorative song in which: 'rich man and poor man went down side by side/ Where Rank made no difference and Death levelled all'.[124] Rank may have made no difference, but St Clair makes it equally clear that it existed, gracing 'Rank' with a capital 'R'.

Social class was, after all, ordained by God. Late Edwardian congregations would have been more than familiar with Mrs Cecil F. Alexander's popular hymn, 'All Things Bright and Beautiful', the third verse of which expounds: 'The rich man in his castle,/ The poor man at his gate,/ God made them high or lowly,/ And ordered their estate.'[125] Divisions of class, then, were both natural and God-given. As Mrs Alexander's hymn concluded, 'The Lord God made them all.'

Finally, we are prompted to look again at St Clair's assertion that 'Rank made no difference'.[126] Clearly, rank aboard the *Titanic did* make a difference at every turn. Even though both inquiries concluded (and recent scholarship agrees) that there was not a *causative* relationship between class and survival on board the *Titanic*, a relationship still clearly existed. The information connecting class and survival rates was readily available in the pubic domain within days of the disaster. Had the popular texts actively examined that relationship, they too may have concluded that nothing was indeed amiss. The point is, however, that they chose not to look at all. The myth of the *Titanic* had millionaire and emigrant equal in the face of death. Even to have questioned that vision would have spoiled the story. The myth, after all, prevailed.

5 'Be British!'

It is time now to add the third dimension to the late Edwardian construct of ideal behaviour as revealed in the myth of the *Titanic*: the dimension of race. Our examination of the popular texts has already revealed that nearly all the stories of individuals acting in an heroic manner involve males who are also members of the upper-middle or upper classes. It will now appear that the ideal hero was also white and Anglo-Saxon. Even when the people involved in 'heroic' behaviour did not in fact belong to these gender, class or racial groups, their behaviour is nevertheless described as if they had, for to die 'like a man' was also to die like an English-speaking gentleman. The fact that the majority of passengers on board the *Titanic* were not British only adds to the mythical power of historical reanimation at work.

At the top of the 'league table' of those from whom manly, dignified and unflinching behaviour was expected were the British. And the epitome of this expectation – which was, of course, mythically fulfilled – was the captain's much quoted and much praised final exhortation to the men: 'Be British!' Even if the men were not all British (and the majority of them were not), they were nevertheless called upon to behave as if they were.

To those of us immersed in the culture of the late twentieth century, the idea of the captain of a sinking ship exhorting the passengers and crew to 'Be British' in the face of disaster (and probably even death) may strike us as almost comically absurd. But in the popular culture of 1912–14, the notion was desperately serious. It constitutes a central feature of the myth of the *Titanic*, and at the same time provides the analyst today with an invaluable insight into the expectations and self-representations of late Edwardian culture.

According to the popular texts, the captain gave the order 'Be British!' in the seconds before the ship finally sank. The *Titanic*, we recall, took over two and a half hours to go down, submerging slowly by the head as passengers and crew made their way either to the lifeboats (if they were lucky) or to the stern in increasing numbers. The cry 'Be British!', then, comes at the most climactic and prominently featured moment in the *Titanic* story. The *Daily Graphic* 'In Memoriam' number reported:

Captain Smith's self-sacrifice and heroism, even after the bridge had disappeared beneath the waves, has been commended by all. Before he was literally washed from his post of duty he called through his megaphone, 'Be British!' to the mass below.[1]

Gibbs describes the same scene in 'The Deathless Story of the Titanic', underlining that this sense of Britishness was historically located in both race and gender:

Captain Smith stood on the bridge, a calm, grave figure, conscious that the end was near. Two words came down from him to the people who were crowding forward:
'Be British!'
It was a call to the old traditions of our race and manhood.[2]

The captain's call was enthusiastically celebrated in song, too. The chorus of Pelham and Wright's jaunty 'Be British' record (plate VII) begins: 'Be British! was the cry as the ship went down', and concludes by calling upon listeners to 'Be British' in giving money to support the widows and orphans of the men who died.[3] Scott's recorded song 'Stand to Your Post', which forms the other side to Scott and Pelham's composition, begins with a recitative which dedicates the song:

in proud remembrance of the heroes who sacrificed their lives for others in obedience to the instinct of their race and the grand old Captain's exhortations: 'Be British!' Hats off please!.[4]

F.V. St Clair's sheet music 'The Ship That Will Never Return' has the captain making the now familiar call from the bridge, and the call meeting with the suitable response: 'Be British – and British were they.' It was a deed that would be remembered 'as long as old England sends ships over the sea'.[5]

Postcards also celebrated the captain's last reported call. Smith's photograph is captioned 'Be British' in the E.A. Bragg of Falmouth 'R.I.P. In Memoriam' card,[6] while a photograph of the *Titanic* on a card published by Debenham of Cowes is flanked by the printed caption: '"Be British." Capt. Smith's last charge to his men.'[7] A picture of Smith on a card published by Tom Harvey of Redruth includes the caption: 'His Last Words Were "Be British" Just Before The Liner Sank.'[8]

To 'Be British' was also to be manly and brave. This is both implicit and explicit in the popular texts, many of which proceed demonstrably combine the two virtues. Captain Smith, according to the *Daily*

Graphic 'In Memoriam' edition, was 'a typical figure of an English sailor'[9] (the words 'British' and 'English' are used interchangeably in the texts), while one of the radio operators was 'composed of that old English valiance that has turned the blood of history into wine'.[10] Smith, according to Philip Gibbs, was: 'the very type of a British sea-captain' and 'brave as a lion',[11] while Stevenson described the Lichfield statue to him as 'an essentially British memorial to a British hero'.[12] And according to Wright's patriotic song, the men aboard the *Titanic*: 'worked like Britons, side by side, all faithful to the last'.[13] Admiral Beresford, speaking at the unveiling of Captain Smith's statue, and quoted in the appropriately titled 'Be British' souvenir publication which commemorated the event, praised the 'lion-hearted' captain for his 'patriotism' in calling 'Be British!' as his final command.[14] J.E. Hodder Williams (of publishers Hodder and Stoughton) had written in praise of Smith in the *British Weekly*, and his remarks were again quoted at length in the commemorative 'Be British' publication. The captain, he wrote, was a family man who loved his dogs, his home and his country:

> 'Be British,' was what we would have expected and wanted him to say. He belonged to the race of the old British sea-dogs. He believed with all his heart and soul in the British Empire. He had added that to his creed. I am glad he recited it at the end.[15]

It is indeed a telling phrase that, according to Williams, 'Be British!' was 'what we would have wanted and expected him to say'. Admiral Lord Charles Beresford, speaking at the unveiling, was seemingly more certain, and certainly equally revealing: 'It was what he did say', he declared, 'and what all who knew him expected he would have said under the circumstances.'[16] The historical evidence that Smith ever actually said 'Be British!' is very slight indeed, however. According to Steward Edward Brown, examined on the ninth day of the British inquiry, the last thing Captain Smith actually said to his remaining crew was: 'Well, boys, do your best for the women and children, and look out for yourselves.' He then returned to the bridge, with his megaphone in his hand. The *Titanic* sank seconds later.[17] Nevertheless, as we saw in Chapter 2, myths frequently conform to cultural wishes and expectations rather than to documentary evidence. Regardless of historical verification, therefore, the plaque on the Lichfield statue of Captain Smith concludes with the simple words: 'Be British'.[18]

What precisely, though, did it mean to 'Be British'? We have seen the expression used in a general sense, and certainly associated with manliness and bravery. To the late twentieth century analyst, however, the concept still seems somewhat amorphous. The late Edwardians do not spell out what was meant or understood by 'being British'. Our best policy, then, is to explore the idea through example and comparison.

A useful example is provided by the *Titanic*'s radio operators, Jack Phillips and Harold Bride, whose 'old English valiance', we recall, even managed to turn 'the blood of history into wine'.[19] Shipboard radio is taken for granted nowadays, but in 1912 it was still something of a novelty. Guglielmo Marconi's wireless Morse code transmitting equipment had only been patented in 1896, and was first installed at sea by the Italian Navy two years later. That summer in Britain, Edward, Prince of Wales, installed a unit aboard the Royal Yacht in order to keep in touch with the Queen. The system was gradually adopted by the larger steamship lines, with the insurers Lloyd's of London actively encouraging its use from 1901. An astute businessman, Marconi arranged it so that his equipment was leased, but never sold, to the commercial shipping lines. The equipment came complete with Marconi company-trained operators, who remained employees of the Marconi International Marine Communications Company and not of the ships upon which they served. Such was the case with Jack Phillips and Harold Bride of the *Titanic*. Phillips, the senior operator, was 25 years old, while Bride was 21. Even by the standards of the day, however, the two operators were not well paid. Phillips received a monthly wage of £4 5 shillings, while the junior Bride earned precisely half that amount. This compared with a wage of £6 a month for the Titanic's engine-room firemen and £5 10 shillings for the coal trimmers.

The *Titanic* had a daytime radio-range of 250–400 miles; at night this could increase to as much as 2,000 miles. The *Titanic* also had the luxury of two operators, who worked shifts so as to provide 24-hour coverage. This was by no means standard practice, however, with many smaller liners carrying only one operator, who closed down at night. Marine wireless technology was not regulated in 1912. In addition to 'official' and navigational messages, the *Titanic* operators also transmitted personal and business communications to and from the ship's private passengers. Such was the combination of radio traffic which was coming and going from the radio room when the *Titanic* struck ice at 11:40 pm on Sunday, 14 April 1912.[20]

At the time of the collision, Phillips was on duty, with Bride scheduled to relieve him at midnight. The junior operator was unaware of the collision until he stepped into the operating room at 11:55 pm. Fifteen minutes later, Captain Smith gave the order to call for assistance. 'It was but a little room, but large enough for heroic virtues,' opined Gibbs in 'The Deathless Story of the Titanic'.[21] Phillips began sending out 'CQD', the preferred international distress call among Marconi operators. Bride, quoted at length in 'The Deathless Story of the Titanic' reported:[22]

> We joked while he did so. We all made light of the disaster. We joked that way while he flashed signals for about five minutes. Then the captain came back.
> 'What are you sending?' he asked. 'C.Q.D.' Phillips replied.
> The humour of the situation appealed to me. I cut in with a little remark that made us all laugh, including the captain. 'Send S.O.S.,' I said; 'it's the new call. It may be your last chance.' Phillips, with a laugh, changed his signal to S.O.S.[23]

Phillips, despite the long hours he had already been working, continued to send out the SOS message, communicating the *Titanic*'s predicament and position to all ships within radio range. 'I brought an overcoat to Phillips', continued Bride, 'it was very cold, and I slipped the coat upon him while he worked.'[24] The ship, of course, continued to sink, and there was no hope of immediate rescue from the ships that had responded to Phillips' SOS calls. Eventually, the last of the lifeboats pulled away. The men remaining at the rails, recalled Officer Lightoller, 'stood as quietly as if they were in church'.[25]

Gibbs let Bride continue the narrative, 'with Phillips as the hero':[26]

> ...how poor Phillips worked through it I don't know.
> 'He was a brave man. I learned to love him that night, for I suddenly felt for him a great reverence, seeing him standing there, sticking to his work while everybody else was raging about. I will never forget the work of Phillips in the last awful fifteen minutes.[27]

Bride told Phillips that the last raft had gone. Then the captain made his final appearance in the radio room:

> 'Men, you have done your full duty. You can do no more. Abandon your cabin now. It's every man for himself. You look out for yourselves. I release you – that's the way it is at this kind of time, every man for himself.'[28]

According to Bride, however, Phillips clung on for another 10–15 minutes, 'sending ... sending ... The water was then coming into our cabin while he worked.'[29] Bride related that he had attached on Phillips' lifebelt because he had been too busy to do it himself. When a stoker 'or somebody from below decks' tried to sneak it away from the still working Phillips, Bride attacked the interloper. 'I did my duty ... I hope I finished him.'[30]

Phillips and Bride then took their chances as the ship finally went under. Phillips ran aft ('that was the last I saw of him'[31]) while Bride managed to cling to an upturned life-raft. Smith gave the order 'Be British!' and of the two operators, only Bride survived to tell the tale. Phillips, according to Gibbs, 'was a hero as great as any on the role of honour. His name is imperishable; his death a glorious tradition.' He was a man who 'did his duty to the uttermost and with a sublime devotion, careless of death'.[32] Bride, the survivor, endured cold and hardship on the open sea before being taken aboard the rescue ship *Carpathia* at dawn. According to his own account, which was greatly used by Gibbs, Bride had had his legs crushed in the life-raft, and was in so much pain that he could hardly climb the ladder to the *Carpathia*. Revived by brandy, he was asked to assist the *Carpathia*'s radio operator, who was under great pressure of work. 'After that, I never left the wireless room, but worked night and day sending official and personal messages.'[33] This was, according to Gibbs, an act of 'real heroism' and 'devotion to duty'; an epic indeed, which would 'go ringing down the ages with deathless music'.[34]

How, then, can we summarize the 'British' qualities demonstrated by Phillips and Bride? Devotion to 'duty' is an insistent and recurring theme: Captain Smith released both men, telling them that they had 'done their duty'; Gibbs praised Bride's 'devotion to duty' on board the *Carpathia*, while Phillips did his duty 'to the uttermost and with a sublime devotion, careless of death.' Bride even claimed that he did his 'duty' in dispatching the would-be thief of Phillips' lifejacket. This devotion to duty combines with a commitment to a solid work ethic. Phillips worked so hard – even though his shift was over – that he had time to put on neither his overcoat nor his lifejacket. Bride had to do it for him 'while he worked', and praised him for 'sticking to his work while everybody else was raging about'. Water was coming into the cabin 'while he worked'. Bride himself, rescued aboard the *Carpathia*, 'never left the wireless room, but worked night and day'. Clearly, they were both depicted as brave and selfless, helping the ship and helping each other.

In addition to devotion to work and to duty, both men kept a calm, tight rein on their emotions: Phillips kept on transmitting 'while everybody was raging about'. The only emotion betrayed is Bride confiding of Phillips: 'I learned to love him that night ...' This was not a mawkish but rather a firm-jawed love, Bride displaying not sentimental affection but 'a great reverence' for his colleague, seeing him standing there, sticking to his work. When Bride lays out the mystery stoker who has attempted to steal his comrade's lifejacket, he does so not in a fit of irrational emotion, but out of a sense of 'duty' and a determination 'not to let that man die a decent sailor's death'.[35] In so doing, he displays an indignant sense of British fair play. It is *Boys' Own* stuff. Finally, the pair display a manly sense of humour in crisis. They joked with each other and 'made light of the disaster'[36] as Phillips sent out the first signals of distress. When Bride advised him to try SOS, the new call, he joshed that: 'It may be your last chance'. It was a remark which, we recall, 'made us all laugh, including the captain.'[37]

According to St Clair's song, the captain gave the order: 'Be British – and British were they'.[38] It is fair to assume, then, that in their devotion to duty, their work ethic, their selflessness, their loyalty, their restrained emotion, their sense of fair play and their sense of humour, Phillips and Bride were indeed being 'British'.

If Phillips and Bride have provided an example of what it meant to 'Be British', the cultural assumptions surrounding 'Britishness' can also be elucidated by comparison with what it meant to be 'Latin', 'foreign' or, especially, 'Italian' in the late Edwardian popular texts. The Italians, indeed, were represented as having behaved particularly badly on the *Titanic*, their conduct typically described as emotional, cowardly, feminine or even wild and bestial. One much-related ingredient of the myth of the *Titanic*, for example, is the story of the man who tried to get into a lifeboat disguised as a woman. The story was told by Fifth Officer Lowe, and reported by Gibbs:

> One Italian in his boat escaped from the *Titanic* disguised as a woman. He had a shawl around him. 'I just picked him up in my arms,' said Mr. Lowe, a stalwart man, 'and pitched him into a lifeboat not so heavily laden as ours.'[39]

Lowe, the Briton, was 'stalwart'; the 'Italian' was hardly a 'man' at all. He was not the only Italian said to have acted improperly, however. According to Filson Young in *Titanic*:

> One band of Italians from steerage ... tried to rush one of the boats, and had to be kept back by force, an officer firing a couple of shots with his pistol; they desisted, and were hauled back ignominiously by the legs.[40]

It is interesting to see Gibbs use the collective term 'band' for the Italians – as though they were a 'band' of thieves or brigands. The Italian women, meanwhile, were 'limp with fright' and had to be lifted bodily into the lifeboats.[41]

In another incident from 'The Deathless Story of the Titanic', Lowe reported having to hold back the 'Italian and Latin people' with gunfire as he was loading the boats. With an image suggestive of wild and dangerous animals, Lowe portrayed them as 'all glaring and ready to spring'. He shouted a warning and let loose a shot along the ship's side. 'I hurt nobody; I fired into space.'[42]

Lowe's disparaging attitude drew protests from the Italian Ambassador to the US. The ambassador took exception to the assumption that anyone behaving badly must have been Italian. Lowe duly apologized, and in a statement asked for the word 'Italian' to be substituted with 'immigrants belonging to Latin races'.[43] In the British popular texts, however, the word 'Italian' remained unchecked. Lowe's assumption clearly rang true in Britain. Even in America, it was deemed acceptable to state broad racial assumptions about 'Latin' people so long as they were not identified with a specific national group which had an ambassador and a large population on the eastern seaboard.

We are able to compare, then, the representations of the British, with their manliness, their devotion to duty, their work ethic, their selflessness, their loyalty, their restrained emotion, sense of fair play and their sense of humour, with that of the Italians. The Italians, we have seen, were undisciplined and emotional to the extent that they had to be restrained with gunfire, while the British needed to be restrained only by their innate sense of duty. The Italians were wild-eyed and ready to 'spring' like beasts; the British, like Lowe, were 'stalwart'. Finally, while the British like Phillips and Bride were equated with 'manly' virtue, one 'Italian' (and in Lowe's mind he was clearly typical) survived only by dressing as a woman. It was a deed which mocked the 'old law of the sea' and which required an abandonment not only of the physical but also the cultural vestiges of manliness. Such a 'man' could only have been 'foreign'.

We can conclude our comparison with the entirely contrasting descriptions of the death of Captain Smith himself. Smith was, according to the *Daily Graphic*, 'a typical British seaman', and all the survivors testified to his 'valour and coolness in the last hour of trial'.[44] According to one survivor, quoted in the *Graphic*, Captain Smith 'stuck to the bridge and behaved like a hero'.[45] The *Graphic* then proceeded enthusiastically to expand upon the story, quoting 'one fireman' who, apparently, chanced to be on the bridge deck at the time. The rising water had now reached the captain's knees, but his face was 'firm' and 'his lips hard set'. The fireman continued that 'it was the intention of the captain to put two little children on a boat'. When he struck the water, though, the cold forced the captain to let go. He must have been swept away from the boats, concluded the fireman.[46] That was the extent of the *Graphic*'s account, but 'The Deathless Story of the Titanic' went further – with additional embellishments. Just as in the *Daily Graphic*'s version, Captain Smith remained on the bridge until the last possible moment, before finally being swept away. A strong swimmer, he remained alive, spotted a lifeboat and

> swam up to it, supporting a baby on his left arm and swimming with his right.
> 'Take the child!' he gasped.
> A dozen hands reached forth to grasp the baby which was taken into the boat. They tried to pull the captain into the boat, but he refused.
> 'What became of Murdoch?' he asked.
> When someone answered that he was dead, 'the captain,' said Mr. Williams, 'released his grasp of the gunwale and slowly sank before our eyes.'[47]

Captain Smith, according to Gibbs' 'Deathless' publication, was

> the very type of a British sea-captain, quiet, with shrewd, keen eyes beneath his shaggy brows, strong in command, gentle in social converse, modest as a simple seaman, brave as a lion, of unblemished honour.[48]

His memorial statue, wrote Stevenson in the 'Be British' souvenir, was 'an essentially British memorial to a British hero'.[49] Admiral Beresford went further: Smith was 'an example of the very best type of British seaman and British gentleman'. He praised him for his 'bravery, his resolution, his chivalrous conduct, and his gallantry'.[50] J.W. Thompson added that Smith had 'died as he had lived, a strict example of the best type of British sailor and English gentleman'.[51] Stevenson himself concluded roundly that Smith represented 'the best that is British'.[52] In this way, the inscription beneath the statue was able to proclaim: 'Bequeathing to his countrymen the Memory and Example of a Great Heart, A Brave Life, and A Heroic Death. Be British'.[53]

We have seen, then, the essentially 'British' behaviour of Bride, Phillips and Smith, and compared it with the ignominious behaviour of the anonymous 'Italians'. There is one further ingredient, however, which needs to be taken into account, for in addition to the committal of these 'British' qualities to the social memory, it must be said that social amnesia has also played its part. There are two aspects of the conduct of the 'heroic' Marconi operators, for example, which were not fêted in the popular texts. First, it was quickly established at the American inquiry that approximately one hour before the *Titanic*'s collision with the iceberg, Phillips had received a warning from the nearby *Californian*: 'We are stopped and surrounded by ice.' Rather than report this important message to the bridge, however, Phillips replied: 'Shut up. I am busy. I am working Cape Race.'[54] Phillips, in other words, was too busy relaying personal messages from passengers via Cape Race on the mainland to attend to a potentially life-saving transmission from another liner. The British inquiry subsequently established that two previous ice warnings had been received by Phillips but not communicated to the bridge.[55] The second of these, concluded the inquiry, 'would perhaps have affected the navigation of the vessel'.[56] Phillips, we recall, was lauded as a 'hero' who was 'composed of that old English valiance that has turned the blood of history into wine'.[57] There is no mention in the popular texts of him failing to deliver ice warnings or telling the *Californian* to 'shut up', even though the details of these acts and omissions were publicly available.

The second case of social amnesia surrounding the Marconi cabin concerns the surviving operator Bride who, it transpired, had sold his story exclusively to the *New York Times*. More than that, however, his exclusive deal was believed in some quarters to have accounted for the notable lack of information emanating from the rescue ship *Carpathia* as it steamed to New York. Official confirmation that the *Titanic* had sunk was not sent until two days after the sinking: even an inquiry from President Taft himself went unanswered. It is possible that both Bride and *Carpathia* operator Cottam were both well aware of the story of another Marconi operator, Jack Binns of the *Republic*. Binns had been on board the *Republic* when it collided with the *Florida* off Nantucket in January 1909. He repaired the damaged Marconi apparatus and transmitted messages for help. Many lives were saved, and the story of 'CQD Binns' was graphically reported in the *New York Times*, transforming Binns from a radio operator into a celebrity and writer on maritime topics. Whether or not that was true, two intercepted messages sent to the *Carpathia* radio room on

18 April remain deeply revealing: '...Marconi Company taking good care of you. Keep your mouth shut and hold your story. It is fixed so you will get big money.' This was followed by: 'Arranged for your exclusive story in dollars in four figures. Mr. Marconi agreeing. Say nothing until you see me.'[58] Bride received $1,000, while Cottam gained $750. At the American inquiry, Senator Smith further discovered that Marconi had a long-standing business connection with the *New York Times*, and that he had managed to get *Times* reporter Jim Speers on board the *Carpathia* when it docked in New York while the rest of the press were kept on shore. Senator Smith felt strongly that public information had been withheld for private gain, and the issue was investigated in open session. In his report to Congress, Senator Smith confirmed his conclusion that information had been 'withheld' for subsequent sale. It was a practice which subjected 'the participants to criticism, and the practice should be prohibited'.[59]

Although details of this less than commendable behaviour by Bride were freely available in the public domain, it does not appear in the British popular texts. Bride remained an untarnished hero. Similarly, Marconi himself remained untainted. His conduct had been publicly pursued by Smith within days of the sinking, but in the British popular texts, there is no hint of this. This is all the more remarkable when one considers that Marconi was Italian. The myth of the *Titanic* was composed of easily distinguishable heroes and villains; presumably the ambiguous status of the real Marconi would unacceptably have clouded the issue.

The final act of social amnesia, however, is reserved for Captain Smith himself. Reading all the tributes to his heroic 'Britishness' it is easy to overlook the fact that for all his bearded authority, shrewd eyes and shaggy brows, he was still the man who ultimately sank the *Titanic*. There is no hint of any culpability in the British popular texts, however. Just like Harold Bride, he remains an unblemished hero who, we recall, 'died as he lived, a strict example of the best type of British sailor and English gentleman'.[60] There remains, however, one possible hint of deliberate amnesia on the plaque at the foot of Captain Smith's memorial statue at Lichfield. The inscription, we remember, praised his great heart, brave life and heroic death, concluding with that famous command: 'Be British'. What the inscription fails to mention, however, is the *Titanic*. There is no mention of it at all. It could be, of course, that it was assumed at the time that anyone seeing the statue would know of the famous Captain Smith and that reference to his command of (and death upon) the *Titanic* would therefore be unnecessary. On the other hand, it may also be possible to interpret the omission as deliberate: by 1914 the popular euphoria surrounding the *Titanic* had begun to die down and the subscribers to the statue did not wish to draw attention to the precise and unfortunate circumstances of their friend's demise. It remains, therefore, a tantalizing hermeneutic conundrum: an interpretive riddle based not upon what had been said, but upon that which had been left unspoken.[61]

Such deftly accomplished acts of social amnesia help to maintain the British at the top of the tree of ideal conduct. It is important to note, however, that although the crew were predominantly British, the majority of the passengers were not. The celebration of 'Be British', then, would seem to create enormous problems, especially as the most celebrated of the deeds among the passengers were committed not by the British, but by Americans. We remember Astor standing back from the boats and lighting his cigarette, the Strauses electing to face death together just as they had faced life, and Guggenheim and his valet changing into evening dress so that they could die 'like gentlemen'. The myth of the *Titanic*, however, was able ingeniously to negotiate the 'British' problem in two ways. First, everyone who behaved well was praised as if they had been British even if they were not. In the words of Wright's song, everyone acted: 'like Britons, side by side';[62] the operative word, clearly being 'like'. It is almost as though those who behaved with manly decorum and dignity were awarded the title of 'Honorary Briton'.[63] Robert Donnelly's sheet music, therefore, is able to include the lines: 'Be British he cried and it can't be denied/ Yankees and Britons together they tried ...'[64] In this way, even the 'Yankees' are able to obey the captain's command and 'Be British'. Similarly, the American Benjamin Guggenheim was roundly praised by Philip Gibbs for donning white tie and tails in the face of death: 'It was the same spirit in which Lord Nelson put on his medals before the battle of Trafalgar.'[65] He faced it like a Briton – and an historically 'great' Briton at that.

There was also a second way round the problem: the Americans in particular could be included by making manly dignity in death a racial rather than just a national characteristic. Those who behaved well could be described as Anglo-Saxon rather than British. 'What a glorious thing it is to know,' began Pelham and Wright's song 'Be British': 'That the breed is just the same/ as it was when the Anglo-Saxon race/ First gained immortal fame'.[66] This joining of Britons and Americans under the umbrella of the Anglo-Saxon race had proved convenient even before the *Titanic* set sail. The *Titanic* was a British-built and registered ship, and the White Star Line a British company. However, the White Star Line was in turn owned by an American conglomerate, headed by an American financier, J. Pierpont Morgan. Additionally (and to an extent, correspondingly), the *Titanic* was, as we recall, heavily marketed in the United States on the grounds of its unparalleled size and luxury. These attributes, it was felt, would appeal particularly to the 'new' money of the American market. It was understandable, then, that the pre-publicity material published by the White Star Line should emphasize what they saw as the common racial heritage of the two countries. A White Star publicity brochure of 1911 boasted: 'It is impossible to overestimate the service rendered to the Anglo-Saxon race by the enterprise of our Shipowners and Shipbuilders.'[67] Indeed, continued the brochure, achievements such as the *Titanic*

> stand for the pre-eminence of the Anglo-saxon race in the Ocean; for the 'Command of the Seas' ... Consequently, these ... Leviathans add enormously to the potential prosperity and progress of the race.[68]

With the demise of the *Titanic*, of course, what ultimately united the Anglo-Saxons was not their pre-eminence at shipbuilding, but rather that, in the words of Pelham and Wright's song, 'Our men knew how to die'.[69] The *Titanic*, then, had provided a welcome test of racial character. According to Young, the disaster was able to determine whether, after 'long years of peace and increase in material comfort ... their race had deteriorated in courage and morale.' Indeed, it was only through such tests that we could periodically 'measure our advance or decline'.[70] The race, of course, was not found lacking, for, it seemed, strength of character was genetic and therefore unaffected by transient comfort and tranquillity. According to the recitative section of Scott's recorded song, the heroes of the *Titanic* 'sacrificed their lives for others in obedience to the *instinct* of their race'(my emphasis).[71] Racial superiority, then, was not learned but innate.

One problem still might have remained, however: Not all the heroes of the *Titanic* were Anglo-Saxon. The celebrated Guggenheim and Straus, for example, were both Jewish (and Straus was an immigrant to boot). To a certain extent, men such as Straus were already included as 'Honorary Britons' or even 'Honorary Anglo-Saxons' on the strength of their impeccable behaviour. But it was Admiral Lord Charles Beresford who perhaps (and probably quite unwittingly) came up with the most convenient umbrella phrase under which to include even the

likes of Isidor Straus. In a letter to *The Times*, later reproduced by
Gibbs in 'The Deathless Story of the Titanic', Beresford praised the
captain, crew and passengers of the ship: 'who were true to the spirit
of manly duty of the English-speaking races'.[72] People such as
Guggenheim and Straus, therefore, could be included in the exemplary racial/heroic group because they were English *speakers*. They
were English by tongue and therefore presumably also in character
and spirit. In this way, all who behaved heroically could be culturally
reanimated to add to the supposed superiority of the British, even
though they were not actually British at all.

Was there no dissent among the broad wave of cultural self-
congratulation which greeted the *Titanic* disaster? Among the cultural
texts it is difficult to find even muted criticism. Gibbs, it is true,
remarked upon what he considered the only frugality on board
Titanic: the lack of lifeboats and rafts. 'Alas! The pity of it!' he
lamented. 'Humanity has paid dearly for that economy.'[73] The *Daily
Graphic* 'In Memoriam' edition similarly contrasted the *Titanic*'s
luxury with the lack of safety equipment. When looking over the won-
drous ship: 'No-one looked at the boats.'[74] The *Graphic*'s criticism
remains slight, however. One inside page of the special edition shows
two photographs of (purportedly) the *Titanic*'s lifeboats on the davits,
the caption to the second of which stated the number on board, their
capacity and the number who were saved. The caption does not
mention the discrepancy between the capacity and the number of
people actually on board. The headline to this page simply announced
'The Much-Discussed Boats'.[75] In view of the indisputable fact that
sufficient lifeboats, properly organized, could have saved everyone on
board the *Titanic*, to describe the boats simply as 'much discussed' is
generous indeed.

As for the celebration of ethnic superiority, there is only one
moment of moderate dissent. Filson Young, discussing the 'heroes' of
the engine room, most of whom died at their posts, observed:

> discipline and conduct like this are proofs, not of the superiority of
> one race over another, but that in the core of human nature itself
> there is an abiding sweetness and soundness ...[76]

It remains a small voice, however, against the overwhelming tide of
racial celebration, to which even Young himself was ultimately a reliable contributor.

As regards any greater dissent from the popular vein, there was
little of it, and it was not to be found within the popular vein itself.

Further, this dissent was allowed to go only so far. The novelist Joseph Conrad was one of the few dissenters, and his views were published in *The English Review* in May and July 1912. In his article: 'Some Reflections, Seamanlike and Otherwise, on the Loss of the Titanic', Conrad criticized both the maritime authorities and the luxurious appointments of the *Titanic*, which were designed to please a 'fatuous hatful of individuals'.[77] Yet while Conrad vented contempt for both officialdom and what he perceived as the idle rich, his stolid support for both captain and crew brought him back into firm compliance with the popular line. The moral remained that whatever the technical deficiencies which the bureaucrats had permitted, the seamen would continue to 'prove themselves truer than steel'.[78] Conrad took pains to separate himself from what he described as 'the penny and halfpenny Press', however. In his subsequent article 'Some Aspects of the Admirable Inquiry',[79] he accused popular journalists of sentimentality in lauding the *Titanic* men as 'heroes'. The majority of people, even 'common people', declared Conrad, would always behave decently in extreme crisis. Journalists seemed unaware of this, 'Hence their enthusiasm'.[80] He would far rather the men had survived to support their families than died heroic deaths. Dismissing the popular press's playing up of the 'Drury Lane aspects of the event', Conrad determined:

> There is nothing more heroic in being drowned very much against your will, off a holed, helpless, big tank in which you bought your passage than in quietly dying of colic caused by the imperfect salmon in the tin you bought from your grocer'.[81]

To the reader today, Conrad's observations may seem to be a welcome antidote to the glorification of the *Titanic* disaster in the popular press. It must be remembered, however, that Conrad's articles did not appear in the popular press: they were aimed at that press from beyond it. The popular, mass-circulation texts remained untouched by Conrad's invective in *The English Review*.

Conrad's indignation, however, was eclipsed by that of George Bernard Shaw. Shaw wrote to the *Daily News and Leader*, accusing the popular texts of 'outrageous romantic lying'. He despised the way in which all men '(except the foreigners, who must all be shot by stern British officers ...)' were made into heroes, and the captain into a 'super-hero'. The captain, indeed, was a 'living guarantee that the wreck was nobody's fault but, on the contrary, a triumph of British navigation'. Consequently, writers who had never heard of Captain

Smith, 'wrote of him as they would hardly write of Nelson'.[82] Was it necessary, he wondered,

> to assure the world that only Englishmen could have behaved so heroically, and to compare their conduct with the hypothetic dastardliness which lascars or Italians or foreigners generally ... would have shown in the same circumstances?'[83]

The upshot of it all, he fumed, was 'ghastly, blasphemous, unhuman, braggartly lying'. It made the British 'vainglorious, insolent, and mendacious'.[84]

This was all too much for Sir Arthur Conan Doyle, who swiftly responded with a point-by-point refutation of Shaw's claims. This was printed in the same newspaper four days later. Shaw, he declared, had used his undoubted genius 'to misrepresent and decry his own people' and only added to the grief of all concerned.[85] Two days later, Shaw responded in turn to Conan Doyle. He disputed the novelist's counter-allegations, and went on to lambast the 'sentimental idiots' who reminded him that Captain Smith went down with the ship. 'I tell them, with the impatient contempt they deserve, that so did the cat.'[86] Conan Doyle closed the correspondence three days after that.[87]

Conrad, Shaw and Conan Doyle were not writers for the 'penny and halfpenny Press' but celebrated literary figures of the day. Their contributions to the *Titanic* debate, therefore, lie outside our examination of the popular texts which narrated the myth of the *Titanic*. I have drawn attention to them here, however, to show that while there was some dissent (certainly from Shaw and partly from Conrad) from the popular mentality of the time, this was dissent and debate among the *literati*, and not the populace. It was remarkable, indeed, that this dissent was exceptional. Shaw himself acknowledged this. 'Did the press really represent the public?' he inquired. 'I am afraid it did.' He concluded, sadly: 'I am in the minority.'[88]

Let us review, for a moment, a few of the disturbing facts about the *Titanic* disaster. The *Titanic* was, at the time, the largest ship in the world. It had the capacity to carry some 3,500 passengers and crew, and was designed to ply the lucrative North Atlantic run between Europe and New York. Its sea trials took place just ten days before its maiden voyage, and lasted no more than 12 hours. During these trials, the ship was not once run at full speed. Many of the crew did not join the ship until hours before its first (and last) commercial voyage. There had been no lifeboat drill, and there was lifeboat capacity for only one third of the ship's capacity.

On the night of 14 April the *Titanic* was cruising at full speed into a known ice-field. That day, the *Titanic* had received five separate ice warnings,[89] but still failed to reduce speed. The binoculars were missing from the lookouts' 'crow's nest', and the captain, having dined at a private dinner party in the company of some of America's leading millionaires, had gone to bed for the night. It was then that the *Titanic* struck ice.

The *Titanic* struck ice in such a way that it was inevitable that it was going to sink. There was never any formal order given to abandon ship, and the loading of the lifeboats was remarkably haphazard. Many were sent away half empty due to lack of organization, still further reducing the number of people who were likely to be saved. A passenger's chances of survival were directly related to his or her social class: 62 per cent in first class, 41 per cent in second class and only 25 per cent in third class.[90] In total of 2,227 people on board, only 705 survived. The remaining 1,522 lost their lives in the middle of a dark, calm and icy Atlantic Ocean.

These stark facts were readily and publicly available at the time. Had the *Titanic* sunk in similar circumstances today, it is almost impossible to imagine the extent of outcry which would have ensued. The dissenting voices of Conrad – and certainly Shaw – would surely have been in the majority. In the British popular culture of 1912–14, however, there is hardly a breath of recrimination. It dwells not on culpability for a completely avoidable disaster, but, rather, celebrates the heroism of everyone concerned. 'As long as the sons of men read the history of heroism,' wrote Gibbs, 'so will this story be remembered.'[91]

I should, perhaps, pause for a moment to make something absolutely clear here: I am not for a moment belittling those who died or the grief of those who mourned for them. Nor am I even disputing that some behaved with extreme bravery and that the *Titanic* disaster did indeed bring about any acts of self-sacrifice. What I am trying to contend is that the *Titanic* was a tragedy – and a wholly avoidable tragedy at that. By emphasizing the triumph in all of this, however, the late Edwardian popular texts succeeded in elevating the one at the expense of the other. Certainly, grief and loss are both remarked upon. 'The tears of those who have to weep for their dead are not yet dry,' lamented Gibbs. 'We are still haunted by that death-ship and hear the great chorus of human agony which rose into the silence of that night of doom.'[92] Indeed, the sinking of the *Titanic* 'stands alone in its awfulness, supreme in its tragedy.' It certainly does sound very terrible, but in the very same page Gibbs turns that phrase round majestically with the simple sentence: 'Yet greater than the tragedy is the glory.'[93] In so doing, Gibbs provides us with perhaps the most significant single sentence of all the *Titanic* texts. Once it has been established that glory has defeated tragedy, then tragedy is left behind – almost dispensed with – and glory is to be allowed full sway. Gibbs is not alone here. Indeed, the popular texts as a group are similarly strewn with such 'transitionary' phrases, sentences or paragraphs. Tragedy is admitted and then, almost symmetrically, replaced with glory. For example, the *Daily Graphic* declared that the *Titanic* provided a scene 'so deep with human anguish yet so lighted with human grandeur'.[94] It expanded that while we should be very sorry for the families of those who died, we should still all be glad because:

> For us, as for them, moreover, there is heartening thought in one thing that can be read into the disaster ... (those who died) have presented us with the most inspiring of spectacles – the inherent nobility of mankind.[95]

The result, therefore, is that although the faces of the bereaved are 'dark with sorrow', they are at the same time 'untouched with the lightest shadow of shame'. For although man has been humbled at sea, he has taken it 'with all the glory and splendour of a victory'.[96] It is an elegant transformation indeed. Filson Young similarly agreed that 1,500 people had died on the *Titanic*, 'but honour and glory have come into their own'.[97] Death may have taken human bodies, 'but he left hearts unconquered'.[98]

Unconquered, the tributes continued. A letter published in the memorial publication for the drowned engineers extolled 'the honour and glory they have cast upon our profession',[99] while another proclaimed: 'Never in our history as a nation, either at land or at sea, has such an example of bravery and fidelity to duty been known.'[100] The *Daily Graphic* was sure that 'nothing has been disclosed which is not to the credit of passengers and crew alike' and quoted a Canadian passenger, Paul Cheveret [*sic*],[101] as saying: 'I take off my hat to the English seamen who went down with the ship and the men who manned the lifeboats. Every man of them was a hero.'[102] 'What a glorious thing it is to know', began the first verse of Pelham and Wright's commemorative song, that 'our men knew how to die'.[103] The Dean of Lichfield Cathedral told those attending the statue unveiling ceremony that the iceberg itself had been 'instrumental in eliciting the supreme expression of the qualities of heart and mind which do most to dignify the human character'.[104] Gibbs was therefore able to claim that 'Human character has revealed itself with all its old qualities of nobility' and has indeed 'gained and held victory over death itself'.[105] He was then able to rise to a rhetorical and emotional crescendo:

> All the great virtues of the soul were displayed upon 'that dim, dark sea, so like unto death' – courage, self-forgetfulness, self-sacrifice, love, devotion to the highest ideals which are the guiding stars of life, beyond the Common reach. Heroism, not tawdry, touched by no falsity of melodrama, but simple, with a divine simplicity, leapt forth, as though in the call of God, like a 'sunburst in the storm of death.'[106]

For Filson Young, it was heroism such as this that provided 'the final crown of glory of this catastrophe'. Indeed, it 'continued and confirmed a tradition of English sea life that should be a tingling inspiration to everyone who has knowledge of it'.[107] Young's belief that the glory of the *Titanic* should be a 'tingling inspiration' to all leads us to discern that it is the triumph rather than the tragedy of the *Titanic* which was thought to be the most worthy of pride of place in the social memory. Once the tragedy had been exorcised, it was the triumph which would live on, narrated and immortalised in myth. As Gibbs put it:

> In all its facts of horror and of heroism, the story of the 'Titanic' will put a spell on the imagination of men ... It must be told, so that our children and our children's children will cherish its memory.[108]

Within days of the sinking, therefore, it was understood that a myth had been made, and that it would be handed down from generation to generation. It was a theme echoed in Pelham and Wright's song 'Be British!', whose second verse ran:

> Thro' the years to come, inscribed in gold,
> On hist'rys page shall be
> The story of how they met their doom
> Out on the icy sea,
> And our children's children all will read
> Throughout the Empire wide,
> These grand old words, and, in days to be,
> Will echo them with pride.[109]

This enduring fame, earned in death and handed down in narrative through the generations, is not unique to the myth of the *Titanic*. In Hellenic literature, it was known as *kleos*, the ancient Greek term for

118   *The Myth of the* Titanic

'fame' or 'glory'. It derived from the word 'kluo' (hear) and so, etymologically, means 'that which is heard'. To the Greeks, then, it also meant the special glory conferred by the inclusion in the tradition of epic poetry.[110] As Gregory Nagy explains, 'The conceit of Homeric poetry is that even a Trojan will fight and die in pursuit of the *kleos* of the Achaeans ... If you perform heroic deeds, you have a chance of getting into Achaean epic.'[111] But *kleos* does more than merely install the hero in epic, it endows upon him something akin to immortal life, for the Hellenic hero, though physically dead, has his reputation, and his honour and his example live after him throughout the generations. This is well understood, for example, by Achilles in *The Iliad* IX, 411–13: if he stays and fights the Trojans instead of merely returning home, he reflects, 'my glory (*kleos*) shall be everlasting'.[112] As Nagy concludes, 'It is to Achilles that the Iliadic tradition assigns the kleos that will never perish.'[113] It is fascinating, therefore, to read this extract from Gibbs in the light of this notion of *kleos*:

> As long as the sons of men read the history of heroism so will this story be remembered ... its deathless drama. Written as it were in letters of gold will be the names of those brave men and women who faced death bravely ... Many poems have already been written on the sinking of the 'Titanic,' but the plain story is itself a poem, of the old and high ideals, of the great traditions of human courage and pity; a poem of brave lives snatching victory out of death.[114]

It is by no means absurd, therefore, to view the myth of the *Titanic* as following in the established tradition of the epic poems of ancient Greece. It also helps us to reflect all the more knowingly upon Gibbs' title: 'The Deathless Story of the Titanic'. In the Hellenic tradition, 'heroes' such as Benjamin Guggenheim chose *kleos* over *nostos* – the longing to return home. By choosing to make a gallant gesture in death, Guggenheim – resplendent in his white tie and tails – chose the immortality of myth rather than the quiet anonymity (or possibly even ignomy) of a safe return. Just like Achilles, his reputation was dearer to him than life itself.

The story of the *Titanic*, of course, was a deeply selective one. The heroism and glory of the *Titanic* were quickly remembered, but the uncomfortable facts surrounding the disaster were forgotten with equal rapidity. This is all the more remarkable in that this heavily partial committal to social memory was done in the face of a far broader range of evidence which was widely available in the public sphere. No sooner had the rescue ship *Carpathia* disembarked the sur-

vivors in New York than a Congressional Committee was set up formally to investigate the loss of the *Titanic*. The hearings, indeed,
began at the Waldorf Astoria hotel the very next day. These hearings
were held under the rigorous chairmanship of Senator Smith, and very
soon revealed the less praiseworthy ingredients in the *Titanic* disaster
in open court: the cursory sea-trials, the scarcity of lifeboats, the lack
of a lifeboat drill, the absence of binoculars, the inexperience of the
crew, the speed of the ship, the warnings of ice, the confusion in the
loading of the boats and the uncomfortable correlation between social
class and survival rate. The British popular texts, however, took from
the hearings (and the contiguous media circus) all that was heroic and
omitted that which was not. In this way, within days of the disaster, the
historical data surrounding the *Titanic* were reanimated to reconstruct
a triumph out of a tragedy. The myth of the *Titanic* was born.

6 'Nearer, My God, to Thee'

One of the most vivid and enduring ingredients of the myth of the *Titanic* is the image of the band playing on as the ship went down. More than that, the myth locates the brave musicians on deck, playing the hymn 'Nearer, My God, to Thee'[1] as their final, solemn offering. Not one of them survived. It is a tale without which no telling of the *Titanic* story is complete.

The story of the band playing on appears towards the end of the greater narrative of the *Titanic*, and is celebrated widely in the late Edwardian texts. Before the *Titanic* struck ice on the night of Sunday, 14 April, the ship was mostly quiet, with the majority of passengers and crew preparing for bed. As Gibbs describes it:

> ...down in the street of this city at sea, mothers were bending over sleeping babies, women were putting off their finery, youth was already in the land of dreams, and old age was praying for a good night's sleep.[2]

The collision was so, seemingly, slight that the majority of the passengers failed to notice it. Most people became aware of the situation only gradually, and only gradually did they begin to appear on deck. In this way, the rhythm of the shipboard narrative is one of activity subsiding into restfulness, followed by a slow awakening which accelerates into curiosity, alarm, despair and – finally – with an almost symphonic resolution into a quiet, calm and dignified acceptance of fate. When we hear the myth of the *Titanic*, then, it is as though the band provide the incidental music.

According to Gibbs, while the lifeboats were being lowered, the band assembled 'on one of the decks' and 'played selections from operas and the latest popular melodies'. Young described them playing 'jolly rag-time tunes' as an accompaniment to the 'bustle and labour of getting off the boats'.[3] The ship, indeed, was 'blazing with light',[4] and to the reader today, the band would seem to have helped create a bizarre party atmosphere as the ship began to sink. Gibbs described the 'merry music floating out above the quiet waters under the star-strewn sky'. It 'set the keynote to this great melody of spiritual devotion to honour and duty'.[5]

Gibbs' allusion to the 'quiet waters' of the traditionally funereal 23rd Psalm reminds us, however, that death was at hand. This was a

state of affairs which became increasingly apparent to everyone as the
ship settled further and further into the sea. This did not deter the
musicians, however. The *Daily Graphic* reported them playing 'secular
music' until they realized that 'Death was near',[6] while Gibbs went so
far as dramatically to assert that 'They played until they were waist
high in water.'[7] It is then that the narrative crescendo reaches its peak.
The emotional climax, however, is neither spectacular nor frenetic.
Rather, it takes place in a suspended moment of quiet dignity when,
like a hurricane seeming to abate in the eye of the storm, everything
involving the ship appears to pause. In the myth of the *Titanic*, this
supremely charged moment arrests all other activity and attention,
uniting the scene from the sloping decks to the distant lifeboats. Gibbs
continues:

> In that dread moment Hartley, the conductor, spoke to his comrades
> and there throbbed out into the darkness, heard by the women in the
> boats far away, the hymn of faith to the Eternal Father.[8]

These 'solemn strains', said Young, 'could be heard coming over the
waters'.[9] When death came, said the *Daily Graphic*, they 'met it with
the strains of "Nearer, my God, to Thee"'.[10] Indeed, continued Gibbs:

> That music, divine as an angelic melody when played by men face to
> face with eternity, was silenced only when the ship reared up in her
> death agony, and then plunged into the depths.[11]

This was enough to ensure all concerned heroic status. The name of
conductor Hartley, declared Gibbs, 'will be remembered always as one
of the greatest heroes of the "Titanic"'.[12] 'The Deathless Story of the
Titanic' went on to dedicate a half-page graphic to Hartley and the
musicians: The score of 'Nearer, my God to Thee' – 'The hymn played
by the band of the "Titanic" as she sank' – is reproduced, complete
with the words to all five verses. A portrait drawing of Hartley is inset,
with the names and addresses of all eight 'Heroic Musicians' listed as
'The brave bandsmen who played "Nearer, my God to Thee" while
the "Titanic" was sinking fast'.[13]

The bandsmen's 'heroism' was celebrated not only in books and
souvenir editions, but also in postcards, in music, in memorial and in
ceremony. The *Daily Mirror*'s front page of 20 April was commercially
reproduced in postcard form: 'Bandsmen heroes of the sinking Titanic
play "Nearer, My God, to Thee!" as the liner goes down to her doom.'
The score and a verse of the 'immortal hymn' were reproduced in
'exact facsimile' of the newspaper edition.[14] It is interesting to note

that the hymn had become 'immortal' within five days of the sinking. The Rotary Photographic Company reproduced four verses and the first four bars of 'The hymn to the strains of which the "Titanic" sunk' [*sic*][15] as their postcard (plate VIII), while Millar and Lang's version gave the entire score of the hymn played by the bandsmen 'as she sank to her doom'.[16] W. Clark of Liverpool and Joe Dixon of Hull both pictured the individual bandsmen on their postcards, complete with extracts from the hymn. Both deemed the musicians 'heroic', while the Dixon card even had crowns depicted over each of the bandsmen's heads. They 'died at their posts like men'.[17] Debenham of Cowes' postcard declared the musicians 'Heroes All' for playing the hymn as 'she went down',[18] while Tom Harvey of Redruth's postcard called them 'British heroes' for playing the same piece as the ship was sinking 'about 2 a.m.'.[19] E.A. Bragg of Falmouth's 'In Memoriam' card gave the words to two verses and concluded: 'Greater Love Hath No Man Than This, That A Man Lay Down His Life For His Friends'.[20] Finally, Bamforth and Company of Holmfirth, Yorkshire, produced a series of six memorial postcards on the theme of 'Nearer, My God, to Thee'. In various combinations they depict weeping angels, a sinking *Titanic*, a score and verses from the hymn, Christ appearing over the waters, a cross and a host of angels ascending through the clouds into heaven. All six contain a direct reference to the words of the hymn.[21]

Not surprisingly, the *Titanic*'s band and their final rendition of 'Nearer, My God, to Thee' were celebrated in music and song. 'The Band Was Playing as the Ship Went Down', for example, was composed and written for piano and voices by Robert Donnelly, and arranged by Percival Langley for sale as sheet music. It could be 'sung in public without fee or licence' – except in music halls and theatres. The cover illustration of the 'ill-fated' *Titanic* was accompanied by an inset portrait of bandleader Hartley. The third verse remarked (somewhat clumsily):

Fancy a band playing knowing that death
Would come in a few minutes' time
Nearer my God to Thee how true these words
To that brave band of men in their prime ...'[22]

The chorus expressed similar sentiments:

And the Band was playing as the ship went down
'Nearer my God to Thee'
Men gave their lives to save those of wives

Out on the ice bound sea
And those hero's playing knowing too well
That in the end they must drown
While some were praying they continued playing as the ship
went down.[23]

Haydon Augarde's 'descriptive musical sketch for the piano', 'The
Wreck of the Titanic', contained no lyrics, except for the section sub-
titled 'Nearer My God To Thee' which, a note on the sixth page of the
score explained, was 'Sung on board the doomed ship'.[24] The recorded
version of Wright's 'Be British' contained a recitative spoken over the
melody to the hymn which included the couplet: 'And though they
found a cold, cold grave, beneath the icy sea,/ Up on high these words
were heard: Nearer, my God to Thee!'[25] At the Royal Albert Hall, the
Orchestral Association staged a 'Titanic Band Memorial Concert' on
'Empire Day', Friday, 24 May. What was claimed to be the largest
professional orchestra ever assembled concluded the proceedings with
a rendition of 'Nearer my God to Thee' orchestrated and conducted
by no less a luminary than Sir Henry Wood.[26] The words of four verses
were included in the programme, as were the names of the eight musicians, bordered in black.[27] The Wigan memorial handkerchief
declared that as the *Titanic* was:

> seen to be settling down preparatory to plunging into the depths,
> the ships orchestra gathered together on deck and played the tune
> of the hymn – 'Nearer my God! to Thee ...'[28]

Although the souvenir publication to the unveiling of the captain's
statue was primarily dedicated to Smith himself, the musicians were
not forgotten. 'We all agree', testified the wife of a crew member, 'that
the brave bandsmen carried out the captain's wish by playing that
hymn "Nearer, my God, to Thee."'[29] The body of bandleader Hartley
was recovered from the sea and buried at Colne in Lancashire on 18
May 1912. A tall monument still marks the grave 'In Loving Memory'
of the man who 'Lost his life in the S.S. Titanic Disaster' (plate IX).
At the foot of the memorial are carvings of a violin and an open
hymn-book revealing the opening bars and refrain: 'Nearer My God
To Thee, Nearer To Thee'.[30]
Hartley became widely known and admired following the disaster.
It will be noted that his grave does not state that he was the bandleader on the *Titanic*, just as the cover to Donnelly's sheet music
identifies him simply as 'Mr. W. Hartley'. Clearly, the public were

expected already to have known. It was, after all, a first-rate story. Once we proceed with a closer analysis of the texts, however, we can see how the details began to change as the story evolved. Gibbs, Young and the *Graphic*, for example, described how the band played mostly rag-time and popular music as the ship was going down. The postcards, the memorial handkerchief and Hartley's grave, however, refer only to the hymn. The majority of their 'performance', then, was gradually forgotten in favour of its shorter but more memorable conclusion. Further, while the more sober among the texts have the hymn played by the band, by the time the story reaches composers Augarde and Wright, the hymn was additionally being sung. This was the hymn, we recall, 'Sung on board the doomed ship', according to Augarde's explanatory note above the appropriate passage from his musical sketch.[31] The recitative to the recorded version of Wright's song declares, we remember, 'Up on high these words were heard: Nearer, my God to Thee!'[32] First, it was simply a tune, but now we have the words being sung, too. In Gibbs' version, it was bandleader Hartley who quietly initiated the playing of the final hymn just as the ship was about to go down. By the time of the 'Be British' publication in 1914, the wife of a crew member was able to write: 'We all agree that the brave bandsmen carried out Captain Smith's wish by playing that hymn.'[33] By now, it was the captain's idea. The crewman's wife was yet more revealing than she had probably intended, however. It seemed now that the story of 'Nearer, My God, to Thee' was one of agreement rather than documented fact.

As we delve further into the details, further discrepancies continue to emerge. The musicians on the *Titanic* were W. Theodore Brailey (piano), Roger Bricoux (cello), John Frederick P. Clarke (bass), Wallace Hartley (bandmaster and violin), John Law Hume (violin), Georges Krins (violin), Percy C. Taylor (piano) and J. Wesley Woodward (cello). All are commemorated together in the popular texts and pictured in postcards such as that of Joe Dixon of Hull with details of their instruments,[34] and with captions, such as in Clark of Liverpool, as 'The Heroic Orchestra'.[35] We notice, however, that this 'orchestra' contained two pianos. This is curious on two counts. First, an eight-piece ensemble is very unlikely to contain two pianos. This is because there was actually no such thing as the 'Titanic Orchestra'. What the ship contained, in fact, was two separate bands of musicians: one a quintet, led by Hartley, and the other a trio, who played in the lounge outside the à la carte restaurant. That would explain the two pianos (and possibly even the two cellos). What it does not explain is what is meant in the popular texts by 'the band'. 'Which band?', one might be tempted to ask. Did one play rag-time and the other hymns?

The second question raised by the curious case of the two pianos is this: how ever did they get them up on deck? The texts make it quite clear that this was where 'the band' played.[36] How else could the hymn have been heard by those in the boats? However, it seems extremely unlikely even in the best of circumstances, let alone on board a ship sinking in the middle of the Atlantic Ocean at dead of night, that eight musicians would struggle to carry two pianos (or even one) out on the deck to entertain the passengers.

The case is exacerbated by the two cellos and even the double bass. As the *Titanic* sank, the decks began increasingly to tilt. Cellos and double basses rest on spikes; the cellos are played from a seated position, and the double bass either from standing or a high stool. On a sloping deck, it would have been extremely difficult to play either of these instruments – certainly as the stern of the ship rose inexorably out of the water. If it was difficult for the cellos and the bass, it must have been impossible for the pianos: even if they had somehow been manhandled on deck, and unless the musicians had somehow devised a speedy method of anchoring them to the floor, they would simply have rolled away down the increasing gradient. That is not all: according to Gibbs, 'they played until they were waist high in water'.[37] Let us presume that the violinists and the bassist played from the standing position. The violinists would probably still have been able to play, but had the water reached bassist Clarke's waist, his instrument would have filled with water. It would have been even worse for the seated cellists and pianists. Quite simply, at least five of the eight musicians would have been physically unable to have played as Gibbs so dramatically described. At the high point of the drama, therefore, when 'Nearer, My God, to Thee' was said to have finally been played, the conditions were those in which it was least likely to have been possible. It is extremely doubtful, then, that 'the band' could have played as popularly described.

A further difficult question remains, however: what exactly were they playing? Reading, listening to and looking at the *Titanic* texts, one might immediately respond, of course, 'Nearer, My God, to Thee'. Once we progress from the level of observation to analysis, however, that conclusion becomes increasingly difficult to support. Certainly, the special editions, postcards, sheet music and other ephemera – to say nothing of Hartley's own grave – unswervingly report it was 'Nearer, My God, to Thee'. It is both reported and commemorated as fact, not supposition. Some give the title, some quote an extract, some even reproduce all five verses. This is, after all, the easiest way to recognize the hymn in print: by the words. Only a minority of the texts (both musical), however, report the hymn as actually being sung. Most relate that it was simply played. Even if it had been sung (by whom?), unless the singers had remarkable powers of both projection and diction, it is highly unlikely that the words sung on deck would have been recognizable to the majority of those who survived to tell the tale: the people several hundred yards out to sea in the lifeboats. It seems far more likely that they would have recognized the tune. This presents us with still greater problems, however.

Although the popular texts do not acknowledge this, there were in fact three different settings of 'Nearer, My God, to Thee' in common use at the time of the *Titanic* disaster. The first tune, 'Bethany', was the work of American composer Lowell Mason (1792–1872). Written in 4/4 time, and in the key of G major, it was the preferred version in the United States (and subsequently rendered in both the American 1953 and 1997 film versions of 'Titanic'.[38]) In Britain, there were two versions in popular use. John Bacchus Dykes' (1823–76) 'Horbury' was written in 3/2 time, in the key of E flat major. This was the preferred version in the Church of England (and featured in the British *Titanic* film 'A Night to Remember' of 1958.[39]) British Methodists, on the other hand, favoured Sir Arthur Sullivan's (1842–1900) 'Propior Deo', written in 4/2 time, in the key of G major. This is the least well remembered of the three. The tune 'Nearer, My God, to Thee', then, would have meant three entirely different things to three different groups of people, all of whom were represented on the *Titanic*.

Which of the two British versions, then, is reproduced in the British popular texts? The answer is that both are reproduced with equal conviction. Neither, however, acknowledges the existence of either of the others. When the score (or part of the score) is reproduced, neither the tune nor the composer is usually given; one needs to be able to read music to detect that completely different tunes are being commemorated as the one played by Hartley and his men as the ship went down.[40] Among the postcards, the (unacknowledged) Dykes setting is reproduced in the *Daily Mirror*, the Rotary and the Millar and Lang versions. Gibbs, too, uses Dykes in 'The Deathless Story of the Titanic'. The Sullivan version, however, is used by Bamforth and Company in their series of six commemorative postcards, and they credit Sullivan with the composition.[41] On record, it is the Dykes version that can be heard playing in the background during the recitative section of Wright's 'Be British', as was the version played at the Royal Albert Hall 'Titanic Band Memorial Concert'. The arrangement (for the vast orchestra) was Sir Henry Wood's, but the programme clearly credits the composition to Dykes. This tribute by fellow professional musicians, then, may seem to be the last word on the tune which Hartley and his colleagues played as the ship went down. The tune engraved upon Hartley's own grave, however, is not Dykes' but Sullivan's (plate X).[42] His family was, after all, Methodist.[43]

If we look closely, then, at the popular texts, we can see that they at the same time both promulgate and undermine the myth of the band playing 'Nearer, My God, to Thee' as the ship went down. Unwittingly, they contain the seeds of their own subversion. In this way, we have been able first to question the very idea of the *Titanic*'s 'band', second to show that it would have been physically impossible for the majority of them to have played as described, and third to contend that discrepancies over which tune was played make it impossible to conclude that any particular tune was played at all. More than that, we have been able to argue these points not from latter-day detective work, but simply from a close reading of the inconsistencies within the late Edwardian texts themselves. If these are apparent to us today, they must have been equally apparent to anyone who cared to look between 1912 and 1914. Look, it seems, they did not. The story was never challenged. The playing of 'Nearer, My God, to Thee' was reported as fact.

On what evidence, then, do the popular texts base their story? If they did have evidence, then they did not divulge it. There is no source quoted in any of the British texts examined to support their assertion about what the band were playing. This is hardly surprising. If, as the popular texts would have us believe, the hymn was the last thing the band played as the ship went down, the vast majority of people in a position to have heard it did not survive to tell the tale. By that stage in the proceedings, practically all those who survived were already some considerable distance from the scene. The key witnesses – the musicians themselves – all died. The majority of surviving witnesses were simply too far away to provide reliable evidence.

What we need, then, is a rare yet reliable witness who left the *Titanic* at the last moment – just as the band were supposed to have been playing the celebrated hymn. Such a witness exists in the form of Marconi operator Bride, who survived by clinging to the overturned collapsible boat B, which was washed from the ship just as it was about to sink. Bride, we recall, survived to give a detailed and exclusive account to the *New York Times* as soon as the rescue ship *Carpathia* reached New York on 18 April. His story was published the following morning while the disaster was still fresh in his mind – and even before he gave testimony to Senator Smith's formal inquiry.

The *New York Times* began with a bold, front page headline: '745 Saw Titanic Sink With 1,595, Her Band Still Playing'. Further page 1 sub-headings declared: 'Band Played As Titanic Sunk' and then 'Ship Sank To Tune of Autumn'.[44] So, according to a witness who was on board up until the last moment, and who was interviewed, in depth, at the first possible opportunity, the band were indeed playing. But what was this 'Autumn' to which it finally sank? Bride continued: 'From aft came the tunes of the band. It was a rag-time tune. Then there was Autumn.' He continued: 'The band was still playing. I guess all of the band went down. They were playing Autumn then.'[45] The *New York Times* did not say what 'Autumn' was. When the story reached Britain, however, an explanation was appended: Gibbs said that 'Autumn' was the name of a hymn tune 'used as a recessional in America'.[46] The band's last tune was now a hymn. Gibbs may have been jumping to conclusions, however, for recent study has disputed this. Lord, for example, has argued that the young British Marconi operator would have been unlikely to have both identified and referred to a hymn ('God of Mercy and Compassion') by the name of its American setting. Rather, he was likely to have known and meant the popular tune 'Songe d'Automne', a waltz that was popular in British dance halls (but not in America) at the time. Composed by Archibald Joyce, it was generally known simply as 'Autumn'. Bride had incorrectly assumed that his American interviewer would have understood what he meant.[47] Everyone agreed that the British band had, after all, been playing popular tunes.[48]

The point of this discussion, however, is not to make a case for what Bride may or may not have meant by the band playing 'Autumn' as the ship went down. The point is, rather, that whatever it was, it wasn't 'Nearer, My God to Thee'. If that was the case in New York, it was also the case in London, where Bride's *New York Times* interview appears to have provided the basis of the lengthy quotations attributed to him in 'The Deathless Story of the Titanic'. This later, British version has him saying: 'From aft came the tunes of the band. There was a rag-time tune, I don't know what, and then there was "Autumn"'.[49] The detail may differ slightly, but the result is the same: the only named witness to the band playing says nothing whatsoever about 'Nearer, My God, to Thee'.

We are bound to ask, then, did *anyone* actually report the band playing that now legendary hymn? The *New York Times* front page was, as we have seen, full of Bride and 'Autumn'. If we turn to page 4, however, we eventually find the cross-heading: 'Band Played "Nearer, My God"'. The body of the column went on to explain: 'Mrs. Dick, who was saved with her husband, told how, as the Titanic finally settled down, the band played "Nearer, My God to Thee".[50] She said:

> What I remember best was that as the ship sank we could hear the band playing 'Nearer, My God, to Thee.' We looked back and could see the men standing on deck absolutely quiet and waiting for the end. Their conduct was splendid, splendid.[51]

Published the morning after the *Carpathia* docked with the survivors, this very probably constitutes the first printed reference to the band playing 'Nearer, My God, to Thee' as the ship went down. There are a number of things to be said about Mrs Dick's claim, however. The first-class passenger Vera Dick, together with her husband Albert, had left the *Titanic* in lifeboat number 3 at approximately 1:00 am. As such, she was among the first to leave. Mrs Dick, therefore, had left the scene a full 1 hour and 20 minutes before the band were supposed to have played the final hymn which she recalled with such apparent clarity. Why, then, did Mrs Dick report having heard 'Nearer, My God, to Thee'? It may be, of course, that this is simply what she did indeed hear, but we have already shown that this was extremely unlikely. It is possible to offer, on the other hand, a much more plausible explanation – an explanation based in social as opposed to individual memory.

On Monday, 22 January 1906, the steamer *Valencia* ran onto rocks off Vancouver Island in British Columbia, Canada. A vessel of the Pacific Coast Steamship Company, it was *en route* from San Francisco to Victoria and then Seattle. Built in Philadelphia in 1882, it grossed 1,600 tons and was carrying over 100 passengers, together with a crew of 65.[52] The passage proceeded uneventfully, following the usual course north for three days before preparing to turn east at around midnight into the Strait of Juan de Fuca and finally docking at Victoria. Unfortunately, due to a navigational error, the *Valencia* overshot the entrance to the strait and ran aground, instead, among the rocks, cliffs and ledges off Pachena Point on the rugged and sparsely populated Pacific side of the island. Although the ship had come to rest only some 20 yards from the shore,[53] that shore comprised a vertical cliff face 100 feet high. The *Valencia* had been holed below the water line, flooding the generators and killing the lights. The captain beached the ship to stop it sinking completely, but it consequently lay helpless on the rocks, taking the full force of the waves which thundered in, unfettered, from the Pacific Ocean.

Although the *Valencia* had been beached only 60 feet from the shore, the habitually boiling seas made it impossible for the passengers to reach land. The *Valencia* had no radio, and it was 15 hours before news reached land that the ship had been wrecked. The ship, meanwhile, began to break apart in the foam and spray. When news of the wreck reached Victoria and Seattle on Tuesday, 23 January, survivors were still clinging on board. Rescuers were dispatched, but were unable to reach the *Valencia* due to its location and the unremitting seas. Rescuers and, increasingly, the public by way of the media, were forced to watch as the passengers and crew began to die. As the ship continued to break up, the remaining passengers and crew – still in agonizing sight of land – were forced higher and higher on the decks and up into the rigging. By Wednesday morning, it was clear that the situation was desperate and that nothing more could be done. It was then, so the story goes, that the women began to sing 'Nearer, My God, to Thee'.

The *Valencia* was lost with more than 100 lives. It was a story reported in graphic and unfolding detail in both the Pacific northwest and on the east coast, too. 'Many Perish in Wreck of 'Frisco Steamship' announced the front page of the *New York Times*. 'Pitiful Scenes Witnessed'. The paper went on to provide a list of both first- and second-class passengers, and detailed incidents such as: 'a little boy running about the deck crying for his mother, who was among the drowned'.[54] Coverage continued in the *New York Times* the following day, and on the Friday it reported that 'Women and children singing "Nearer, My God, to Thee" shivered and clung together on the hurricane deck.' Indeed, 'The women had taken off their petticoats and burned them as a signal in a vain effort to attract passing vessels.'[55] Back in the northwest, the *Pacific Monthly*'s March edition boasted: 'The first complete account published of the recent disaster off the West coast of Vancouver Island'.[56] Here, a journalist, Clarence H. Baily, described how, as wind, waves and rocks tore relentlessly at the *Valencia* under the shadow of an 'awesome' cliff, 'a half-score women lifted up their voices in song'. They had faced death for two days, but the brave women, after 'long hours of agony that crazed strong men, tremulously sang "Nearer My God, to Thee"'.[57] Some of the women who sang the hymn:

> had seen their children and their husbands drowned before their eyes. Some of the men who heard it had seen their wives and babies dashed to death against the rocks.[58]

One group of men attempted to paddle a life raft away through the turbulent sea. As they looked back to the ship they saw a group of women and children gazing towards the raft, 'and over the roaring of the waters the strains of the song faintly floated: "E'en tho' it be a cross that raiseth me"'.[59] Eventually, the life-raft was picked up with 18 survivors. They were all, reported Baily, 'well-nigh crazed' by the memory of:

> the brave faces looking at them over the broken rail of a wreck and of the echo of that great hymn sung by women who, looking death smilingly n the face, were able in the fog and mist and flying spray to remember: 'Nearer, My God, to Thee'.[60]

The *Titanic*, then, was not the first sinking ship upon which 'Nearer, My God, to Thee' is reputed to have been rendered at the last: the *Valencia* had preceded it by six years.[61] How, though, can we link this with the British reporting of the *Titanic*? When the rescue ship *Carpathia* picked up the *Titanic* survivors, it took them to New York. It is hardly surprising, then, that the New York newspapers had the first pick of the survivors' stories. It would have taken at least five days for any British passengers to return home, while many of the crew were detained in the United States to give evidence at the American inquiry. Consequently, the British press depended principally upon American reports for their own news. We have noted, for example, that much of Bride's *New York Times* interview was reproduced, almost verbatim, in 'The Deathless Story of the Titanic'. It was in that same edition of the *New York Times* that Mrs Dick claimed that she had heard 'Nearer, My God, to Thee'. By the time the news had crossed the Atlantic, Mrs Dick's brief page 4 account of the band had eclipsed Harold Bride's front-page exclusive. Whether or not it was true, it was clearly a far better story. Mrs Dick was soon forgotten, but Hartley's hymn became immortal.

Why, though, had Mrs Dick reported hearing 'Nearer, My God, to Thee' when she was in a very poor position reliably to have done so? Vera Dick was a Canadian from Calgary, Alberta, the neighbouring province to British Columbia, where the *Valencia* had gone down so dramatically six years previously. It is entirely likely, then, that she knew of the *Valencia* story. It had been widely reported in the press on both sides of the continent, and the subsequent inquiries prolonged controversy in the Pacific northwest. So infamous, indeed, was the disaster that almost 90 years later, Michael Neitzel was able to refer to it as the 'most shameful incident in Canadian maritime history',[62] while a number plate from a *Valencia* lifeboat still hangs in the Vancouver Maritime Museum.[63] We will never know whether Vera Dick heard, thought she had heard, or thought she ought to have heard 'Nearer, My God, to Thee' as the *Titanic* went down. On the balance of evidence, however, it is most unlikely that this actually took place. Again, we cannot prove it, but it is much more feasible and likely that Mrs Dick's memory in this instance was social rather than personal, and based on the *Valencia* disaster before being projected upon the *Titanic*. In her memory and experience, this was just the sort of thing that was done as a ship went down. The public did not need persuading. Just as 'Be British!' was 'what we would have expected and wanted' Captain Smith to have said as his final words,[64] so 'Nearer, My God, to Thee' was just what was required as the *Titanic* sank. The fact that it was not true was hardly the point. The late Edwardians agreed with Mrs Dick.

What was it about this hymn that made it so appropriate to the myth of the *Titanic*? It could hardly have been the tune, as three different versions were in circulation. The answer, of course, lies in both its title and refrain: 'Nearer, My God, to Thee'. The hymn was written in 1841 by Sarah Flower Adams (1805–48). It comprises five verses, the first of which begins with – and each of which concludes with – the words: 'Nearer, My God, to Thee'.[65] There is no chorus. The hymn is essentially one of bitter-sweet consolation in death. No matter how bad things may be, the consolation is that the singer, even though she or he be dead, is consequently nearer to God. In each verse, a grim circumstance is concluded with the same consolatory sentiment. In the first verse, the singer is nearer to God, 'E'n though it be a cross/That raiseth me'. The reference to the cross identifies it as a Christian hymn, and finds consolation in the most awful and central death in Christian mythology: the crucifixion of Christ himself. Even if the singer were to experience the same death (physically or, more likely, metaphorically), 'Still all my song shall be,/Nearer my God to Thee,/Nearer to Thee'. The imagery proceeds from desolation to ascension into heaven. In the second verse, the sun has gone down and darkness has fallen. Rest is 'a stone'. In the third, however, 'Steps unto Heav'n' appear, and angels beckon the singer nearer. In the fourth, the singer is duly awoken from 'stony griefs' and is 'bright with Thy praise'. Finally, the singer flies upwards 'on joyful wing/Cleaving the sky', and still 'all my song shall be,/Nearer, my God, to Thee,/ Nearer to Thee'.

This, then, is a song about singing in the face of death, sung now in the face of death itself. The mood is no longer conditional. Its acceptance of death is total: 'still *all* my song shall be ...' (my emphasis). And, in the tradition of Christian belief (in common with many others, both 'developed' and 'primitive'), it denies the finality of death itself.

It goes without saying (as Barthes might have put it) that late Edwardian Britain was a theistic society. On the face of it, therefore, the supposed playing of this hymn represents a devoutly religious, Christian society celebrating the decorous acceptance of death while at the same time denying its finality. It understood the involvement of a divine being in the sinking of the *Titanic* as beyond the necessity of discussion. Once we begin to examine the role of the divine in the greater myth of the *Titanic*, however, we start to detect a far deeper ambivalence towards the perceived involvement of God in late Edwardian British society.

In the myth of the *Titanic*, the role of God varies from the benevolent to the wrathful. For good or ill, however, he (God is always male in the popular texts) is usually an interventionist God, taking an active and personal interest in the *Titanic* and everyone aboard it. The benevolent God gives character, comfort and consolation. According to Gibbs, God was responsible for the heroism of those on board. It was a heroism which, 'with a divine simplicity, leapt forth, as though in the call of God, like a "sunburst in the storm of death."'[66] In the *Daily Graphic*, the selflessness of the *Titanic* men was 'the last gift of God' in time of death. Indeed, they 'died as we would have them die, as we would like to have died ourselves had God steeled our hearts with a similar courage'.[67] Shortly after the disaster, a message from Captain Smith's widow, Eleanor, was posted outside the White Star offices in Southampton. Bordered in black, it was duly reproduced in Gibbs beneath a picture of her with her only child, Helen.[68] 'May God be with us and comfort us all,' wrote Mrs Smith.[69] The story of the *Titanic*, declared Gibbs, was one of 'spiritual significance'. It was a story of men 'going to their God' with a hymn of faith.[70] They may have died, horribly, but they were now with God. In this way, the finality of death was denied. The Duchess of Sutherland agreed. Speaking at the unveiling of the captain's statue, and quoted in the subsequent souvenir, she observed that those who had died in the sea would surely 'take the wings of the morning' and 'see the face of God'.[71] They were not altogether dead, therefore, but merely somewhere else, in visual contact with God himself. God was pleased to see them, too, for according to Gibbs: 'God welcomed many souls that night.'[72] Their being with God was not the end of the story, however, as the hymn which they sang in the face of death would 'go echoing forever across the eternal sea'.[73]

God did not merely welcome people to him, however; in some cases he had taken a personal interest in getting them there himself. According to John Hay in the 'Be British' souvenir, Captain Smith was one of those so chosen. In taking Smith's life, he wrote, 'God has seen fit to take to Himself one of the noblest lives He ever created!'[74] The Bishop of Willesden appeared similarly convinced of the personal involvement of God in the life and death of Captain Smith. His death was a lesson of how man 'could fulfil that which God has given him to do, as our friend Captain Smith undoubtedly did. (Loud applause).'[75] This leaves the less devout mind with something of a problem, though. What, precisely, had God given Captain Smith to do? Sink the *Titanic*? Whatever it was supposed to have been, the captain 'undoubtedly did' it. Presumably, the Bishop was referring to the captain's selflessly doing his duty right to the end. But, if Captain Smith's behaviour was God-given, what about the collision of the *Titanic* with an iceberg and the subsequent death of nearly 1,500 (presumably) innocent people? Was that God-given, too?

The question of why a benevolent, omnipotent, interventionist God might allow terrible things to happen is not a new one. The Bishop of Willesden even thought it a good one but, for all the applause, he failed to provide what many today would consider a persuasive answer. In the event, he explained that it was out of such trials of faith with God that 'we might still gain a truer, more real and lasting trust in Him'.[76] Exactly how the icy death of 1,500 men, women and children might make for 'a truer, more real and lasting' trust in God, the Bishop did not say. If he believed that, in the face of such evidence, trust was all that was left, he kept his opinion to himself.

At the end of the unveiling of the statue to Captain Smith, the Bishop, along with the other dignitaries and spectators, made the short walk to evensong at Lichfield Cathedral, where they sang the hymn 'God Moves in a Mysterious Way'.[77] It is not a hymn which echoes with conviction. We cannot be sure whether the loss of the *Titanic* caused many people to question their faith, albeit privately. We can detect no mass movement towards agnosticism in 1912, but if the *Titanic* disaster (to say nothing of the world war that was shortly to follow) did not cause people to abandon their belief in God, it may have led some of them, at least, to wonder whether their God was fully responsible for everything that happened on earth. It is a view to which Owen Chadwick subscribes in *The Secularization of the European Mind in the Nineteenth Century*. According to Chadwick, the religious reaction to the sinking of the *Titanic* revealed 'a distancing of God from the detail of human disaster: a determination not to hold God responsible for human error in the design of elaborate machinery'.[78] This is an important concept in the light of our observation of an emerging ambivalence in the perceived role of God in the *Titanic* disaster. On the one hand, it would be possible to argue that if God was not wholly involved in the detail of the disaster, he was no longer perceived as omnipotent. Such a position enabled people to thank God for his welcome gifts of character, comfort and consolation, while absolving him from responsibility for the disaster itself. A counter-interpretation, however, might be that God had lost none of his power. Rather, if the *Titanic* had sunk on its maiden voyage, it was because God had specifically wanted it to do so. This dichotomy between partial and full responsibility suggests, therefore, that the late Edwardian God had two conflicting personalities: the gentle and redemptive God of the New Testament, and the powerful and vengeful God of the Old.

It is this second, angry God that we find in Filson Young's *Titanic*. Indeed, Young's book begins with an extensive quotation from the Old Testament book of Job, XLI. 'I will not conceal his parts, nor his power,' begins Job, and continues:

> Out of his mouth go burning lamps, and sparks of fire leap out./ Out of his nostrils goeth smoke, as out of a seething pot or cauldron./ His breath kindleth coals, and a flame goeth out of his mouth.'

This was a wrathful, omnipotent God without fear: 'he is a king over all the children of pride.' This, then, was the God who had sunk the *Titanic*. But what had caused this God to be so particularly enraged? Young supplied the answer, echoing the dark, Old Testament tones of the prophet. Man, in his pride, had created:

> a ship so monstrous and unthinkable that it towered high over the buildings and dwarfed the very mountains beside the water. It seemed like some impious blasphemy that man should fashion this most monstrous and ponderable of all his creations into the likeness of a thing that could float upon the waters.[79]

The *Titanic*, then, was an unnatural monster. Like the golem of Jewish mythology, or the gothic creation of Dr Frankenstein, it was an aberrant being in the guise of nature. Yet the 'impious blasphemy' of the 'thing' was not so much its likeness to nature, but rather its challenge to nature itself. For in the myth of the *Titanic*, the *Titanic* was to become 'the unsinkable ship', a ship which 'God himself' would be unable to sink. It is this most powerful component of the *Titanic* myth which now concerns our final chapter.

7 'The Unsinkable Ship'

Greater even than the band playing 'Nearer, My God, to Thee' is the myth of the *Titanic* as 'the unsinkable ship'. Even today, we could be forgiven for taking this literally; it permeates contemporary popular culture just as it did in 1912. For many people, for example, James Cameron's film 'Titanic' has been the mass provider of information about the ship. Released in Britain in 1998, it is a film whose historical accuracy has been widely assumed. When heroine Rose DeWitt Bukator's mother looks up at the ship from Ocean Dock at Southampton and remarks, 'So this is the ship they say is unsinkable', we can be forgiven for assuming that this is exactly what everyone did say. 'It *is* unsinkable,' confirms Rose's fiancé, 'God himself could not sink this ship.'[1]

The same notion persists in contemporary literature, too. Beryl Bainbridge's *Every Man for Himself*, shortlisted for the Booker Prize in 1996, is a novel set aboard the *Titanic*. Here, her fictional narrator laments for the captain in the ship's final moments: 'the unthinkable was in process and his unsinkable vessel' was about to submerge.[2]

The purpose of the feature film and of literature is not necessarily historical accuracy. Documentary films do carry with them the aura of authenticity, however. People going to see the Imax documentary 'Titanica' on both sides of the Atlantic will have seen the publicity slogan: 'The Unsinkable Ship. The Unthinkable Disaster'. The advertising for the 'Titanica' season at the National Museum of Photography, Film and Television in Bradford went on to claim that the experience was 'so real you'll think you're there'.[3] The leaflet for the same film shown on the Imax screen at Vancouver, Canada in 1997 added: 'Titanic … the unsinkable liner that sank …'[4] To consumers of film, literature and even documentary in the 1990s, therefore, the *Titanic* was still indeed 'unsinkable'.

Non-fiction publications on the *Titanic* have traditionally taken a similar line – a line that remains the most persistent and commonly held view. Walter Lord, who wrote the seminal work on the *Titanic*, referred to it as the 'unsinkable ship' in *A Night to Remember* of 1956.[5] He even titled a chapter 'God Himself Could Not Sink This Ship'.[6] In the revised edition of 1976, Lord said that the White Star Line themselves had claimed the *Titanic* to be unsinkable,[7] and that the claim had been repeated in travel brochures.[8] 'The Titanic was unsinkable,' he narrated. 'Everybody said so.'[9] Lord's assertions have been echoed by subsequent writers. In *The Maiden Voyage* of 1969, Geoffrey Marcus claimed that 'everyone knew' that the *Titanic* was supposed to be unsinkable, and that a seaman had even observed as the *Titanic* lay at its dock in Southampton: 'God himself could not sink this ship.'[10] Southampton, indeed, was full of talk of her 'unsinkability'.[11] Terry Coleman in *The Liners* of 1977 explained why there as no panic after the *Titanic* hit the iceberg: 'The Titanic was unsinkable. The builders had said so. Practically everyone believed she was as unsinkable as a railway station.'[12] In 1990 Charles Pellegrino, in *Her Name Titanic*, even had the conviction to reconstruct a conversation between the *Titanic*'s designer Thomas Andrews and his wife as they looked over the building of the giant liner: She: 'And you say she'll be unsinkable?' He: 'Safer than a lifeboat.'[13] Paul Heyer claimed in *Titanic Legacy* of 1995 that the builders considered the *Titanic* to be 'a virtual giant lifeboat',[14] while the following year, Steven Biel in *Down with the Old Canoe* again subscribed to the view that the *Titanic* was 'supposedly unsinkable'.[15]

It may seem, therefore, that received opinion both was and is that the *Titanic* was widely proclaimed and believed to have been the 'unsinkable' ship. This is not the whole story, however, for there has also emerged a contrary view which directly contradicts this: the revised belief that no one ever called the *Titanic* 'unsinkable' at all until after the event. This was an opinion first put forward by Philip Howard discussing language and metaphor in an article for *The Times* in 1981. He stated: 'I can find no contemporary evidence that the Titanic was regarded as virtually unsinkable until after she had sunk.' Nobody, he continued, 'was writing about unsinkability' until after the event. The belief had been created retrospectively because it made a far more impressive metaphor. 'The word unsinkable appears for the first time in *The Times* on the day after the disaster,' he claimed.[16] Howard's article was, perhaps, an intoxicating piece of 'bubble bursting', and to an extent his claim became the accepted opinion among the informed minority who thought they 'really knew', and considered the belief that the *Titanic* was proclaimed unsinkable to be just another *Titanic* 'myth' in the pejorative sense.[17] It was a view even taken up by the American-based Titanic Historical Society. As late as the summer of 1992, an informational 'Did You Know?' display board at their Massachusetts headquarters and museum declared: 'The builders and designers of Titanic did not call her "unsinkable". This appellation was given to her by the press and media after the sinking and became an accepted cliché.'[18] Similarly, an article appeared in a 1993 edition of *The Atlantic Daily Bulletin*, the official journal of the British Titanic Society. This article, titled 'Twelve Popular Myths Concerning the Titanic Disaster', stated that the White Star Line never claimed that the *Titanic* was unsinkable, and attributed the belief to an old interview with the captain, concluding: 'it was the Press which coined the phrase "unsinkable" when they misquoted him.'[19]

Inevitably, perhaps, there has also emerged a body of opinion which places itself somewhere between these two extremes. This middle ground is built upon analysis of a technical article in a special edition of *The Shipbuilder* magazine in 1911, which reported that the sophisticated system of water-tight compartments aboard the *Titanic* did indeed render the vessel 'practically unsinkable'.[20] This should be by no means the end of the story, however, for the discovery of the phrase 'practically unsinkable' in a trade journal leads itself to a range of conflicting interpretations. These differing theories (which often overlap) can be grouped and summarized as follows: (1) *The Shipbuilder* article was just one among many claims of the *Titanic*'s unsinkability, including those found in advertisements. As such, it served to give the technical seal of approval to the travel brochures' claims, and so the unsinkability of the *Titanic* was widely believed by the public even before the maiden voyage.[21] (2) *The Shipbuilder* may have pronounced the *Titanic* 'practically unsinkable', but the owners and builders themselves never did.[22] (3) Despite the owners and builders never having made such a claim, articles such as that in *The Shipbuilder* nevertheless led to it still being widely believed by the public before the *Titanic* set sail.[23] (4) *The Shipbuilder*'s qualifier 'practically' – as in 'practically unsinkable' – was lost as the idea spread.[24] (5) That the *Titanic* was unsinkable was the considered opinion of the experts at the time, but it was still not a claim made publicly in White Star advertising. The idea that the *Titanic* was believed to be unsinkable entered the public domain in the hours of uncertainty immediately after garbled news reports broke that the liner was in trouble. This was due to the White Star Line's American Vice-President in New York telling reporters: 'We have absolute confidence in the Titanic. We believe that the boat is unsinkable.'[25]

None of these existing theories is entirely accurate, and none of them is complete. By returning to the original texts, we will now be able to see not only how the myth of the *Titanic*'s unsinkability emerged, but how this was culturally adapted to become a story of hubris and nemesis worthy of ancient Greece. This in turn will demonstrate the 'universal' component in the myth of the *Titanic*.

The sources of the *Titanic*'s alleged unsinkability can in fact be traced back to not one but three nationally available publications, one from 1910 and the other two from 1911.[26] The first is both the least substantial and the least well known. Published in approximately September 1910,[27] it is a small, folding, illustrated, pre-publicity leaflet showing the *Titanic* and its 'sister' ship the *Olympic* in various stages of construction at Belfast, together with an artist's impression of the completed ships. The leaflet describes them as 'ocean palaces' and concludes: 'as far as it is possible to do so, these two wonderful vessels are designed to be unsinkable'.[28] This is a long way from widely publicizing the *Titanic* as 'unsinkable' for two reasons. First, it will be noted that the phrase 'as far as it is possible to do so' is a very significant qualifier to any claim of outright unsinkability. Indeed, it betrays the underlying assumption that it is in fact impossible to build an unsinkable ship. The White Star Line, the phrase implies, have simply done the best they can in approaching a goal which they admit to be unreachable. Second, there is only one known copy of this brochure in existence, and its discovery was published for the first time in the spring of 1993.[29] This suggests that there were very few printed. Indeed, a typographical error in the spelling of the word: 'Titanic' on the second page possibly suggests that this was a proof copy which was never in fact mass produced.[30] For both reasons of content and of circulation, then, it seems reasonable to conclude that the leaflet could not have been responsible for a widespread, pre-maiden voyage belief that the *Titanic* was unsinkable.

The two remaining sources date from the following year. The first is a fully illustrated publicity brochure: 'White Star Line Royal and United States Steamers Olympic and Titanic'.[31] It includes photographs of both ships in various stages of completion, together with artists' impressions of the public rooms, passenger accommodation and the finished ships. The brochure is divided into three parts: the first deals with the hull and is very technical in content, the second deals with the decor and is superlative in tone, and the third section deals with the propelling machinery and is again much more technical. It is in the first part that the idea of unsinkability arises. The brochure here explains that the hull of the *Titanic* is divided by 15 watertight bulkheads, and designed so that 'any two compartments may be flooded without in any way involving the safety of the ship'.[32] An entire page is then devoted to the 'Electrically Controlled Watertight Doors' which divide the compartments:

> Each door is held in the open position by a suitable friction clutch, which can be instantly released by means of a powerful electric magnet controlled from the Captain's bridge, so that, in the event of an accident, or at any time when it may be considered advisable, the Captain can, by simply moving an electric switch, instantly close the doors throughout, practically making the vessel unsinkable.[33]

Many of the same comments may be made about this as for the preceding brochure. While it does again dispel the misconception that the owners and builders never made *any* sort of claim for the *Titanic*'s unsinkability, it does again fall short of a claim for total infallibility. We note that the *Titanic* was designed to stay afloat with only two of its 16 compartments flooded. There is no claim for the other 14. Further, it is then claimed that the ship is thus rendered 'practically' (and not 'totally') unsinkable. Then there is the question of how loudly and how widely this (moderated) claim was made. We note first that this claim to unsinkability is found among the body of the text on an inside page, and not in any way prominently, such as on the front cover. The only claim made there is for the *Titanic*'s superlative size. And while it is not known how many of these brochures were in fact printed and circulated,[34] it is known that many other White Star publicity brochures, leaflets, posters and advertisements were produced and that not one of them save the 1910 leaflet already described made any similar claim.[35] Their emphasis is uniformly on size and luxury – in which the White Star Line were indisputably ahead of their rivals. Again, therefore, it seems reasonable to conclude that this brochure did not lead to the British public at large believing the *Titanic* to be unsinkable before the maiden voyage.

Finally, there is *The Shipbuilder* special number of 1911.[36] *The Shipbuilder* was a regular trade publication aimed at both shipbuilders and their suppliers. Published in Newcastle upon Tyne and London, this special number cost two shillings, was 130 pages long, painstakingly detailed and fully illustrated with both photographs and technical drawings – including fold-out plans of the ship. No fitting was left undescribed. A section on the hull described the system of watertight compartments, which was 'so arranged that any two main compartments may be flooded without in any way involving the safety of the ship'.[37] The description of the system of watertight doors is described as 'usual in White Star vessels' and continues:

Each door is held in the open position by a suitable friction clutch, which can be instantly released by means of a powerful electro-magnet controlled from the captain's bridge, so that in the event of an accident, or at any time when it may be considered advisable, that captain can, simply by moving an electric switch, instantly close the emergency doors throughout and make the vessel practically unsinkable.[38]

Three things are worthy of note here. First, the system of bulkheads, subdivisions and emergency doors is described as 'usual' in White Star vessels. Second, the wording is almost exactly the same as in the White Star brochure described above, except that the phrase 'practically making the vessel unsinkable' has been slightly changed to 'and make the vessel practically unsinkable'. Nevertheless, this is still a very qualified claim. Third, *The Shipbuilder* was a technical, trade publica-tion and not a mass circulation daily newspaper. At two shillings, this special number cost 24 times the price of a popular newspaper such as the *Daily Graphic*. These three points combine to tell us that the watertight system on board the *Titanic* was not thought to be unique, that its safety claims were limited, and that even if they were remark-able, they were made in a publication that was designed for specialists and not for the public at large. No other technical article or publica-tion made any sort of claim for the *Titanic*'s unsinkability.[39] Again, therefore, it seems reasonable to conclude that on the strength of this publication, the population as a whole were unlikely to have thought of the *Titanic* as a unique, unsinkable ship before its maiden voyage. It is additionally telling that a full-page, White Star Line advertisement inside the front cover of *The Shipbuilder* special edition describes the *Olympic* and *Titanic* only as the 'largest steamers in the world'. Again, there is nothing about them being unsinkable.

In the light of this evidence, therefore, it seems almost impossible that the *Titanic* was generally held to have been unsinkable before it in fact sank. Once news of the disaster broke, however, it was an entirely different story: it was as though the *Titanic* had been universally hailed as unsinkable all along. The *Titanic*, according to Gibbs in 'The Deathless Story of the Titanic', 'had been called a thousand times "unsinkable"'.[40] Indeed, he continued rhetorically: 'The "Titanic" could not sink.' 'The "Titanic" is unsinkable.' These words were repeated again and again by men of expert knowledge.[41] So, within days of the sinking, three obscure and very qualified claims had become viewed as a thousand, repeated and compounded by innumerable experts. It is not surprising, then, that the post-disaster texts imply that the passengers and crew of the *Titanic* all thought of the ship as unsinkable, and that this affected their behaviour as the disaster began to unfold. According to Young, for example, although the passengers were aware that the ship had stopped mysteriously at dead of night, they pondered simply: 'It was rough luck, to be sure: they had not thought they would soon have a chance of proving that the Titanic was unsinkable.'[42] As the ship began to go down at the head, things became visibly worse, but Young continues: 'everyone was walking about and saying that the ship was unsinkable'.[43] Such a belief, however, began to have serious consequences, as the *Daily Graphic* 'In Memoriam' issue reported:

> Confidence in the unsinkableness of the liner appeared to have been responsible for the loss of a number of lives. Passengers refused to enter [life] boats, thinking they were safe as they were …[44]

Gibbs said that this was particularly true of the women, who had 'a pitiful faith in the unsinkable strength of the "Titanic"'.[45] It was only the order to lower away that brought about 'the terrible admission that this immense vessel, which had been called "unsinkable," was sinking'.[46]

How, then, had these writers so quickly come to report that the *Titanic* had been so widely hailed and so widely believed to have been unsinkable? This can, to an extent, be explained by the working practices of the press, especially the general rule that journalists conduct research in response to rather than in anticipation of unexpected events. This was the case with the *Titanic*.[47] When companies and commercial organizations want publicity for a forthcoming product or venture, they typically bombard the media with unsolicited press releases, photographs and other information in the hope of free and favourable editorial coverage. Much of this material is typically ignored as being of limited news value. Some of it may be kept, however, either because no one can be bothered to throw it away, or occasionally on the off-chance that it might, one day, become of interest. Additionally, news organizations typically keep files of cuttings and other information for consultation when need be. This is how many journalists quickly obtain 'background' information for breaking stories: obituaries, for example, can rapidly be assembled in this way. The *Titanic* was one such story: information which had been filed or forgotten suddenly became of extraordinary value. Articles, supplements and even promotional brochures which had been left unconsidered or even completely unread were now ransacked for every fascinating detail.[48] And even the most lacklustre, workaday journalist could not help but have leaped with excitement at the discovery that the *Titanic* had – even once – been described as 'practically unsinkable'.

The extreme probability that *The Shipbuilder* special number and the 1911 publicity brochure were rediscovered in this way is supported by an examination of the texts. Both Gibbs' 'Deathless Story' and the *Daily Graphic* 'In Memoriam' issue, published five days after the sinking, give detailed descriptions of the *Titanic*'s bulkheads and watertight doors and conclude that this had the effect of 'practically making the vessel unsinkable'.[49] Gibbs attributes the phrase to what he describes as the 'official description' of the *Titanic*, while the *Daily Graphic* makes no kind of attribution at all. Both descriptions, however, appear to be direct paraphrases of the White Star publicity brochure of 1911.[50]

Some of the journalists of 1912 probably discovered the printed 'unsinkable' references for themselves while performing hasty research. Even the least diligent among them, however, would have been spurred on to do so by comments made by Philip A.S. Franklin,[51] the vice president of the White Star Line in New York. Several hours had elapsed between the news first breaking that the *Titanic* was in trouble and the revelation that it had actually sunk. It was during this period of intense uncertainty and speculation on the morning of Monday, 15 April that Franklin announced in New York: 'We place absolute confidence in the *Titanic*. We believe that the boat is unsinkable.'[52] This time, the qualifier 'practically' had been omitted. And this time, the world's media was listening. 'Manager of the Line Insisted Titanic Was Unsinkable Even After She Had Gone Down', declared a front-page sub-headline in the *New York Times* the following morning.[53] The second page detailed Franklin's astonishment:

> Mr. Franklin called her unsinkable, and last night when he knew at last that the pride of his line was beneath the ocean he could not seem to comprehend that the steamer had sunk.
>
> 'I thought her unsinkable,' he declared. 'and I based by [*sic*] opinion on the best expert advice. I do not understand it.'[54]

That the *Titanic* was said to be unsinkable had suddenly and dramatically entered the public consciousness, but by now the *Titanic* had already sunk.

Franklin's words may have inspired the media to speak of the *Titanic*'s 'unsinkability' as news of the disaster began to filter though. For a while, some even appear to have believed him.[55] But within days of the news that the *Titanic* had actually sunk, these same words were being quoted again in memorial editions by the likes of Philip Gibbs and Filson Young. This time, however, they were quoted not reassuringly but ironically. For Gibbs, Franklin's statement was 'dreadfully ironic',[56] while Young reproduced one of Franklin's most optimistic statements in full before rhetorically observing: 'Still that same word, "unsinkable," which had now indeed for the first time become a true one: for it is only when she lies at the bottom of the sea that any ship can be called unsinkable.'[57]

We are now beginning to discern both a growth and a transformation in the notion of the unsinkability of the *Titanic*. It began with a very few, weak seeds left sown but unnoticed in some peripheral literature. Once the *Titanic* hit the iceberg, however, these few 'seeds' were discovered and multiplied and grew in strength. It was then that they began to be viewed ironically. In their final transformation, the *Titanic*'s claims to unsinkability were to become the pestilential cause of its sinking.

Let us pause for a moment, though, to review the changing language used to describe the *Titanic* and its alleged unsinkability. Initially, the *Titanic* was designed to be unsinkable: 'as far as it is possible to do so'. Once disaster struck, however, the *Titanic* had been called 'a thousand times unsinkable' and the original claims were then reread with 'dreadful irony'. By this stage, then, it was retrospectively believed that the *Titanic* had always been held and hailed by everybody to have been 'the unsinkable ship'. But this irony was now to turn to an even darker shade: the story of the 'unsinkable' *Titanic* was to be transfigured into a myth of hubris and nemesis worthy of a Greek tragedy.

Before we return to the *Titanic* texts, however, it is important first to make clear what is understood by the terms hubris and nemesis. This leads us into a brief, explanatory excursion though some myths of a previous era.

Hubris is a kind of arrogance or pride which leads one to overreach oneself, typically by attempting to defy the gods. Nemesis[58] is the result – the retributive justice which inevitably follows. In this way, one may foolishly try to assume knowledge, power or position which is the prerogative of the gods, but one is sure consequently only to meet with draconian punishment. And because in Greek mythology the gods were at one with the elements, hubris would include any attempt to conquer nature. Hubris could be shown in a multiplicity of ways: the ability to invent things was regarded as an attribute of the gods, and invention was also associated with navigation and exploration. In this way, according to Françoise Graziani, 'The audacity of the first person to "put up a sail hoisted on a plank into the sea" was a challenge to the gods' and so the navigator was often compared 'to the great hubristic figures of ancient mythology'.[59] Nemesis, on the other hand, is illustrated in the original myth of Narcissus, who according to Yves-Alain Favre, 'was punished for having sought to escape the laws that apply to all'[60] It was the role of Nemesis to 'punish those who seek to escape the common lot'.[61] Icarus was one such character: his father Daedalus made him wings, but he flew so close to the sun that the wax which held them together melted and he fell to his death in the sea. Most famous of all those who exhibited hubris, however, was Prometheus, who, in the *Theogony* of Hesiod, stole the secret of fire from the gods and gave it to mortals. Nemesis, of course, ensued, and Prometheus' punishment was to be tied to a pillar and have his liver eaten out by an eagle – only to have the liver grow again each night and be eaten away again each following day. In the *Works and Days*, Hesiod goes further by supplying the moral: 'It is utterly impossible to escape the intrigues of Zeus.'[62] Hesiod's lesson then, according to Raymond Trousson, was one of 'submission to the divine will'.[63] It was Aeschylus' *Prometheus Bound*, however, which provided the best-known version of the story. According to Aeschylus, man's greatest fault was hubris: succintly defined by Trousson as 'an excess of ambition or pride which led to overreaching'.[64] In Aeschylus' tragedy, Prometheus not only steals the secret of fire, but after being punished by being nailed to a mountain peak, further refuses to divulge an important secret to Zeus and, in his pride, demands an even worse punishment. Zeus, of course, obliges him with an earthquake which swallows him whole. It is true that in *Prometheus Bound*, Prometheus is treated with some sympathy: the gift of fire was of great technological value to man, but he had still overstepped the divine order, and so his nemesis was inevitable.[65]

There is, of course, one final point to note: Prometheus was a Titan,[66] the son of the Titan Iapetus, one of a group of twelve huge and enormously strong mythological characters who deposed their father and put one of themselves on the throne. The Titans, after a mighty struggle, were in turn defeated by Zeus and succeeded by the gods of Olympus. It will not go unnoticed, therefore, that Prometheus, who so epitomized hubris, was himself Titanic.

If we look for words such as 'hubris', 'nemesis', 'Prometheus,' 'Titan' or even 'Greek' in the British popular texts from 1912 to 1914, we have a very hard time finding them.[67] It seems highly improbable, then, that these late Edwardian sources would have deliberately alluded to such classical themes because they made for clever literary references. Although the specific classical *terms* may be missing, however, the *concepts* run rampant throughout the popular texts. The word 'hubris' does not appear in any of the *Titanic* texts examined, but 'pride', its nearest English translation, is used both frequently and insistently. The *Titanic*, according to the *Daily Graphic*, set out on its maiden voyage 'in an atmosphere of pride'.[68] For Gibbs it was the 'proudest of the world's ships'.[69] But this was not pride in the positive sense – as in (say) taking pride in one's work. Rather, this was pride in its negative sense, the pride, the conceit even, that elevates one beyond one's rightful place. It is the pride of the deadly sins. It is with this in mind that Young's *Titanic* begins with the extract from Job XLI, reminding his readers that God is 'king over all the children of pride'.[70] This, then, is the censorious tone with which Gibbs reports that the *Titanic* had 'gone forth in her pride'.[71] Young's condemnations escalated yet further. Not only were those aboard the liner 'proud', they were 'preoccupied with the source of their pride'.[72] The *Titanic* had sailed 'in her pride and her shame'.[73]

The *Titanic*'s pride was technological. Daedalus made wings so that he and Icarus might fly; Prometheus stole the secret of fire from the gods. The *Titanic*'s pride was equally audacious: it was a ship that could not sink. As Young related, the designers of the great ship no longer thought it 'vulnerable' to the high seas. 'In their pride they had said "the Titanic cannot spring a leak"'.[74] Its technological strength was rapturously yet ironically applauded in the memorial issues. The *Daily Graphic* said it was 'the mightiest, finest product of human brains in the matter of ships to sail the sea'.[75] Philip Gibbs saw it as the 'greatest liner in the world ... the most astonishing achievement in naval architecture and marine engineering'.[76] And according to the 'Wigan' memorial handkerchief, it 'represented the last word in ocean going science'.[77]

In the myth of the *Titanic*, the pride of science – and the particular pride of the ship itself – is seen as its attempt to overcome nature. Gibbs reported:

> 'The "Titanic" could not sink.' 'The "Titanic" is unsinkable.' These words were repeated again and again by men of expert knowledge, who rejoiced in the belief that science had conquered over Nature and that the sea would be cheated of further sacrifice.[78]

This extract from Gibbs is additionally revealing: he uses a capital 'N' on nature, so as to personify it as though 'she' were a goddess in the Olympian mould.[79] Additionally, the sea is portrayed as an entity requiring 'sacrifice' – just like the petulant and demanding gods of ancient Greece. To deny further sacrifice was to 'cheat' a god. The prognosis, then, was hardly good for a ship that had 'boasted conquest over nature',[80] and the stage was ominously set for the revenge of what Young described as 'the waters she was to conquer'.[81]

The certainty that hubris would be followed by nemesis is underlined by the frequent close and sequential pairings of the two concepts in the popular texts. There is a distinct and inescapable symmetry about it: nature, challenged, would swiftly and inevitably exact retribution. This is what happened with the *Titanic* – and the point is often made within a single sentence, as in this example from the *Daily Graphic*, where the:

> last word in ship construction, equipped with every last device making for safety, for an aid in case of need, met at her maiden issue with the sea a challenge that broke her utterly and took her in a toll with over twelve hundred of the lives she carried.[82]

The bigger the ship, so the argument seemed to go, the bigger the consequence. 'She was named Titanic, and she has been Titanic in her sorrow,' lamented the *Daily Graphic*.[83] Indeed, the same issue described the *Titanic*'s vast 'displacement of water' as it first triumphantly set sail from Southampton, but noted in the following paragraph that the 'cheering is now hushed into sobbing', for within a week of that departure, 'the displacement of the Titanic has been so tremendous that she has drenched the bosom of the world in an ocean of tears.'[84] As Young added with similar hubristic symmetry, the *Titanic*, 'with the fires burning in her luxurious rooms, had plunged into the icy depths of death'.[85]

When nature took 'her' revenge, it was almost as if 'she' had taken it personally in return for the *Titanic*'s hubristic affront. Again, nature is personified. Gibbs heard 'the dreadful voice of Nature pronouncing her doom'.[86] This was not a gentle and benevolent but an angry and vengeful nature. If this was going to be a trial of strength ('there is nothing that man can build that nature cannot destroy',[87] observed Young), nature's retribution would be spectacular. According to the *Daily Graphic*:

> The forces of nature shook themselves free from the chains from which man would bind them, burst in all their power from the limits in which he would confine them, and dealt him a blow which has sent mourning through two nations.[88]

It was a reminder which the *Daily Graphic*, appropriately, termed 'cat-aclysmic'.[89] The imagery of cataclysm was also employed by Gibbs, describing the memorial service for the *Titanic* dead in St Paul's Cathedral on 19 April. Here, he wrote, the welling sound of the massed military drums made it sound as though:

> all the winds of heaven were rushing over the heads of the people, as though the sea were rising in fury. Then came the boom of great guns, the echo of tremendous thunder and great crashes as though the sky were rent.[90]

Nature was leaving no doubts as to 'her' authority. The *Titanic*, as the *Daily Graphic* had it, 'lay somewhere tangled in the old sea forest',[91] and human pride (said Gibbs), 'which had boasted conquest over nature, now was humbled and afraid'.[92]

An important point will be noted from the texts. The act of hubris described is portrayed as committed not by the particular individuals who built the *Titanic*, but by western civilization and even mankind itself. Consequently, nature's lesson is visited upon mankind as a whole: the responsibility is entirely collective. This underlying assumption is frequently revealed: we recall, for example, that *Daily Graphic* quotation in which the forces of nature shook themselves free from the chains with which 'man' would bind them, and, in return, dealt 'him' a terrible blow.[93] This, the *Graphic* continued, was a cataclysmic reminder not to congratulate 'ourselves' too well.[94] According to Gibbs, this was a blow to 'all our human pride',[95] while Young reflected that 'it was like some impious blasphemy that man should fashion this most monstrous and ponderable of all his cre-ations' in such an arrogant way.[96] It was a blasphemy committed, then, not by Harland and Wolff, nor even the White Star Line, but by mankind as a whole.

This important concept is underlined by the vast and overt metaphorical significance that was also imposed upon the *Titanic* in late Edwardian popular culture. Gibbs grandly asserted in 'The Deathless Story of the Titanic' that: 'Within the high steel walls of the "Titanic" all that civilisation means, all that human life means, was here gathered up',[97] while Young crisply concurred that the *Titanic* was 'a microcosm of civilized society'.[98]

The *Titanic*, then, was a lesson for everyone. Man, in his pride, had sought to defy nature and challenge the universal order by building an 'unsinkable' ship. Retribution was both inevitable and swift. On its very first voyage, the unsinkable liner was pierced by an iceberg and sunk in two and a half miles of dark and freezing water. Fifteen hundred people died.

We can see, therefore, that the belief that the actual *Titanic* was the great unsinkable ship was essentially retrospective, but that it soon became a vital and fundamental ingredient of the *Titanic* myth. The reason for this is that it served somehow to make sense of an arbitrary event, to imbue it with meaning. As we recall from Chapter 2, one of the prime functions of myth is to create order out of a seemingly random universe, to make meaning out of the meaningless. Culture, as Clifford Geertz has said, is a 'web of significance' which man himself has spun.[99] The *Titanic* hit an iceberg: it was a probability calculated by insurance companies at the time at a million to one.[100] But this was not the significance that late Edwardian society required: like a family grieving over a sudden, premature and unexpected death, the laws of probability did not provide an acceptable answer to the question 'Why?' The myth of the unsinkable ship provided an explanation. The signifier *Titanic* had thus been made to signify.

We have seen that the *Titanic* only really came to be thought of as the unsinkable ship once it had sunk, and we have discerned this from a careful analysis of the late Edwardian texts. We have seen also that the historical data were reanimated to make a myth of the *Titanic*, and that in so doing, significance was imposed upon a signifier to make a sign. The relationship between the signifier and the signified was not, therefore, inevitable. The facts were culturally reassembled to make a meaning, and mythogenesis took place. The argument, then, is strong. By concluding our analysis with a 'control experiment', we can now make our case incontrovertible.

For this experiment, we will need a ship designed and built to the same specification as the *Titanic*, constructed by the same makers at the same yard and even, for good measure, in adjacent berths. This 'control' ship needs to have been built with exactly the same safety features and for which exactly the same claims of unsinkability (or not) were made before its maiden voyage. It will precede the *Titanic* into service by several months, and we will even give it the same captain for the maiden trip to the same destination. We will then see if it is hailed as 'the unsinkable ship' and if, indeed, nature at any time seeks retribution for such audacity and presumption.

Fortunately for us, this is no idle speculation. Precisely such a ship existed: the *Titanic*'s almost identical 'sister' ship the *Olympic*, designed as one and built side by side under the same gantry at Harland and Wolff of Belfast. The *Olympic* and *Titanic* were conceived of from the start as 'sister' ships.[101] The idea to build them both was conceived by the White Star Line in 1907: the trans-Atlantic passenger trade, we remember, was lucrative yet competitive, and all the rival shipping companies sought to provide a regular, weekly trans-Atlantic service, and to achieve this effectively, it would be logistically necessary to have a total of three ships plying the route at any given time, so as to provide a dependable 'ferry' service.[102] White Star believed that this would be best accomplished with three ships of identical speed and capacity, and so the grand scheme was launched to build three such ships almost at once: the *Olympic* Class of liners. The *Olympic* and the *Titanic* were to be constructed first on adjoining slipways under the same, giant gantry. The *Olympic* was shipyard order number 400, the *Titanic* number 401. The *Olympic* would be completed several months before the *Titanic*, after which its slipway would become free for work to begin on the third of the trio, the *Gigantic*.[103]

The *Olympic* and the *Titanic* were the biggest ships ever built. At 45,000 tons gross, they were considerably larger than the existing record-holders *Lusitania* and *Mauretania*, which weighed in at 32,000 tons. The White Star duo had exactly the same dimensions. The *Olympic* was launched on 20 October 1910; the *Titanic* on 31 May 1911. The two ships were almost identical both inside and out, sharing exactly similar hulls, construction and propulsion. The similarity of the two – in some ways they were more like twins than 'sister ships' – is confirmed by the technical articles, the publicity material and even the surviving photographs of the two. In the trade and technical journals, the *Olympic* and *Titanic* were almost invariably described as one. The point is underlined even by the titles of these articles, for example: 'The Olympic and Titanic',[104] 'The White Star Liners Olympic and Titanic' (three different articles shared this title),[105] and 'Electric Lifts on the Olympic and Titanic'[106] in *The Engineer*. The supplement 'The White Star Line' in the same publication[107] similarly treated the two liners as one and the same. It was the same story in *The Shipbuilder*, especially with the 130-page special number 'The White Star Liners "Olympic" and "Titanic"'[108] of the summer of 1911. In all these publications, every point that is made, every device that is illustrated and every room that is portrayed, apply equally to the *Olympic* as to the *Titanic*. *The Shipbuilder* special number, for example made it clear:

> The progress of work in connection with the Titanic is illustrated by the photographs we have used for that purpose in the case of the

Olympic, the vessels having, as already stated, been built on adjoining berths.[109]

The same can be said of the publicity material as well as the technical articles. There were no special brochures for either the *Olympic* or the *Titanic* – they were always publicized and indeed depicted as one, typically, as in the case of a White Star Line brochure from 1911 titled: 'White Star Line Royal and United States Steamers "Olympic" and "Titanic"'.[110] Such was the similarity that the artist's illustrations used on the covers made no indication of which of the two ships was portrayed. There was no distinction: it was as though they were one and the same.[111]

Photographs of the two ships also look practically identical. To the expert eye, there are slight differences around the first-class promenade on A deck, the forward section of which was enclosed on the *Titanic* as a last-minute modification following experience with the *Olympic* at sea.[112] Until this modification was made – just three weeks before the *Titanic* left Belfast for sea trials – it was virtually impossible to tell them apart. But even once the modification was made, confusion still existed, and many photographs purporting to be of the *Titanic* were in fact of the *Olympic*. This was a common feature of the 'In Memoriam' postcards which were hurriedly published after the sinking, which frequently show the wrong ship (plate XI).[113] The similarities still held true even 80 years after the event: the cover of the Christie's auction catalogue for 'Titanic Memorabilia' in 1992 is in fact a photograph of the *Olympic*.[114] The similarities between the two ships were such, indeed, that Gardiner and Van Der Vat were able to construct their much publicized 'conspiracy' theory of 1995, which speculated that the *Titanic* had not actually sunk: it had been switched with the *Olympic* as part of an audacious insurance fraud.[115]

The most important similarity for us, though, remains this: before the *Titanic* sank, exactly the same claims of unsinkability (or otherwise) were made of both ships. When *The Shipbuilder*, for example, reported that the emergency doors 'make the vessel practically unsinkable',[116] it was a (qualified) claim made equally of the *Olympic* and the *Titanic*, as the special issue was devoted equally to the 'sister' ships. Consequently, the *Olympic* was 'the unsinkable ship' just as much as the *Titanic*. Indeed, if either of the two was the original 'unsinkable ship' it was the *Olympic* because the *Olympic* was the first and – at the time – the better known.

Until the maiden voyage of the *Titanic*, the only significant difference between the two ships was their public profile. As the second of two 'sisters', the *Titanic* was, if anything, the poorer relation – both in the eyes of the White Star Line and in the ensuing publicity. An article in *The Engineer*, purportedly about 'The White Star Liners Olympic and Titanic' was really all about the *Olympic*, and added, almost as an after-thought: 'The work on the Titanic is also proceeding very rapidly.'[117] Even a White Star publicity brochure betrayed a similar focus by concluding: 'The foregoing details apply of course to the "Titanic" as well ...'[118] When the *Olympic* was launched on 20 October 1910, its hull was painted off-white so that it would show up better in press photo-graphs. The *Titanic*'s hull, launched seven months later, was left as it was. It was the launch of the *Olympic* that received by far the greater share of media attention. For the launching of the *Titanic*, *The Engineer* reported simply that 'the second of the two White Star liners is now afloat' and continued: 'The arrangements were exactly the same as those made in the case of the Olympic.'[119] *The Times* took a similar line, rele-gating the launch of the *Titanic* to page 9.[120] Once the *Titanic* had entered the water, the attending VIPs were taken by launch to the *Olympic* which was standing by, and thence to Liverpool, where the elder 'sister' was opened to inspection by the public. The same thing happened at Southampton, where, according to *The Shipbuilder* special edition, 'the vessel was visited by some thousands of people, prior to sailing with a full complement of passengers'.[121] The *Titanic*, on the other hand, was never opened to the public, and set sail with spare capacity.

Let us return now to our idea of the control experiment. The *Olympic* and the *Titanic* were structurally and mechanically identical ships, built by the same yard, owned by the same line and even captained by the same man.[122] Their maiden voyages were both from Southampton to New York. The only difference – the only significant variable – is that the *Titanic* sank and the *Olympic* did not. It was for this reason alone that the *Titanic* is remembered as 'the unsinkable ship'. By rights, this appellation should have been given to the *Olympic*, and if hubris had been committed and nemesis deserved, it was the *Olympic* – the first and better-known of the two – which should have been dispatched to the ocean floor by the wrathful and revengeful forces of nature. But no one called the *Olympic* (plate XII) unsinkable because it stayed afloat until 1937, when, having earned the sobriquet 'Old Reliable',[123] it was unceremoniously scrapped in Scotland. It was the second-string *Titanic* which became mythologized as 'the unsinkable ship' in order – retro-spectively – to construct meaning out of an arbitrary event.

Conclusion

On 28 January 1986, an emotional Ronald Reagan appeared live on American television. This time, the old actor seemed genuinely shaken. His task was to try to explain to the American public why the space shuttle *Challenger* had exploded just 73 seconds after take-off, killing everyone on board.[1]

It was not just that the latest mission into space had gone horribly – and publicly – wrong; it was also that there had been a civilian school-teacher among the crew, and her pupils had watched it happen, together, live on television at school.

'I know it's hard to understand,' said the president, 'but sometimes painful things like this do happen. It's all part of the process of exploration and discovery. It's all part of taking a chance and expanding man's horizons.' The future, he declared, did not belong to the faint-hearted. 'It belongs to the brave.'[2]

He ended his broadcast with the final image of seven astronauts who, in a now much-quoted conclusion: '"slipped the surly bonds of earth" to "touch the face of God."'[3]

Many people, especially Americans, still vividly remember not only the *Challenger* disaster, but also President Reagan's simple but vividly emotional television address to the nation. It was a hugely effective piece of rhetoric, written immediately after the explosion and delivered live on American TV late that very afternoon. It was, perhaps, 'The Great Communicator's' finest rhetorical hour.

To some people, however, the president's remarks had something of a familiar ring to them. President Reagan's famous space shuttle eulogy: 'The Future Does Not Belong to the Fainthearted' was in fact, written for him by a professional speechwriter. There is nothing particularly unusual about this: many of President Kennedy's most famous words, for example, were written for him, too.[4] On this occasion, Reagan's speech was written by a regular contributor Peggy Noonan.[5] Noonan herself relates the story of the writing and delivery of the speech: she was at work, as usual, in the White House when news came in that the *Challenger* had exploded. She switched on her word-processor and began writing immediately. She concluded – and Reagan was word-perfect in his delivery –

'We will never forget them, nor the last time we saw them – this morning, as they prepared for their journey, and waved goodbye, and 'slipped the surly bonds of earth' to 'touch the face of God'.[6]'

On the printed page, we can see the quotation marks, around the final line, which, as Peggy Noonan freely admits, was borrowed from a single-stanza Second World War poem called 'High Flight', written by a former fighter pilot, John Gillespie Magee Junior, subsequently and popularly known as 'The Pilot Poet'.

Magee was a Spitfire pilot in the Royal Canadian Airforce. He wrote 'High Flight' on 3 September 1941, a little over three months before he was killed in a mid-air collision over Lincolnshire, at the age of 19. His 14-line poem describes the exhilarating and liberating experience of flight, recounting experiences which 'you have not dreamed of'. It begins: 'Oh! I have slipped the surly bonds of Earth ...' and concludes: '... Put out my hand and touched the face of God.'[7]

So, the mystery is solved: Reagan's remarks were in fact written by a professional speechwriter who had borrowed the most memorable lines from a dead poet.[8] Yet, to the student of the *Titanic*, even if he or she has never heard of John Gillespie Magee, let alone his poem, those lines should now have a familiar ring.

On a hot, summer's day in July 1914, Millicent, Duchess of Sutherland, rose to speak at the ceremony at Beacon Park, Lichfield, to unveil a statue of Edward John Smith, captain of the *Titanic*. She praised the heroic bravery of all on board, and sought to find consolation in their deaths. She said:

> Do you remember how the Psalmist sings that those who dwell in the uttermost parts of the sea shall take the wings of the morning?
> Surely on the wings of the morning, they shall see the face of God.[9]

It is quite a coincidence: two distinct eulogies using distinctly similar rhetoric and images to describe two famous disasters. Both President Reagan and the Duchess of Sutherland used images of release, one from earth, the other from water: the *Challenger* astronauts had that morning 'slipped the surly bonds of earth', while the *Titanic*'s passengers and crew had left 'the uttermost parts of the sea' to take 'the wings of the morning'. Both the *Titanic* and the *Challenger* dead ended up touching or seeing the 'face of God'. In both cases, then, the eulogist has sought to soften the blow of violent, probably painful and certainly dramatic death with the consolation of divine release from

earthly constraints. The image of the 'morning' is offered by both
speakers, suggesting beginnings rather than ends. Seeing – or even
touching – the face of God is the final, glorious reward.

Startlingly similar though the rhetoric may be, the speeches themselves are not directly connected. Although we can trace Ronald
Reagan through Peggy Noonan and back to John Gillespie Magee, it
is hugely unlikely that any one of these three was familiar with a
eulogy given by a British duchess at a statue unveiling ceremony 70
years previously; a eulogy preserved in a Staffordshire local history
archive.

If it is unlikely that Ronald Reagan, Peggy Noonan or John Magee
had heard of the Dowager Duchess of Sutherland, it is chronologically
impossible that the Dowager Duchess had ever heard of any one of
them.

Yet even when we, quite sensibly, dismiss any possibility of a *conscious* connection between the two events and the two eulogies, we
still cannot help but be impressed by a string of coincidences between
them.

Both speeches used the idea of God as a consolation and death as a
release. Both glossed over human error (which featured in both disasters) to concentrate, instead, on the human valour of everyone concerned: remarkably, ice warnings were ignored in the build-up to both
the *Titanic* and the *Challenger* tragedies.

The most important connection, however, exists in the public consciousness: the *Challenger*, just like the *Titanic* disaster, came quickly
to represent popular cultural crisis-points in the perceived relationship between man, God, nature and technology. If the rhetoric is the
same, it is because the meaning of the two events was popularly construed to be the same.

We are by now familiar with the story of the *Titanic*. The space
shuttle *Challenger*, with its seven-strong crew, was scheduled to make
its tenth journey into space on 20 January 1986. Shuttle launches into
space had come to be seen as fairly routine events, as the use of the
term 'shuttle' betrays. It might have seemed as if the astronauts were
going to New York or Washington rather than out into dark and
weightless space.

The lift-off from NASA's Florida launch-pad 39-B was postponed
until Saturday, 25 January, following a delay with one of the other
three space shuttles. Then, a dust-storm out in the Atlantic provoked
another 24 hour wait. Sunday's rain led to Monday, when mechanical
problems again delayed the launch. Ice formed on the shuttle and the

gantry overnight, but on Tuesday, 28 January, despite telephone warnings from an engineer, the countdown continued. Seventy-three seconds after lift-off, a sealant ring failed and the shuttle exploded, live, on television, killing everyone on board. Back at the White House, Peggy Noonan turned on her computer.

The *Challenger* never claimed to be infallible, but as Ronald Reagan quietly told his national television audience, 'We've grown used to the wonders of this century ... We've grown used to the idea of space'.[10] So confident were both NASA and the American public about their technological progress that they had chosen on this occasion to put their first ordinary citizen into orbit: New Hampshire high school teacher Christa McAuliffe. It was going to be, in the words of NASA publicity, 'the ultimate field trip'. Her parents, together with 18 third-graders from Concord, had flown down to Florida to witness the launch. Back at McAuliffe's high school, pupils and colleagues watched the launch together on TV. Many of us today still remember the stark, television image of those two, white, bifurcating vapour trails, standing out against a clear blue sky.

The *Titanic* met its demise at sea; the *Challenger* in the air. Both disasters happened during periods of enormous national self-confidence: the *Challenger* during the Reaganite 1980s in the United States, the *Titanic* in the last Edwardian summer before the outbreak of the First World War in Europe. Yet the rhetoric of both disasters can be traced back way beyond the current century.

Millicent, Duchess of Sutherland, referred to 'the Psalmist' in her eulogy. She was in fact referring to Psalm 139, verses 9 and 10: 'If I take the wings of the morning, and dwell in the uttermost pasts of the sea; Even there shall thy hand lead me, and thy right hand shall hold me.'[11] References to 'the face of God', as alluded to by Reagan, Magee and the Duchess of Sutherland, recur throughout the Bible, especially the Old Testament. Job 33, verse 26, for example, says: 'He shall pray unto God, and he will be favourable unto him: and he shall see his face with joy: for he shall render unto man his righteousness.'

However, seeing the face of God, is, in Old Testament terms, something of a mixed blessing, for it was generally held that no man could see the face of God and live: 'And Manoah said unto his wife, "We shall surely die, because we have seen God"' (Judges 13: 22). Seeing the face of God, then, was a final, ecstatic vision for the *Challenger* and *Titanic* victims, a glorious and bittersweet consolation in death.

As we saw in the last chapter, societal articulations of this complex relationship between man, God and nature, are by no means limited to Judeo-Christian traditions. We recall the story of Daedalus, the architect and inventor of Greek mythology who made wings held together by wax so that he and his son Icarus could escape King Minos' labyrinth. Icarus, however, flew too near the sun; his wings melted and, just like the *Challenger*, he fell to his death from the sky into the sea. Similarly, we remember the myth of the Titan Prometheus, who, in a supreme act of hubris, stole the secret of fire from the gods, and gave the technological gift to man.

Our brief look at the case of the space shuttle *Challenger* serves to remind us that the *Titanic* was not the last event to be subject to the forces of mythologization. By referring to the myths of Icarus and Prometheus, we can see that we continue today to share common concerns with civilizations separated from us by both time and space. Further, we can see that we continue to articulate these concerns by way of myth. Both the *Challenger* and the *Titanic* are tales of hubris – and of nemesis – in the modern world constructed, by a process of *bricolage* from the cultural materials at hand. They are modern myths, related in popular culture.

Let us remind ourselves how appropriately we are using the term 'myth'. In Chapter 2, I described the functional theory of myth, and showed how according to theories such as those of Malinowski, myths served both to serve and to articulate the interests of particular social groups. In chapters 3, 4, and 5, I proceeded to show how the myth of the *Titanic* in late Edwardian popular culture encoded attitudes towards gender, class and race in narrative form. An analysis of these attitudes revealed the presumed supremacy of the upper-class, Anglo-Saxon male. This was followed by a description of historical theories of myth, and showed how according to theories such as those of Hill and Rappaport, myths embraced a complex negotiation between the actual and the imaginary in the particular experiences of particular peoples. Although the experiences were particular, however, the process in which the historical data were reanimated in the interests of cultural rather than historical 'truth' turned out to be common across particular times and peoples. In Chapters 3 to 7, we saw exactly such a process taking place with the myth of the *Titanic*: it was based on a real ship and a real event, but within hours of the sinking, the physical *Titanic* was eclipsed by the mythical as a complex process of mythogenesis began. Finally, I described Lévi-Strauss' structural theory of myth, and showed how, in addition to merging actual and imaginary experience, this theory revealed myth as serving to construct order out of an arbitrary world.

In this investigation, I have attempted to use a specific case study to make a universal point. In doing so, I have followed the methodological tradition of authorities such as John Grierson and Clifford Geertz, supported by thinkers such as Hegel and Kant. Grierson, the socially purposive documentary film-maker and theorist, drew on Kantian and Hegelian philosophy to make the distinction between the 'real' or 'noumenal' and the 'phenomenal'.[12] The 'real' was abstract and general truth, the underlying reality between diverse human experience. The 'phenomenal', on the other hand, was the local, the empirical and the particular, and Grierson advocated the use of the phenomenal in pursuit of the real, the real providing his ultimate aim, his ultimate destination. In this way, he was able, for example, to make specific films about herring fishermen or night mail trains in order to make broader and more important points about society – and indeed the human condition – as a whole.

Similarly, the anthropologist Clifford Geertz has made celebrated case-studies of, for example, cockfighting in Bali and ritual sheep-stealing in Morocco, not simply because he finds them inherently interesting, but more so because, as a social anthropologist, he is more significantly concerned with the broader understandings to which analysis of specific case studies such as these can lead us. They are, as Geertz himself says, 'particular attempts by particular peoples to place these things in some sort of meaningful, comprehensive frame'.[13] His aim, like mine, is to find any sort of specific and phenomenal clue to universal human experience, whether that experience or those concerns are articulated through sinking ships, fighting cocks, melting wings or exploding space rockets. They are all, to paraphrase Geertz, 'stories we tell ourselves about ourselves'.[14] The stories, then, have both temporal and universal dimensions. At a temporal level, they give us insight into the specific experiences, concerns, attitudes and beliefs of particular societies. At a universal level, they demonstrate features, uses and needs common to cultures seemingly divided by both time and space. They point, therefore, to a shared aspect of the human experience. In this way, the myth of the *Titanic*, encoded abstract concepts in concrete form to give us both an insight into late Edwardian, British cultural attitudes, and to show how the late Edwardians reanimated the historical data surrounding the physical *Titanic* to create a myth which not only constructed a triumph out of a tragedy, but at the same time manufactured meaning out of meaninglessness.

This analysis has, therefore, provided us not only with an understanding of late Edwardian *mentalités*, but also, and more importantly, an understanding of the relationship between popular culture and modern myth. Rather than reviling both popular culture and the academic study of it, it persuades us to take popular culture seriously, for an analysis of popular culture can provide inroads and insights into areas which a study of merely high or élite culture alone cannot adequately illuminate. In this way, the intelligent and rigorous study of popular culture can, if we are both wise and discriminating, lead us towards a deeper understanding of real, universal truths about the nature of human experience. Finally, this study persuades us that in seeking an understanding of culture and values, we need to pay serious attention to representations (and even erroneous representations) and not simply to what we may previously have thought of as 'facts'.

What, though, is the point of all this? The point is two-fold. First, and unashamedly, I believe in the intrinsic value of knowledge. As Thomas Nagel has argued, knowledge is valuable regardless of any additional, practical benefits to which it may or may not immediately lead. In this way, 'The mere existence of understanding, somewhere in the species, is regarded by many as worthy of substantial sacrifices.'[15] The usefulness of knowledge, therefore 'cannot be measured by its practical effects'.[16]

Thought and knowledge – even at their most seemingly abstract and theoretical, however, may still have a vital social use. As R.G. Collingwood has shown, work within the college walls could and indeed should have a practical and constructive effect on life beyond them. For according to Collingwood, we all live in a world not of facts but of thoughts; therefore, if you can change the moral, political and economic theories which are generally accepted by the world in which an individual lives:

> you change the character of his world; and that if you change his own 'theories' you change his relation to that world; so that in either case you change the way in which he acts.[17]

Academic thought – even in something so apparently trivial as a case-study of two years of representations of the *Titanic* – could lead, therefore, to an improved state of societal self-awareness. Adorno argued that the situation could be likened to a metaphorical prison in which thinking alone offered the prospect of escape. In this way:

> When the doors are barricaded, it is doubly important that thought not be interrupted. It is rather the task of thought to analyze the

reasons behind this situation and to draw the consequences from these reasons. It is the responsibility of thought not to accept this situation as finite. If there is any chance of changing the situation, it is through undiminished insight.[18]

For as Adorno has said, the truly critical thinker never gives up, and so 'whoever refuses to permit his thought to be taken from him has not resigned'.[19]

We need to go even further, however. Not only must we defy resignation, we must also accept the challenge of dangerous thought – even when the insight that we thus achieve is one that exposes our need to fashion meaning from a meaningless world.

Notes

INTRODUCTION

1. Some changes in maritime regulation and procedure did result from the *Titanic* disaster. These will be described in Chapter 1.
2. A total of 4,375 people are believed to have died in the Philippines ferry disaster, compared with 1,490 on the *Titanic*. The precise figures for those lost and saved on the *Titanic* are a matter of some marginal dispute: in this study I have used those figures accepted by the British government inquiry of 1912, for the reasons explained in the following chapter.
3. Children at American grade schools and summer camps still sing 'It Was Sad When the Great Ship Went Down' (US traditional).
4. For example: 'Waiter, I know I asked for ice, but this is ridiculous!'
5. For example, on 21 December 1993, US Vice President Al Gore introduced the announcement of a Clinton administration package of legislative and administrative proposals on telecommunications by telling the story of the radio operators on the *Titanic*. Source: Transcript of Vice Presidential address at the National Press Club Luncheon, Washington, DC. Meanwhile, metaphorical allusions to the *Titanic* remain legion in politics. For example, late and inadequate action is frequently compared to 'rearranging the deckchairs on the *Titanic*'.
6. Fictional casualties of the *Titanic* include Edward and Edith in Noel Coward's play *Cavalcade*, and Lady Marjory Bellamy of BBC Television's 'Upstairs, Downstairs'. Fictional survivors include the assorted dwarves of 'Time Bandits', directed by Terry Gilliam, Handmade Films, UK, 1981.
7. Beryl Bainbridge, *Every Man for Himself* (London, 1996).
8. 'Titanic' opened at the Lunt-Fontanne theatre, New York City, on 23 April 1997. The book was by Peter Stone, music and lyrics by Maury Yeston, and directed by Richard Jones. Production costs were estimated at $10 million.
9. 'Titanic', directed by James Cameron, Twentieth Century Fox/Paramount Pictures, USA, 1997. The film was released in the USA in 1997 and the UK early in 1998.
10. The *Titanic* feature films to date are: 'Atlantic', directed by E.A. Dupont, British International Pictures/Süd Film, UK, 1929; 'Titanic', directed by Herbert Selpin and Werner Klinger, Tobis Films, Germany, 1943; 'Titanic', directed by Jean Negulescu, Twentieth Century Fox, USA, 1953; 'A Night to Remember', directed by Roy Ward Baker, The Rank Organisation, UK, 1958; 'SOS Titanic', directed by Billy Hale, EMI Films, UK, 1979; 'Titanic' directed by James Cameron, Twentieth Century Fox/Paramount Pictures, USA, 1997. Additionally, 'Raise the Titanic', directed by Jerry Jameson, Martin Starger Productions for ITC, USA, 1980, concerns an entirely fictitious attempt to salvage the ship during the 'Cold War'.

11. 'Titanic: Adventure out of Time' marketed on CD-ROM in the UK from March 1997 by Cyberfix GTE Entertainment.

12. Rick Archbold and Dana McCauley, *Last Dinner on the Titanic: Menus and Recipes from the Great Liner* (London, 1997). Journalist Erica Wagner hosted a dinner party, based on the book, to 'commemorate' the 85th anniversary of the disaster. The result was reported in a full-page feature in *The Times*. See Erica Wagner, 'Dinner as the Ship Went Down' in *The Times*, 14 April 1997, p. 16.

13. Tim Radford, 'Titanic Iceberg Is Innocent' in *The Guardian*, 17 September 1993, p. 1. This is just one example of continuing media interest in the *Titanic*.

14. The American Titanic Historical Society was originally called Titanic Enthusiasts of America and today has nearly 5,000 members world-wide. A second American organization, Titanic International, has begun in competition to its predecessor, while the British Titanic Society has over 800 members.

15. Recent exceptions are Heyer's account of media coverage of the *Titanic* and Stephen Biel's study of the disaster in North American culture. See Paul Heyer, *Titanic Legacy* (Westport, Connecticut, 1995) and Steven Biel, *Down With the Old Canoe* (New York, 1996).

16. Robert Darnton, *The Great Cat Massacre and Other Episodes in French Cultural History* (London, 1984).

17. Roger Chartier, *Cultural History* (Cambridge, 1988).

18. Chartier (1988), p. 107.

19. Paul Fussell, *The Great War and Modern Memory* (Oxford, 1975; first paperback edition, 1977).

20. This expression is used by Fred Inglis in his discussion of Fussell in Fred Inglis, *Media Theory* (Oxford, 1990), p. 184.

21. Fussell (1977), p. ix.

22. Beau Riffenburgh, *The Myth of the Explorer*, Polar Research Series (London and New York, 1993), p. 3.

23. For an example of the sociology of representation in both theory and practice see Stuart Hall, ed., *Representation: Cultural Representations and Signifying Practices* (London, 1997). Representation is, according to Hall, a key 'moment' in the 'circle of culture'. Hall (1997), p. 1. The term 're-presentation' is also term used by Chartier, which he defines as 'the production of classifications and exclusions that constitute the social and conceptual configurations proper to one time or place'. Chartier (1988), p. 13.

24. Hall (1997), p. 15.

25. This study does not attempt an account of the political economy of the media during that period, nor does it engage itself with the sociology of reception of late Edwardian popular culture. These are both valid courses of inquiry, but lie beyond the deliberate focus of this examination.

26. Some authorities such as Jonathon Rose, take the Edwardian period as extending as far as 1919. See Jonathon Rose, *The Edwardian Temperament, 1895–1919* (Athens, Ohio, 1986).

27. T.S. Eliot, *Notes Towards the Definition of Culture* (London, 1948), p. 41.

28. Eliot (1948), p. 31. I am aware, of course, of the dangers of extending the concept of culture so far that it loses any real or particular meaning. My point here (as indeed was Eliot's) is simply to remind us of the greater dangers of constricting that definition.
29. Colin MacCabe, 'Defining Popular Culture' in *High Theory/Low Culture: Analysing Popular Television and Film*, edited by Colin MacCabe, Images of Culture (Manchester, 1986), p. 8.
30. Eugene Weber, *France: Fin de Siècle* (Cambridge, Massachusetts and London, 1986), p. 4.
31. James Monaco, *How to Read a Film* (New York and Oxford, 1981), p. 211.
32. Robert Warshow *The Immediate Experience* (New York, 1962), p. 28.
33. John Brinkerhoff Jackson, *Discovering the Vernacular Landscape* (New Haven, 1984) pp. ix–xii.
34. See especially T.W. Adorno and M. Horkheimer, 'The Culture Industry as Mass Deception' in *The Dialectic of Enlightenment* translated by John Cumming (London, 1979).
35. T.W. Adorno, *Notes on Literature*, Volume II (New York, 1992), p. 245.
36. Inglis (1990), p. 6.
37. Ludwig Wittgenstein, *Culture and Value*, translated by Peter Winch (second edition, Oxford, 1980), p. 80.
38. Siegfried Kracauer, *From Caligari to Hitler* (Princeton, NJ, 1947, fifth printing, 1974), p. 5.
39. Kracauer (1947), p. 272.
40. John Dunn, 'Practising History and Social Science on 'Realist' Assumptions' in *Political Obligation in its Historical Context* (Cambridge, 1980), pp. 81–111, 110–11.
41. Clifford Geertz, 'Deep Play: Notes on the Balinese Cockfight' in *The Interpretation of Cultures* (London, 1975), p. 452.
42. Adorno (1969), p. 348.
43. Geertz (1973), p. 16.
44. Walter Benjamin, *The Origin of German Tragic Drama*, translated by John Osborne (London, 1977).
45. Geertz (1973), p. 444.
46. Geertz (1973), p. 444.
47. The term derives from the Greek 'hermeneus': an interpreter.
48. Geertz (1973), p. 453.
49. Geertz (1973), p. 5.
50. Terry Eagleton, *The Crisis of Contemporary Culture* (Oxford, 1993), p. 17. Eagleton claimed, in the same lecture, that because cultural theory threatened the current division of academic labour, it was considered to be a nuisance by the 'Establishment' (p. 17).
51. Henry Louis Gates, originally quoted in a letter to Harvard alumni and alumnae from Jeremy R. Knowles, 20 September 1996. Permission to requote granted in author's correspondence with Gates, 1 November 1996.
52. It is reasonable, I think, to suspect that a significant item on the agenda of male survivors' accounts in particular is the justification of their own survival in a context which applauded the concept of 'women and

children first' and which had correspondingly heaped odium upon male survivors with flimsy excuses for saving their own skins. J. Bruce Ismay, the Managing Director of the White Star Line, for example, survived and was pilloried in the press, effectively lost his job, and lived out the rest of his life as a recluse in Ireland.

53. Interview with survivor Eva Hart, conducted at her home at Chadwell Heath, Essex, 21 October, 1990. Miss Hart died in 1996.
54. John Kenneth Galbraith, *A Tenured Professor: A Novel* (London, 1990), p. 50.
55. The complex variety of theories of myth is both acknowledged and investigated in the chapter in question.

1   A BRIEF HISTORY OF THE *TITANIC*

1. Michael Davie, *The Titanic: The Full Story of a Tragedy* (London, 1986), p. 9.
2. Any ship carrying more than 50 steerage passengers sailing from a British port to ports outside Europe was classified by the Board of Trade as an 'Emigrant Ship'. As such, form 'Surveys 27', 'Report of a Survey of an Emigrant Ship' was completed for the *Titanic* on 12 April 1912, while form 'Surveys 32', 'Certificates of Clearance of an Emigrant Ship' was completed by emigration officers as the *Titanic* left each of its ports of call in Europe. See Public Record Office reference MT 9/920 F (No. 356).
3. First-class fares remained generally stable, but steerage rates fluctuated considerably due to keen competition. C.R. Vernon Gibbs in *British Passenger Liners of the Five Oceans* (London, 1963), p. 540, gives examples of fares and describes a 'rate war' which temporarily reduced Liverpool to New York fares to £2.
4. For useful introductions to the economy of trans-Atlantic carriage, see Davie (1986), especially pp. 6–16, and Terry Coleman *The Liners* (Harmondsworth, 1977).
5. The figures I have given here are for Gross Registered Tonnage (GRT) which reflects not the weight but the enclosed volume of the ship. This is the standard form of measurement for merchant vessels. The precise figures for individual ships vary due to modification and date of measurement.
6. Technically, the *Titanic* was owned by the Oceanic Steam Navigation Company (Ltd), a British registered company usually known as the White Star Line. Ultimately, OSNC was controlled by the American-based International Mercantile Marine, headed by financier J. Pierpoint Morgan.
7. Anon, 'Launch of the Titanic' in *The Times*, 1 June 1911, p. 9.
8. White Star Line publicity brochure: 'White Star Line Royal and United States Mail Steamers "Olympic" & "Titanic" 45,000 Tons Each The Largest Vessels in the World.' (Liverpool, 1911), p. 31.

9. Gibbs (1963), p. 260.
10. White Star Line publicity brochure: 'The World's Largest & Finest Steamers new Triple Screw S.S. "Olympic" and "Titanic"' (October 1911), unpaginated.
11. Publicity brochure: 'White Star Line Royal and United States Mail Steamers "Olympic" & "Titanic" ...' p. 33.
12. Publicity brochure: 'White Star Line Royal and United States Mail Steamers "Olympic" & "Titanic" ...' p. 37.
13. Publicity brochure: 'White Star Line Royal and United States Mail Steamers "Olympic" & "Titanic" ...' p. 39.
14. The White Star liner *Adriatic* boasted a similar 'plunge bath'. See the White Star Line publicity brochure 'The World's Largest & Finest Steamers ...' (1911), unpaginated.
15. Publicity brochure: 'White Star Line Royal and United States Mail Steamers "Olympic" & "Titanic" ...' p. 47.
16. Publicity brochure: 'White Star Line Royal and United States Mail Steamers "Olympic" & "Titanic" ...' p. 51.
17. Publicity brochure: 'White Star Line Royal and United States Mail Steamers "Olympic" & "Titanic" ...' p. 54.
18. Publicity brochure: 'White Star Line Royal and United States Mail Steamers "Olympic" & "Titanic" ...' p. 54.
19. The *Titanic* did not contain the large, open, dormitory-style accommodation normally associated with 'steerage' class. While some such accommodation had been originally planned, it was not included in the final specification for the ship. See John P. Eaton and Charles A. Haas, *Titanic: Triumph and Tragedy* (Sparkford, Somerset, 1986 and 1992), p. 74. Eaton and Haas's deck plans reflect these later developments.
20. Seminal *Titanic* researcher Walter Lord used the terms interchangeably in *A Night to Remember* (London, 1956); also the illustrated and revised edition (London, 1976).
21. 'Shipping Casualties (Loss of the Steamship "Titanic.") Report of a Formal Investigation into the circumstances attending the foundering on 15th April, 1912, of the British Steamship "Titanic," of Liverpool, after striking ice in or near Latitude 41° 46′ N., 50° 14′ W., North Atlantic Ocean, whereby loss of life ensued.' Parliamentary Command Paper cd. 6352 (1912), p. 15. Subsequent references will be given as British Inquiry Report (1912). Some of the *Titanic*'s accommodation could be used for either of two classes of passengers, as the inquiry noted (p. 15).
22. British Inquiry Report (1912), p. 15.
23. British Inquiry Report (1912), p. 23. Exact passenger and crew figures for the *Titanic* are still a matter of debate. The American inquiry produced slightly different figures. See '"Titanic" Disaster Report of the Committee on Commerce United States Senate Pursuant to S. Res. 283' 62nd Congress, 2nd Session, Report No. 806 (1912), p. 6. Subsequent references will be given as American Inquiry Report (1912). The differences in the figures are explained by discrepancies such as stowaways, deserters, passengers joining and leaving in France and Ireland, and inaccuracies in the passenger list. The minutiae do not concern us here.

24. Passengers embarking at Queenstown sailed for a slightly reduced £6 10 shillings.
25. Source: the *Daily Graphic* 'Titanic In Memoriam Number', 20 April 1912, p. 8. The US dollar price for the most expensive accommodation (parlour suite with private promenade) was $4,350 in high season. Source: 'White Star Line First Class Passage Rates' (New York office) issue number 1, January 1912.
26. Madeleine Astor's condition was only euphemistically referred to by the press at the time.
27. He is now believed to have been travelling with his mistress, a certain Madame Aubert of Paris. See Lynch and Marschall (1992), p. 41.
28. Quoted in Wyn Craig Wade, *The Titanic: End of a Dream* (London, 1980), p. 35.
29. Gardiner and Van Der Vat (1995) question the impartiality of the Admiralty's investigation, suggesting it smacked of an 'efficient "stitch up" and pre-emptive strike by the Navy'. See Robin Gardiner and Dan Van Der Vat, *The Riddle of the Titanic* (London, 1995), p. 15.
30. When entering and leaving busy ports, ships were required to take on board a pilot, who took temporary control on the bridge. If the ship was involved in any sort of any accident during this time, it was the pilot and not the captain who was therefore held responsible.
31. The command of the *Olympic* passed to the splendidly named Captain Herbert James Haddock.
32. PRO reference MT 9/920 F (No. 356).
33. The similar suite on the starboard side was taken at Cherbourg by Mr and Mrs Thomas Cardeza, for which they paid £512 6 shillings.
34. British Inquiry Report (1912), p. 29.
35. British Inquiry Report (1912), p. 29. It is, of course, unlikely that Lightoller was word perfect in his recollection of his conversation with the captain. The reported conversation is, however, taken verbatim from the inquiry report.
36. Ultrasound investigations have since suggested a series of six slits 'the width of a man's palm'. This was still big enough, however, for the ocean to rush in faster than 'a modern fireman's hose'. See Quentin Letts, 'Six Narrow Slits That Sank the Titanic' in *The Times*, 9 April 1997, p. 16.
37. This useful analogy is used by Gardiner and Van Der Vat (1995), p. 94.
38. British Inquiry Report (1912), p. 37.
39. British Inquiry Report (1912), p. 38. The exact number of people in each boat remains a matter of dispute, the evidence being unreliable.
40. The precise number is not known. The British inquiry concluded only one (British Inquiry Report [1912] p. 69.), but later research (see, for example, Don Lynch and Ken Marschall, *Titanic: An Illustrated History* [London, 1992]) has suggested considerably more.
41. British Inquiry Report (1912), p. 42. The American inquiry produced marginally different figures (American Inquiry [1912], pp. 5–6), but the breakdown by class and gender in both reports reveals an almost identical pattern.
42. Anon, 'New Liner Titanic Hits An Iceberg; Sinking By The Bow At Midnight; Women Put Off In Lifeboats; Last Wireless At 12:27 Am Blurred' in the *New York Times*, 15 April 1912, p. 1.

43. Anon, 'All Saved from Titanic After Collision' in the New York *Evening Sun* (final edition), 15 April 1912, p. 1.

44. Speech to the Senate of the United States, Tuesday 28 May 1912, as transcribed and included in the Government Printing Office (Washington, 1912) publication of the American Inquiry Report (1912), pp. 69–82, p. 69.

45. Speech to Senate, American Inquiry Report (1912), p. 70.

46. Speech to Senate, American Inquiry Report (1912), p. 70.

47. Speech to Senate, American Inquiry Report (1912), p. 71.

48. Cited in Wade (1979), p. 175. Wade provides the best available description and analysis of the Senate inquiry.

49. Gardiner and Van Der Vat (1995), p. 195.

50. Gardiner and Van Der Vat (1995), pp. 177–8.

51. Gardiner and Van Der Vat (1995), p. 202.

52. For logistical reasons, the inquiry also sat for two days at the Caxton Hall, Caxton Street, Westminster on 1 and 3 July.

53. British Inquiry Report (1912), p. 10.

54. British Inquiry Report (1912), p. 24.

55. British Inquiry Report (1912), pp. 24–5.

56. British Inquiry Report (1912), pp. 26–8.

57. British Inquiry Report (1912), p. 29.

58. British Inquiry Report (1912), p. 30.

59. British Inquiry Report (1912), p. 30.

60. British Inquiry Report (1912), p. 30.

61. British Inquiry Report (1912), p. 30.

62. British Inquiry Report (1912), p. 30.

63. British Inquiry Report (1912), p. 30.

64. British Inquiry Report (1912), p. 39.

65. British Inquiry Report (1912), p. 39.

66. British Inquiry Report (1912), p. 41.

67. Peter Padfield, *The Titanic and the Californian* (London, 1965).

68. Leslie Reade, *The Ship That Stood Still* (Sparkford, Somerset, 1993).

69. British Inquiry Report (1912), p. 46.

70. British Inquiry Report (1912), p. 47.

71. British Inquiry Report (1912), p. 48.

72. British Inquiry Report (1912), p. 61.

73. British Inquiry Report (1912), p. 87.

74. British Inquiry Report (1912), p. 1.

75. Davie (1986), p. 184.

76. Lynch and Marschall (1992), p. 182.

77. Lynch and Marschall (1992), p. 188.

78. Geoffrey Marcus, *The Maiden Voyage* (London, 1969), p. 274.

79. Gardiner and Van Der Vat (1995), p. 246.

80. Ballard's account of the discovery and exploration of the *Titanic* wreck site is fully described in Robert D. Ballard, *The Discovery of the Titanic* (London, 1987, revised edition, 1989).

81. Robert D. Ballard, 'Epilogue to the 1989 Edition' in *The Discovery of the Titanic* (London, 1989), p. 214.

82. Jon Thompson, director of the Memphis Wonders series of exhibitions, quoted in Alex Duval, 'Survivors Sail into Titanic Row on Disaster Spin-Offs' in the *Guardian*, 5 April 1997, p. 16.

83. See R. Barry O'Brien, 'Inquiry Captains all on Different Courses' in the *Daily Telegraph* 3 April 1992, p. 8.

84. Cited in R. Barry O'Brien, 'Titanic Inquiry Fails to End Row Over Rescue That Never Came' in the *Daily Telegraph*, 3 April 1992, p. 8.

85. Inspector Captain Thomas Barnett, a retired nautical surveyor who did most of the reappraisal, believed that the *Californian* was between 5 and 10 miles away from the *Titanic*, essentially as supposed in 1912. Captain de Coverly, who wrote the final report, found, however, the distance to be between 17 and 20 miles, and as Deputy Chief Inspector of Marine Accidents, his view officially prevailed. Captain Barnett also believed that the *Californian* kept the *Titanic* under observation until it sank, while Captain de Coverly concluded this was another, unidentified vessel. Captain Peter Marriott, Chief Inspector of Marine Accidents, supported his deputy rather than Captain Barnett in a letter to Malcolm Rifkind, Transport Secretary at the time of the publication of the re-examination report. Captain Barnett was not named in the report. The disagreements between the parties responsible may well explain why, although Captain Barnett delivered his findings in the spring of 1991, the report was not published until April 1992. See O'Brien (1992, 'Inquiry Captains All on Different Courses'), p. 8.

2 MYTH AND THE *TITANIC*

1. Percy S. Cohen, 'Theories of Myth' in *Man*, volume 4 (1969), pp. 337–53, p. 337.

2. Claude Lévi-Strauss, *The Savage Mind*, The Nature of Human Society Series (London, 1972), p. 258. See also Cohen (1969), p. 352.

3. Cohen (1969), p. 352.

4. Alan Hamilton, 'Sunk at Last: Some Myths About the Titanic' in *The Times*, 15 April 1982, p. 10.

5. Marcus (1969), p. 7. Marcus refers to the 'true facts' again on p. 284.

6. Terence Turner, 'Ethno-Ethnohistory: Myth and History in Native South American Representations of Contact with Western Society' in *Rethinking History and Myth*, edited by Jonathan D. Hill (Urbana, Illinois and Chicago, 1988), pp. 235–81, pp. 235–6.

7. Peter Burke, 'History as Social Memory' in *Memory*, edited by Thomas Butler (Oxford, 1989), pp. 97–113, pp. 103–4.

8. This discussion of theories of myth acknowledges Stephen-Hugh Jones's seminar series on myth at the Department of Social Anthropology, University of Cambridge, Spring 1992.

9. Cohen (1969), p. 338.

10. B. Malinowski, 'Myth in Primitive Psychology' (1929) in *Magic, Science and Religion and Other Essays* (New York, 1954), pp. 93–148, p. 117.

11. See Cohen (1969), p. 344.

12. Malinowski (1954), p. 144.

13. Cohen (1969), p. 344.

14. Malinowski (1954), p. 146.

15. See Cohen (1969), p. 344.
16. Malinowski (1954), p. 125.
17. Malinowski (1954), p. 125.
18. Malinowski (1954), p. 125.
19. We note the use of the word 'primitive' in the title of his essay.
20. M.I. Finley, 'Myth, Memory and History' in *The Use and Abuse of History* (London, 1986), cited by Joanne Rappaport in *The Politics of Memory*, Cambridge Latin American Studies (Cambridge, 1990), p. 12. I used: M.I. Finley, 'Myth Memory and History' in *The Use and Abuse of History* (London, 1986), pp. 11–33.
21. Rappaport (1990), p. 12.
22. E.R. Leach, *Political Systems of Highland Burma*, London School of Economics, Monographs in Social Anthropology, no. 44 (London, 1954, reprinted 1964, this edition 1970).
23. Leach (1954), p. 265.
24. Leach (1954), p. 277.
25. Rappaport (1990), pp. 12–13.
26. Rappaport (1990), p. 189.
27. Jonathan D. Hill, 'Myth and History' in *Rethinking History and Myth*, edited by Jonathan D. Hill (Urbana and Chicago, 1988), pp. 1–17, p. 5.
28. Hill (1988), p. 10.
29. Turner (1988), p. 237.
30. Turner (1988), pp. 251–2.
31. This is, of course, a very brief summary of a complex investigation. Should a detailed example of Lévi-Strauss's 'oppositional' method be required, an excellent one can be found in Claude Lévi-Strauss, 'The Story of Asdiwal' in *The Structural Study of Myth and Totemism*, translated by Nicholas Mann, edited by Edmund Leach (London, 1967), pp. 1–47. Here, Lévi-Strauss finds and describes the oppositions not only in the myth of Asdiwal, but also in and between the story of his son Waux. The paradoxes uncovered include the geographic, economic, sociological and cosmological.
32. See Claude Lévi-Strauss, 'The Structural Study of Myth' in *Structural Anthropology*, translated by Claire Jacobson and Brooke Grundfest Schoepf (London, 1968), pp. 206–31, p. 229. Also Lévi-Strauss (1967), p. 29. See also Cohen (1969), p. 346.
33. Claude Lévi-Strauss, 'The Comparative Religions of Nonliterate Peoples' in *Structural Anthropology II*, translated by Monique Layton (London, 1978), pp. 60–7, p. 65.
34. Lévi-Strauss (1968), p. 230.
35. Lévi-Strauss (1968), p. 230.
36. Lévi-Strauss (1978), p. 65.
37. Lévi-Strauss (1978), p. 65.
38. Lévi-Strauss (1978), p. 62.
39. Lévi-Strauss (1978), p. 65.
40. Malinowski (1954), p. 146.
41. Lévi-Strauss (1967) pp. 4–7. Lévi-Strauss took this version from Franz Boas, *Tsimshian Texts (New Series)*, American Ethnological Society, Volume III (Leyden, 1912), pp. 71–146.

42. Lévi-Strauss (1967), p. 30. Of course, many other myths could be used to illustrate this argument, but since this is unlikely to be a contentious issue, I will rest at this one good example and not labour the point.
43. Lévi-Strauss (1967), pp. 7–13.
44. Lévi-Strauss (1967), p. 13.
45. Lévi-Strauss (1967), p. 13.
46. Roland Barthes, *Mythologies*, translated by Anette Lavers (New York, 1972, 23rd printing, 1990), p. 128.
47. Homer, *The Iliad*, translated by Richard Lattimore (Chicago, 1951), p. 225, lines 255–9.
48. Burke (1989), p. 110.
49. Nathaniel Hawthorne, *The Scarlet Letter* in collected novels edition (New York and Cambridge, 1983), p. 149. I owe awareness of this quotation to Mike Weaver's presentation at the Royal Academy on 8 December 1989. Weaver was discussing the special relationship of photography to reality.
50. Hill (1988), p. 10.
51. Ernst Bloch, *The Principle of Hope*, three volumes, translated by Neville Plaice, Stephen Plaice and Paul Knight (Oxford, 1986), pp. 794–838.
52. Bloch (1986), p. 813.
53. Vincent Geoghegan, *Utopianism and Marxism* (London, 1987), p. 88.
54. Chartier (1988), p. 6.
55. Slavoj Žižek, *The Sublime Object of Ideology* (London and New York, 1989), p. 70.
56. Lévi-Strauss (1967), p. 30.
57. See Dan Sperber, 'Claude Lévi-Strauss' in *Structuralism and Since*, edited by John Sturrock (Oxford, 1977), pp. 19–51, pp. 40–2.
58. Geoghegan (1987), p. 2.
59. Geoghegan (1987), pp. 1–2.
60. Geertz (1973), p. 446.
61. Lévi-Strauss (1967), p. 30.
62. Cannell (1990), pp. 667–86.
63. Cannell (1990), p. 682.
64. Lévi-Strauss (1967), p. 21.
65. Richard Wolin, *Walter Benjamin: An Aesthetic of Redemption* (New York, 1982), p. 76.
66. Graham McCann, 'Biographical Boundaries: Sociology and Marilyn Monroe' in *The Body*, edited by Mike Featherstone, Mike Hepworth and Bryan S. Turner, Theory, Culture and Society (London, 1991), pp. 325–38, p. 334.
67. Rappaport (1990), p. 16.
68. Rappaport (1990), p, 16.
69. Thomas Gilovich, *How We Know What Isn't So: The Fallibility of Reason in Everyday Life* (New York, 1991), p. 99.
70. Philip M. Taylor and Michael Sanders, *British Propaganda During the First World War 1914–18* (London and Basingstoke, 1982), p. 147.
71. F.S. Stevenson, (ed.), *'Be British' Captain E.J. Smith Memorial A Souvenir of July 29th, 1914* (Lichfield, Staffordshire, 1914), pp. 30–1.
72. Nikos Kazantzakis, *The Last Temptation of Christ*, translated by P.A. Brien (New York, 1960), p. 476.

73. Kazantzakis (1960), p. 477.
74. Thomas Keneally, *Schindler's Ark* (London, 1982), pp. 248–9.
75. See Leo Lowenthal, *The Arts in Society* (Englewood Cliffs, NJ, 1964), p. 125; Martin Jay, *The Dialectical Imagination* (London, 1973), pp. 136–8.
76. See Cohen (1969), pp. 340–3.
77. Cohen (1969), p. 340. See also Bloch (1986), pp. 57–61 on the 'collective unconscious'.
78. Lévi-Strauss (1967), p. 30.
79. See Dan Sperber, 'Claude Lévi-Strauss' in *Structuralism and Since*, edited by John Sturrock (Oxford, 1977), pp. 19–51, pp. 40–2.
80. See Sperber (1979), p. 34.
81. Roland Barthes, 'Soap Powders and Detergents' in *Mythologies*, p. 36. Sophisticated, modern advertising, of course, does sometimes consciously exploit psychology to make us buy. This still does not invalidate it for the student of popular culture looking for societal values. The fact that an advertiser may deliberately exploit (say) patriotism to sell soup can still be most revealing of an audience if that call to patriotism does indeed sell the soup. It reveals patriotism as an active societal value. American advertising since Reagan has made increasing use of patriotism reflecting a significant change since Vietnam and Jimmy Carter when patriotism was hardly used in advertising at all.
82. Chartier (1988), p. 6.
83. Chartier (1988), p. 44.
84. See Graham McCann, 'Ernst Bloch, The Utopian Function of Art and Literature' in *Radical Philosophy*, Autumn 1988, p. 47. John Dunn used the expression 'overshoot' in a not dissimilar context in Dunn (1980), p. 108.
85. For more on the unconscious element in popular culture, see Eliot (1948), pp. 94 and 106; Siegfried Kracauer, *From Caligari to Hitler* (Princeton, NJ, 1947, fifth printing), p. 6; Leo Lowenthal, 'On Sociology of Literature' in *Literature and Mass Culture* (New Brunswick, NJ, 1984), p. 268; Chartier (1988), p. 6.
86. Eliot (1948), p. 94.
87. Cited by Pierre Brunel, *Companion to Literary Myths, Heroes and Archetypes*, edited by Pierre Brunel, translated by Wendy Allatson, Judith Hayward and Trista Selous (London, 1992), p. xi.
88. Graham McCann has observed that myth is strong in generality but weak in detail. See Graham McCann, *Marilyn Monroe* (Cambridge, 1988), p. 110.
89. Ruth Benedict, *Patterns of Culture* (London, 1935, fifth impression, 1952), p. 2.
90. Benedict (1935), p. 2.
91. Benedict (1935), p. 183.
92. Benedict (1935), p. 183.
93. Fenella Cannell, 'Concepts of Parenthood: The Warnock Report, the Gillick Debate and Modern Myths' in *American Ethnologist*, volume 17, no. 4 (Washington, DC, 1990), pp. 667–86, p. 670.
94. Cannell (1990), p. 667.
95. The only notable exception was provided by George Bernard Shaw. He was prepared to admit, though, that his was a lone dissenting opinion.

'Did the press really represent the public?' he asked. 'I am afraid it did.' See George Bernard Shaw, letter to the *Daily News and Leader*, 14 May 1912, p. 6. Shaw's dissent will be discussed more fully in Chapter 5.

96. Clifford Geertz, 'Found in Translation: On the Social History of the Moral Imagination' in *Local Knowledge* (New York, 1983), pp. 36–54, p. 41.
97. Geertz (1973), p. 448.
98. Malinowski (1954), p. 101.
99. Malinowski (1954), p. 110.
100. Malinowski (1954), p. 138.
101. Malinowski (1954), p. 144.
102. Don Cupitt, *What is a Story* (London, 1991), p. 45.
103. Don Cupitt, *The Time Being* (London, 1992), p. 36.
104. Cupitt (1992), p. 40.
105. Richard Howells, 'And the Band Played on ...' in *The Times Higher Education Supplement*, 24 April 1992, p. 17. Vincent Crapanzano uses the phrase 'meaning out of the meaningless' in a derogatory context in an attack on the methodology of Clifford Geertz in Vincent Crapanzano, 'Hermes' Dilemma; The Masking of Subversion in Ethnographic Description' in *Writing Culture*, edited by James Clifford and George E. Marcus (Berkeley, 1986), pp. 51–76, p. 51. I use the same expression, not the same argument. Michael Harrington, meanwhile, wrote that a myth 'could give meaning to the meaningless and make sense out of senseless events' in an article for the *Sunday Telegraph*, in which he compared the assassination of President Kennedy to, among other things, the sinking of the *Titanic*. It may be noted that my article on the myth of the *Titanic* (Howells, 1992), which drew similar conclusions, pre-dated Harrington's by seven months. See Michael Harrington, 'Dead to the Truth' in the *Sunday Telegraph*, 22 November 1992, p. 31.
106. Geertz (1973), p. 5.
107. Geertz (1973), p. 30.
108. Geertz (1973), p. 443.
109. Geertz (1973), p. 443.
110. Lévi-Strauss (1967), pp. 27–9. See also David Pace, *Claude Lévi-Strauss* (Boston, 1983), p. 163.
111. Lévi-Strauss (1967), pp. 15 and 16.
112. Lévi-Strauss (1968), p. 229.
113. Malinowski (1954), p. 98.
114. Turner (1988), p. 274.
115. Marcus Raskin, 'JFK and the Culture of Violence' in *The American Historical Review*, volume 97, no. 2, (1992), pp. 487–99, p. 490.
116. Gilovich (1991), p. 9.
117. Gilovich (1991), p. 10.
118. Gilovich (1991), p. 21.
119. Gilovich (1991), p. 23.
120. Gilovich (1991), p. 50.
121. Harrington (1992), p. 31.
122. Harrington (1992), p. 31.

123. Gilovich (1991), p, 76.
124. Gilovich (1991), p. 78.
125. Benedict (1935), p. 23.
126. My term, not hers.
127. Benedict (1935), p. 23.
128. Cupitt (1991), p. ix.
129. Cupitt (1991), p. 77.
130. Cupitt (1991), pp. 99–100.
131. Cupitt (1991), p. 106.
132. Cupitt (1991), p. 107.
133. Pierre Maranda, 'The Dialectic Metaphor: An Anthropological Essay on Hermeneutics' in *The Reader in the Text*, edited by Susan Suleiman and Inge Crossman (Princeton, NJ, 1980), p. 192. See also Pierre Maranda, *Mythology* (London, 1972), p. 8.
134. Žižek (1989), p. 71.
135. Coleman, (1977), p. 84.
136. Gibbs (1963), p. 246.
137. Geertz (1973), p. 448.
138. Howells (1992), p. 17.
139. Lévi-Strauss (1966), p. 16. Cited by Cohen (1969), p. 347.

3 'WOMEN AND CHILDREN FIRST!'

1. Harold Begbie, untitled poem in 'The Deathless Story of the Titanic', a special publication of *Lloyd's Weekly News* authored by Philip Gibbs (1912), p. 1. Subsequent references will be given as Gibbs (1912).
2. Gibbs (1912), p. 22.
3. 'The White Star Liners "Olympic" and "Titanic"' in *The Shipbuilder*, 6, Special Number, Midsummer 1911, pp. 1–130.
4. The *Daily Graphic* (1912). The *Daily Graphic* was amalgamated with the *Daily Sketch* in 1926.
5. Gibbs began his career on Fleet Street, and served as war correspondent to the *Daily Chronicle* during the First World War. He published prolifically, his output including novels, travelogues and biographies. He was knighted in 1920.
6. The *News of the World*'s circulation in 1910, by comparison, is estimated at 1,500,000. Source: David Butler and Anne Sloman, *British Political Facts 1900–1975* (London, 1975), p. 389.
7. *Lloyd's Weekly News*, 28 April 1912, p. 16.
8. *Lloyd's Weekly News*, 12 May 1912, p. 8.
9. *Lloyd's Weekly News*, 19 May 1912, p. 18; and 26 May 1912, p. 16.
10. As with 'The Deathless Story of the Titanic', records do not reveal the circulation figures for this special number.
11. Newspapers at the time were often secretive about their actual circulations. In 1908, the Advertisers' Protection Society estimated the daily circulation of the *Daily Graphic* as 40,000. This compares, for example, with

The Times estimated daily circulation of 60,000 that same year. See John Cunningham, 'National and Daily Newspapers and their Circulations in the UK, 1908–1978' in *Journal of Advertising History* volume 4, February 1981, pp. 16–18, p. 17. Wadsworth's much cited paper: 'Newspaper Circulations 1800–1954' does not give any figures for the *Daily Graphic*. See A.P. Wadsworth, 'Newspaper Circulations 1800–1954', a paper of the Manchester Statistical Society, (Manchester, 1955).

12. The *Daily Graphic* 20 April 1912, p. 9.

13. The *Daily Graphic* 22 April 1912, p. 9.

14. Lawrence Beesley, *The Loss of the RMS Titanic: Its Story and Its Lessons* (London, 1912) also (Boston, 1912).

15. Archibald Gracie, *The Truth About the Titanic* (New York, 1913), re-issued as *Titanic: A Survivor's Story* (Chicago, 1986).

16. As this was an American publication, I have not considered it one of my central texts.

17. Many of these American publications did not carry full authorship credits and publication details, often simply announcing themselves as 'Official Edition'. A good collection is held by the Titanic Historical Society and by the Marine Museum at Fall River, Massachusetts. Examples include: Marshall Everett, *Nearer My God to Thee: The Story of the Wreck of the Titanic: The Ocean's Greatest Disaster* (no date and place of publication given); Logan Marshall, *The Sinking of the Titanic and Great Sea Disasters: Thrilling Stories of Survivors with Photographs and Sketches* (no date and place of publication); Thomas H. Russell (ed.), *Sinking of the Titanic: The World's Greatest Sea Disaster, Official Edition* (no date and place of publication).

18. Filson Young, *Titanic* (London, 1912).

19. Alexander Bell Filson Young, of Irish descent, was literary editor of the *Daily Mail* and also served as the *Manchester Guardian* correspondent for the South African War. His many and varied publications included *The Complete Motorist* (1904) and *Cornwall and a Light Car* (1926). From 1926 he was an advisor on programmes to the BBC.

20. Bown and Simmons refer to a 'national craze' for collecting picture postcards during the Edwardian era. Their booklet provides the definitive publication (to date) on postcards of the *Titanic*. See Mark Bown and Roger Simmons, *R.M.S. Titanic: A Portrait in Old Picture Postcards* (Loggerheads, Shropshire, 1987). Another relevant publication which draws upon picture postcards of the period is Paul Louden-Brown, *The White Star Line: An Illustrated History 1870–1934* (Coltishall, Norfolk, 1991).

21. Paul Pelham and Lawrence Wright (composers), 'Be British', The Lawrence Wright Music Company (London, nd, presumably 1912). Coloured lantern slides illustrating the song were available from the publisher.

22. F.V. St Clair (composer), 'The Ship That Will Never Return', E. Marks and Son (London, 1912).

23. Robert Donnelly (composer), 'The Band Was Playing as the Ship Went Down', Rossi and Spinnelli Ltd (London, nd, presumably 1912).

24. For an illustrated guide to all Southampton's *Titanic* memorials, see Brian Ticehurst, *The Titanic: Southampton's Memorials* (Poole, Dorset, 1987, revised and reprinted, 1992).
25. F.S. Stevenson, (ed.), *'Be British' Captain E.J. Smith Memorial A Souvenir of July 29th, 1914* (Lichfield, 1914), p. 5.
26. Stevenson (1912), p. 5.
27. Stevenson (1912), p. 7.
28. B. Scott (composer), 'Stand to Your Post' ('In remembrance of the "Titanic"'), sung by Ernest Gray, catalogue number 289, coupled with L. Wright (composer), 'Be British' ('In remembrance of the "Titanic"'), sung by Ernest Gray, catalogue number 290, 78 rpm record, The Winner label (UK, 1912).
29. Wright (1912). The sheet music of this version (described earlier) credits Paul Pelham as co-writer and co-composer. In the sheet version, the corresponding line is given as: 'When your country to you pleaded/ you gave freely what was needed,/ To those they left behind.' The printed music, however, instructs the 'charitable' line of the recorded version to be substituted 'Where collections are made'. Another (small) difference between the printed and recorded versions is that the exclamation mark in the title of the printed version is omitted from the label in the recorded version.
30. Scott (1912).
31. Anon, 'In Memory of the Captain, Crew and Passengers ...' (memorial paper handkerchief), published by the Palatine Printing Co. (Wigan, 1912). Examples of this seemingly unusual piece of ephemera are held at The Maritime Museum, Southampton; The Wesleyan Chapel, Etruria, Stoke-on-Trent; and the Marine Museum at Fall River, Massachusetts. Some sources refer to this as a paper napkin rather than a handkerchief.
32. Royal Opera House Covent Garden Disaster Fund Matinee Programme, Royal Opera (London) 14 May 1912.
33. Royal Albert Hall Titanic Band Memorial Concert Programme, The Orchestral Association (London), 24 May 1912.
34. Stevenson (1914). Contributors towards the cost of the memorial included Dr H.M. Butler, Master of Trinity College, Cambridge.
35. An exception might be C.H. Lightoller's *The Titanic and Other Ships* (London, 1935). While this does contain interesting material on the *Titanic*, the book is essentially Lightoller's life story; much more space is devoted to the 'other ships' than to the *Titanic* itself. Lightoller was second officer on the *Titanic*, and his further adventures at sea included the rescue of British troops from Dunkirk. His book proved to be a very limited commercial success.
36. Gibbs (1912), p. 1.
37. Published in 1912, reproduced in Bown and Simmons (1987), p. 60.
38. Wright, recorded version (1912).
39. Gibbs (1912), p. 38.
40. Gibbs (1912), p. 14.
41. Jas. Adamson (ed.), 'Institute of Marine Engineers Vol. XXIV Memorial to the 'Titanic' Engineering Staff (London, 1912), p. 7.

42. Gibbs (1912), p. 28.
43. Gibbs (1912), p. 10.
44. Scott (1912).
45. Stevenson, (1912), p. 11.
46. Titanic Engineers' Memorial, East Park, Southampton.
47. Published in 1912 by E.A. Bragg of Falmouth reproduced in Bown and Simmons (1987), p. 56.
48. The *Daily Graphic* (1912), p. 3.
49. Wright (recorded version) (1912).
50. One notes similar use of the word in the British tabloid press during the Falklands war of 1982. Seemingly, one needed only to have been present in the war zone in order to be dubbed a 'hero' on one's return.
51. The exact circumstances of the death of Captain Smith have never been discovered. The five versions which have circulated in popular culture since are contradictory, and none has been supported by hard evidence, including the story of him saving the child. We recall from Chapter 2, however, that the existence of different and often contradictory versions is typical of myth.
52. Gibbs (1912), p. 16.
53. Gibbs (1912), p. 16.
54. Gibbs (1912), p. 10
55. Gibbs (1912), p. 10.
56. Young (1912), p. 112.
57. Young (1912), p. 116.
58. Op. cit.
59. Gibbs (1912), p. 12.
60. Scott (1912).
61. St Clair (1912).
62. Pelham and Wright (1912).
63. Haydon Augarde, 'The Wreck of the Titanic' (sheet music for piano), The Lawrence Wright Music Co. (London, 1912).
64. The *Daily Graphic* (1912), p. 9.
65. The *Daily Graphic* (1912), p. 8.
66. Gibbs (1912), p. 10.
67. Scott (1912).
68. Stevenson (1914), p. 6.
69. Postcard published by E.A. Bragg of Falmouth, 1912, reproduced in Bown and Simmons (1987), p. 56. Memorial at East Park, Southampton.
70. The *Daily Graphic* (1912), p. 3.
71. Op. cit.
72. Gibbs (1912), p. 14.
73. Young (1912), pp. 196–7.
74. Gibbs (1912), p. 11. The story is also related by Young (1912), p. 125, and his conduct is praised in the *Daily Graphic* (1912), p. 3.
75. Pelham and Wright (1912).
76. The *Daily Graphic* (1912), p. 8.
77. The *Daily Graphic* (1912), p. 9.
78. The *Daily Graphic* (1912), p. 3.
79. The *Daily Graphic* (1912), p. 8

80. St. Clair (1912).
81. Gibbs (1912), p. 22.
82. Young (1912), p. 117.
83. Young (1912), p. 178.
84. British Inquiry Report (1912), p. 39. These figures do not include the numbers of people believed to have been picked up in the water once the lifeboats had left the ship. An additional 107 male crew members were reported to have gained entry to the boats in order to row and take general charge. The precise figures, like so much of the minutiae concerning the *Titanic*, have since been subject to scrutiny and question. There is no dispute about the general proportion, however. I have kept to the British inquiry figures in this discussion as a matter of consistency. They were certainly the most available to public and experts alike in 1912.
85. British Inquiry Report (1912), p. 37.
86. British Inquiry Report (1912), p. 38.
87. For hostility to Ismay in the United States, see particularly Davie (1986), pp. 109–21.
88. Wade (1979), p. 41.
89. Gracie (1913), p. 322.
90. British Inquiry Report (1912), p. 40.
91. It is possible that, because the *Graphic* was published only one day (20 April 1912) after the American inquiry had begun, it was genuinely unaware of the controversy surrounding Ismay.
92. Gibbs (1912), p. 13.
93. Young (1912), p. 145.
94. Young (1912), p. 189.
95. Young (1912), p. 190.
96. Captain Rostron of the rescue ship *Carpathia*, for example, declared Ismay 'mentally very ill' in the immediate aftermath of the sinking. See Wade (1979), p. 243.
97. Women in Britain achieved limited suffrage in 1918 and full suffrage in 1928.
98. Cited in Wade (1979), p. 65.
99. Clark McAdams, 'Enough Said' in the *St Louis Post-Dispatch*, 22 April 1912, p. 10. Cited in Biel (1996), pp. 30–1.
100. Cited in Wade (1979), p. 65. For more on American suffragettes and the *Titanic* see Wade (1979), pp. 291–4; Biel (1996), pp. 29–33 and 100–7, and Ann E. Larabee, 'The American Hero and His Mechanical Bride: Gender Myths and the Titanic Disaster' in *American Studies*, volume 31, no. 1, Spring 1990, pp. 5–23. Neither British nor American *Titanic* literature takes up the British suffrage issue. Clearly, there is room for further scholarship here.
101. Barthes (1990), p. 11.
102. The *Daily Graphic* (1912), p. 8.
103. Gibbs (1912), p. 2 and the *Daily Graphic* (1912), p. 9.
104. See, for example, Gibbs (1912), pp. 17 and 38.
105. Young (1912), p. 132.
106. Gibbs (1912), p. 27.

107. Young (1912), p. 164.
108. Young (1912), p. 21.
109. Marcel Duchamp, 'The Bride Stripped Bare by her Bachelors, Even', mixed media, 1923, the Philadelphia Museum of Art.
110. 'The Last Emperor', directed by Bernardo Bertolucci, Thomas, UK/Italy, 1987.
111. The *Daily Graphic* (1912), p. 8.
112. The *Daily Graphic* (1912), p. 8.
113. In Jewish folklore, an artificially created human being. Frankenstein's monster continues in this tradition, both in concept and in consequence.
114. The subtitle of Shelley's novel was, of course, 'The Modern Prometheus'. The connection between Prometheus and the myth of the *Titanic* will be examined in Chapter 7.
115. Young (1912), p. 189.
116. Young (1912), pp. 15–16.
117. Young (1912), p. 17.
118. Young (1912), p. 17.
119. Young (1912), p. 19.
120. Young (1912), p. 18.
121. Young (1912), p. 20.
122. The casting of the *Titanic* as the 'mechanical bride' in American culture is well discussed by Larabee's important article (op. cit.) to which acknowledgement is freely given.
123. William Shakespeare, *Macbeth*, Act 1, scene V.

4   'WE SHALL DIE LIKE GENTLEMEN'

1.   Gibbs (1912), p. 8, reported Guggenheim's fortune as £20 million.
2.   Gibbs (1912), p. 4.
3.   Gibbs (1912), p. 4.
4.   Gibbs (1912), p. 4.
5.   Leo Lowenthal, 'The Triumph of Mass Idols: Rise of Biography as a Popular Literary Type' in *Literature and Mass Culture*, Communication in Society, Volume I (New Brunswick, New Jersey, 1984), pp. 203–28, p. 206. Lowenthal was writing in 1944.
6.   Gibbs (1912), p. 4.
7.   Gibbs (1912), p. 10.
8.   Gibbs (1912), p. 12. The story is repeated, in condensed form, in page 18, in a feature box under the heading 'Some Incidents of the Disaster'. The quotation attributed to Guggenheim differs slightly: 'If anything happens to me, tell my wife I have done my best in doing my duty.' Gibbs (1912), p. 18.
9.   Gibbs (1912), pp. 11–12.
10. The story of Guggenheim is widely retold in the secondary literature, for example, John P. Eaton and Charles A. Haas, *Titanic: Destination Disaster: The Legends and the Reality* (Wellingborough,

Northamptonshire, 1987), p. 8; Marcus (1969), p. 160; and Wade (1980), p. 52. The details vary, but the point is the same.

11. Donnelly (1912).
12. Gibbs (1912), p. 28.
13. The age at which Smith left school is not known. Some sources say he was 14, but the point is, nevertheless, taken. He was a man of little formal education.
14. Source: Captain Smith's birth certificate, Hanley Central Library, Stoke-on-Trent. See also Gary Cooper, *The Man Who Sank the Titanic? The Life and Times of Captain Edward J. Smith* (Alsager, Stoke-on-Trent, 1992), pp. 166–7.
15. Stevenson (1914), p. 18. A similar phrase, 'English gentleman', was used by J.W. Thompson and reported by Stevenson (1914), p. 27.
16. Gibbs (1912), p. 38.
17. Stevenson (1914), p. 19.
18. Scott (1912).
19. Publisher unknown, almost certainly 1912. Collection M. Bown, reproduced in Bown and Simmons (1987), p. 86.
20. Gibbs (1912), p. 10.
21. Gibbs (1912), p. 26.
22. Gibbs (1912), p. 38.
23. Stevenson (1914), p. 18.
24. The *Daily Graphic* (1912), p. 8.
25. The *Daily Graphic* (1912), p. 8.
26. The *Daily Graphic* (1912), p. 8.
27. Gibbs (1912), p. 10.
28. Gibbs (1912), p. 28.
29. Publisher unknown, almost certainly 1912, collection M. Bown, reproduced in Bown and Simmons (1987), p. 86.
30. Stevenson (1914), p. 10.
31. Stevenson (1914), p. 11.
32. Stevenson (1914), p. 15.
33. Stevenson (1914), p. 31.
34. Stevenson (1914), p. 11.
35. Stevenson (1914), pp. 18–19.
36. Mark Girouard argues that the period from the late eighteenth century to the First World War saw a self-conscious revival of medieval-style chivalry among English gentlemen. This involved not only codes of social conduct, but also styles of art and architecture. See Mark Girouard, *The Return to Camelot: Chivalry and the English Gentleman* (New Haven and London, 1981), passim.
37. Gibbs (1912), p. 4.
38. See, for example, Cooper (1990), p. 134; Donald Hyslop and Sheila Jemima, 'The "Titanic" and Southampton: The Oral Evidence' in *Oral History*, volume 18, no. 1 (1991), pp. 37–43, p. 41; Walter Lord, *The Night Lives On* (Harmondsworth, 1987), p. 17; Marcus (1969), p. 94; Žižek (1989), p. 70.
39. See Lynch and Marschall (1992), p. 176; Eaton and Haas (1987), p. 100.
40. Wade (1980), p. 253.

41. Wade (1980), p. 49.
42. Gibbs (1912), p. 26.
43. Young (1912), p. 75. Young persistently used the word 'steerage', for what the White Star line preferred to call 'third-class' accommodation.
44. Young (1912), p. 75.
45. Young (1912), p. 76.
46. Young (1912), pp. 76–7.
47. Young (1912), pp. 78–9.
48. Gibbs (1912), p. 11.
49. Gibbs (1912), p. 25.
50. The *Daily Graphic* (1912), pp. 4–5.
51. The case of the crew is clearly different as so many were called to give evidence at the subsequent enquiries. They quickly became celebrities after the event.
52. See Lynch and Marschall (1992), p. 41.
53. Gibbs (1912), p. 11.
54. Young (1912), p. 125.
55. See Lynch and Marschall (1992), pp. 36–7.
56. 'List of First Class Passengers Royal and U.S. Mail S.S. "Titanic"', White Star Line, April 1912. Unpaginated. The passenger list was distributed on board and included 'Information for Passengers' such as how to send telegrams or reserve deck chairs.
57. Gibbs (1912), p. 28.
58. 'White Star Line United States and Royal Mail Steamers First Class Passage Rates' (New York, January 1912), p. 3.
59. 'White Star Line United States and Royal Mail Steamers First Class Passage Rates' (New York, January 1912), p. 2.
60. 'White Star Line Olympic Titanic' brochure (New York, 1911), unpaginated.
61. Young (1912), p. 48.
62. Young's publishers, Grant Richards Ltd, sold books at five or six shillings each, compared with the penny and twopence charged for the *Daily Graphic* special edition and 'The Deathless Story of the Titanic' respectively.
63. Gibbs (1912), p. 12.
64. Gibbs (1912), p. 12.
65. Stevenson (1914), p. 18.
66. Gibbs (1912), p. 38.
67. 'Lord Charles Beresford's Tribute to the "Black Squad"' in Gibbs (1912), p. 38. The tribute originally appeared as a letter to *The Times*.
68. Inscription on the Engineers' Memorial, East Park, Southampton. This large and impressive memorial remains in excellent condition today.
69. Gibbs (1912), p. 38.
70. The British Inquiry Report (1912), p. 23, gives the number of first-class passengers as 325, compared with 285 in second-class.
71. Young (1912), p. 75.
72. Gibbs (1912), p. 4.
73. Davie (1986), p. 44.
74. Young (1912), p. 162.

75. The *Daily Graphic* (1912), p. 3.
76. Gibbs (1912), p. 8.
77. Young (1912), p. 92.
78. Young (1912), p. 94.
79. Gibbs (1912), p. 8.
80. Young (1912), p. 48.
81. Young (1912), p. 118.
82. Young (1912), p. 17.
83. Young (1912), p. 75.
84. Young (1912), p. 110.
85. The *Daily Graphic* (1912), p. 8.
86. St Clair (1912), verse three.
87. Gibbs (1912), p. 26.
88. Gibbs (1912), p. 26.
89. Young (1912), p. 119.
90. Young (1912), p. 119.
91. Gibbs (1912), p. 12.
92. Times, of course, have changed. Survival and class is a concern of commentators today, but it was not in Britain in 1912–14.
93. Gibbs (1912), p. 12.
94. '"Titanic" Disaster Report of the Committee on Commerce United States Senate Pursuant to S. Res. 283 Directing the Committee to Investigate the Causes Leading to the Wreck of the White Star Liner "Titanic"'. Senate Report No. 806, 62nd Congress, 2nd Session (Washington, 1912), p. 13. Subsequent references will be given as 'American Inquiry Report (1912)'.
95. American Inquiry Report (1912), p. 5.
96. Young (1912), pp. 203–4. Young also gives the figures for the crew.
97. Young (1912), p. 119.
98. Young (1912), p. 119. Survival rates on the *Titanic* are also discussed in Wayne Hall, 'Social Class and Survival on the S.S. Titanic' in *Social Science and Medicine*, no. 22, volume 6, 1986, pp. 687–90.
99. British Inquiry Report (1912), p. 5. The simple term 'class' used by the inquiry suggests that for the investigators, social class and class of accommodation were one and the same thing.
100. British Inquiry Report (1912), p. 5.
101. There are slight differences between the two sets of figures, but these are very minimal and do not affect my argument here.
102. British Inquiry Report (1912), p. 70.
103. British Inquiry Report (1912), p. 70.
104. British Inquiry Report (1912), p. 40.
105. Young (1912), p. 75.
106. See Davie (1986), p. 28.
107. The American Inquiry Report (1912), pp. 58–65, produced a list of third-class passengers, dividing them into geographical groups which (roughly) can be taken to indicate the proportion likely to have spoken English.
108. British Inquiry Report (1912), p. 70.
109. Lynch and Marschall (1992), p. 118.

110. British Inquiry Report (1912), pp. 40–1.
111. British Inquiry Report (1912), p. 40. Lynch and Marschall concur. See Lynch and Marschall (1992), p. 118. Lord, too, is in agreement: it was not that there was any policy to hold back the third-class passengers. Rather, 'there was no policy at all. Some gates were open; some were closed. Some passengers were assisted, some were stopped; others were left to shift for themselves.' See Lord (1986), p. 114.
112. See Wade (1980), p. 21. The normally stringent US customs and immigration formalities were suspended for the survivors of the *Titanic*. See Gardiner and Van Der Vat (1995), p. 158.
113. I am grateful to Charles A. Haas of the Titanic International Society for sharing his knowledge of New York immigration procedures with me. Correspondence with Charles A. Haas, 10 May 1998.
114. The British Inquiry Report noted that the *Titanic* had been constructed in compliance with 'American Immigration Laws.' British Inquiry Report (1912), p. 10.
115. Lord (1976), p. 130.
116. Lord (1986), p. 203.
117. Lord (1976), p. 130.
118. *Formal Investigation into the Loss of the S.S. 'Titanic'. Evidence, Appendices and Index* (24 June 1912), day 29, p. 736. This is the full transcript of the inquiry, and was published by HMSO in addition to the shorter report. Subsequent references to the full document will be given as 'British Inquiry Evidence).
119. Lord (1976), p. 130.
120. The *Daily Graphic* (1912), p. 8.
121. The *Daily Graphic* (1912), p. 8.
122. Gibbs (1912), p. 1.
123. Gibbs (1912), p. 26.
124. St Clair (1912), verse three.
125. Mrs Cecil F. Alexander, hymn: 'All Things Bright and Beautiful', 1848, verse three. The hymn was included, for example, in *The Church Hymnal for the Christian Year* (London, 1917), and so was in current use in 1912. The hymn still remains popular today, although the third verse is, tellingly, usually omitted.
126. St Clair (1912), verse three.

5 'BE BRITISH'

1. The *Daily Graphic* (1912), p. 9.
2. Gibbs (1912), p. 14.
3. Pelham and Wright (1912).
4. Scott (1912).
5. St Clair (1912).
6. Op. cit. See Bown and Simmons (1987), p. 56.
7. Published by Debenham, Cowes, Isle of White (1912), and reproduced in Bown and Simmons (1987), p. 58.

8. Published by Tom Harvey, Redruth, Cornwall (1912); reproduced in Bown and Simmons (1987), p. 57. It is interesting to note that the captain's date of birth is given incorrectly on this card: it demonstrates how quickly such memorabilia was produced, with little time to lose on checking details of fact.

9. The *Daily Graphic* (1912), p. 8.

10. The *Daily Graphic* (1912), p. 8.

11. Gibbs (1912), p. 4.

12. Stevenson (1914), p. 10.

13. Wright (1912).

14. Stevenson (1914), p. 18.

15. Stevenson (1914), pp. 30–1.

16. Stevenson (1914), p. 18.

17. British Inquiry Evidence (1912), minutes 10585–8, p. 220. The order 'Be British' does not appear in either the British or American inquiry transcripts or reports. Nor are any reliable witnesses quoted in the press. That Smith shouted 'Be British!' is always reported without attribution. See also Cooper (1992), p. 136.

18. Statue to Captain Smith at Beacon Park, Lichfield, Staffordshire, unveiled 1914. See also Stevenson (1914), p. 24.

19. The *Daily Graphic* (1912), p. 8. It is not clear to which individual operator the *Graphic* referred. From the context, however, we can surmise that it is Phillips.

20. An excellent account of the Marconi system and its role within the *Titanic* disaster is provided by Heyer (1995), especially pp. 27–55, to which this section is indebted.

21. Gibbs (1912), p. 9.

22. Much of Bride's account also appears in Young (1912), who makes use of a number of identical quotations. Their mutual source appears to be the *New York Times*, the importance of which will be discussed later in the body of the text.

23. Gibbs (1912), p. 10. The call CQD was preferred by Marconi operators at the time, despite international attempts to establish the new SOS as standard. It became standard only after the *Titanic* disaster, partly due to the publicity surrounding the incident. See, for example, Heyer (1995), p. 34.

24. Gibbs (1912), p. 10.

25. Gibbs (1912), p. 14.

26. Gibbs (1912), p. 14.

27. Gibbs (1912), p. 14. The same quotation appears in Young (1912), p. 134.

28. Gibbs (1912), p. 14. See also Young (1912), pp. 135–6.

29. Gibbs (1912), p. 14.

30. Gibbs (1912), p. 14. See also Young (1912), p. 137.

31. Gibbs (1912), p. 14.

32. Gibbs (1912), p. 9.

33. Gibbs (1912), p. 22.

34. Gibbs (1912), p. 22.

35. Gibbs (1912), p. 14.

36. Gibbs (1912), p. 10.
37. Gibbs (1912), p. 10.
38. St Clair (1912).
39. Gibbs (1912), p. 12. The same story is narrated by American survivor Colonel Archibald Gracie in Gracie (1913), p. 157. In Gracie's version, Lowe further supposes that the man was wearing skirts. Gracie drew this addition from Lowe's evidence to the American inquiry.
40. Young (1912), p. 117.
41. Young (1912), p. 117.
42. Gibbs (1912), p. 12. In Gracie's version, Lowe actually describes them as 'like wild beasts, ready to spring'. See Gracie (1913), p. 156.
43. See Wade (1980), p. 198.
44. The *Daily Graphic* (1912), p. 9.
45. The *Daily Graphic* (1912), p. 9.
46. The *Daily Graphic* (1912), p. 9.
47. Gibbs (1912), p. 16. According to Stevenson's version, Smith did not die in the sea, but even managed to swim back to the bridge, where he remained to the last. See Stevenson (1914), p. 26.
48. Gibbs (1912), p. 4.
49. Stevenson (1914), p. 10.
50. Stevenson (1914), p. 18.
51. Stevenson (1914), p. 27.
52. Stevenson (1912), p. 31.
53. The statue and its inscription remain in Beacon Park, Lichfield, Staffordshire.
54. American Inquiry Report (1912), p. 7.
55. A message from the *Amerika* via *Titanic* to the Hydrographic Office in Washington was properly relayed to Washington by Phillips but then 'put aside', while a warning from the *Mesaba* direct to *Titanic* 'does not appear to have been delivered to the master or any of the officers'. Had it reached the bridge, the inquiry concluded, it 'would perhaps have affected the navigation of the vessel'. British Inquiry Report (1912), pp. 27–8.
56. British Inquiry Report (1912), p. 27.
57. The *Daily Graphic* (1912), p. 8.
58. Cited in Heyer (1995), p. 47. Heyer argues that while these messages arrived as late as 18 April, the operators had already been withholding information in hope or anticipation of such a deal, which was now given official sanction by Marconi himself.
59. American Inquiry Report (1912), p. 18.
60. J.W. Thompson, quoted in Stevenson (1914), p. 27.
61. Visitors to the statue today will notice a second plaque identifying Smith as captain of the *Titanic*. This is a later addition.
62. Wright (recorded version) (1912).
63. Biel (1996), p. 48, uses the phrase: 'honorary Anglo-Saxons' in his account of the disaster in American culture.
64. Robert Donnelly, 'The Band Was Playing as the Ship Went Down' (sheet music) (London, not dated, but almost certainly 1912).
65. Gibbs (1912), p. 12.

66. Pelham and Wright (1912).
67. White Star Line publicity brochure: 'White Star Line Royal and United States Mail Steamers Olympic and Titanic' (Liverpool, 1911), p. 3.
68. 'White Star Line Royal and United States Mail Steamers Olympic and Titanic' (publicity brochure) 1911.
69. Pelham and Wright (1912).
70. Young (1912), p. 195.
71. Scott (1912).
72. Gibbs (1912), p. 38. Lord Beresford was also a warmly-received speaker at the unveiling of the Lichfield statue to Captain Smith.
73. Gibbs (1912), p. 4.
74. The *Daily Graphic* (1912), p. 8.
75. The *Daily Graphic* (1912), p. 6.
76. Young (1912), p. 202.
77. Joseph, Conrad 'Some Reflections, Seamanlike and Otherwise, on the Loss of the Titanic' in *The English Review*, Volume XI, May 1912, pp. 304–15, p. 308.
78. Conrad (1912), p. 315.
79. Joseph Conrad, 'Some Aspects of the Admirable Inquiry' in the *English Review*, Volume XI, July 1912, pp. 581–95, p. 595.
80. Conrad 'Some Aspects ...' (1912), p. 595.
81. Conrad 'Some Aspects ...' (1912), p. 595. A literary analysis of Conrad's *Titanic* articles can be found in J.H. Stape, 'Conrad Controversial: Ideology and Rhetoric in the Essays on the Titanic' in *Prose Studies*, volume 11, no. 1 (1988), pp. 61–8. Stape explains that Conrad lost the manuscript of his short story 'Karain' on the *Titanic* (p. 61). The thrust of Stape's argument, however, is to reveal Conrad's 'nuanced stylistic performance' (p. 61).
82. George Bernard Shaw, 'Some Unmentioned Morals', letter to the *Daily News and Leader*, 14 May 1912, p. 9.
83. Shaw (14 May 1912), p. 9.
84. Shaw (14 May 1912), p. 9.
85. Sir Arthur Conan Doyle, letter to the *Daily News and Leader* (20 May 1912), p. 9.
86. Shaw, letter to the *Daily News and Leader* (22 May 1912), p. 9.
87. Sir Arthur Conan Doyle, letter to the *Daily News and Leader* (25 May 1912), p. 9.
88. Shaw (14 May 1912).
89. The number of warnings received has been a matter of dispute. The American inquiry noted three, the British five, and Walter Lord (1976) seven. I have continued to use the British figures in this analysis, in the interests of context and consistency.
90. British Inquiry Report (1912), p. 42.
91. Gibbs (1912), p. 28.
92. Gibbs (1912), p. 1.
93. Gibbs (1912), p. 1.
94. The *Daily Graphic* (1912), p. 8.
95. The *Daily Graphic* (1912), p. 8.
96. The *Daily Graphic* (1912), p. 8.

97.   Young (1912), p. 191.
98.   Young (1912), p. 195.
99.   Adamson (1912), p. 11.
100.   Adamson (1912), p. 12.
101.   The correct spelling is Chevré.
102.   The *Daily Graphic* (p. 3).
103.   Pelham and Wright (1912).
104.   Stevenson (1912), p. 6.
105.   Gibbs (1912), p. 1.
106.   Gibbs (1912), p. 1.
107.   Young (1912), p. 197.
108.   Gibbs (1912), p. 2.
109.   Pelham and Wright (1912).
110.   Greek epic poetry was, of course, originally an oral form, hence 'that which is *heard*'.
111.   Gregory Nagy, *The Best of the Achaeans* (Baltimore, 1979), pp. 16–17.
112.   Homer, *The Iliad*, translated by Richard Lattimore (Chicago, 1951), p. 209.
113.   Nagy (1979), p. 29.
114.   Gibbs (1912), p. 28.

6   'NEARER, MY GOD, TO THEE'

1.   The punctuation and capitalization of the hymn title varies from source to source. When quoting from the texts, I have maintained the original form used in each case.
2.   Gibbs (1912), p. 8.
3.   Young (1912), p. 151.
4.   Young (1912), p. 151.
5.   Gibbs (1912), p. 11.
6.   The *Daily Graphic* (1912), p. 3.
7.   Gibbs (1912), p. 14.
8.   Gibbs (1912), p. 14. 'Eternal Father' is most likely a conscious reference to the opening of the well-known maritime hymn 'For Those in Peril on the Sea' which begins: 'Eternal father, strong to save …'.
9.   Young (1912), p. 151.
10.   The *Daily Graphic* (1912), p. 3.
11.   Gibbs (1912), p. 2.
12.   Gibbs (1912), p. 10.
13.   Gibbs (1912), p. 15.
14.   Publisher unknown. Reproduced in Bown and Simmons (1987), p. 65.
15.   Rotary Photographic Company (1912).
16.   Millar and Lang 'National' series postcard (1912).
17.   W. Clark of Liverpool, postcard (1912) and Joe Dixon of Hull, postcard (1912).
18.   Debenham of Cowes, postcard (1912).
19.   Tom Harvey of Redruth, postcard (1912).

20. E.A. Bragg of Falmouth, postcard (1912). Bown and Simmons (1987, p. 56) note that 'In Memoriam' postcards were published as soon as within three days of the disaster.
21. Bamforth and Company, Ltd, series of six postcards (1912).
22. Robert Donnelly, composer, 'The Band Were Playing as the Ship Went Down', published by Rossi and Spinelli Ltd, (London, n.d., but almost certainly 1912).
23. Donnelly (1912).
24. Haydon Augarde, 'The Wreck of the Titanic', musical sketch for piano, published by the Lawrence Wright Music Co. (London, 1912).
25. Lawrence Wright, 'Be British!' recorded version, 'The Winner' label, 1912.
26. Wood was also founder of the 'Promenade' concerts, now presented annually by the BBC.
27. Annotated programme, 'The "Titanic" Band Memorial Concert' (London, 1912), unpaginated.
28. Memorial paper handkerchief (Wigan, 1912).
29. Stevenson (1912), p. 27.
30. Colne was Hartley's home town, although at the time of the *Titanic*'s maiden voyage, he gave his address as Dewsbury, Yorkshire, to where the family had moved. The names of four other members of his family were later added to the memorial. At the time of the author's visit in 1998, fresh flowers had been left at the grave.
31. Augarde (1912).
32. Wright (1912).
33. Stevenson, (1912), p. 27.
34. Joe Dixon of Hull, postcard (1912).
35. W. Clark of Liverpool, postcard (1912).
36. See for example, Gibbs (1912), p. 11, and the Wigan handkerchief (1912).
37. Gibbs (1912), p. 14.
38. 'Titanic', directed by Jean Negulesco, 20th Century Fox USA, 1953 and 'Titanic', directed by James Cameron, 20th Century Fox /Paramount Pictures, USA, 1997.
39. 'A Night to Remember', directed by Roy Ward Baker, The Rank Organization, UK, 1958.
40. Augarde (1912) uses yet another setting in his 'descriptive musical sketch'.
41. Of the six Bamforth cards, only the first of the series reproduces any of the score. The rest use only the words.
42. Personal visit to Hartley's grave, Colne, Lancashire, April 1998.
43. Hartley and his family were Independent Methodists and worshipped at the Bethel Chapel while they lived in Colne.
44. The *New York Times*, 19 April 1912, p. 1.
45. The *New York Times*, 19 April 1912, p. 1.
46. Gibbs (1912), p. 14.
47. Lord (1987), pp. 140–1. Lynch and Marschall (1992), p. 115, concur.
48. That the band (in some or other combination) were playing was agreed by witnesses such as Steward Edward Brown and Stewardess Annie

Robinson at the British Inquiry. They were not asked, and did not volun-
teer, however, what was being played. See British Inquiry Evidence,
minutes 10589–93, p. 221; and minutes 13313–14, p. 281.
49. Gibbs (1912), p. 14.
50. The *New York Times*, 19 April, 1912, p. 4.
51. The *New York Times*, 19 April, 1912, p. 4.
52. The exact number of passengers is not known.
53. Survivors gave the distance as between 15 and 30 yards. More recent
dives to the wreck have suggested between 15 and 20. See Michael C.
Neitzel, *The Valencia Tragedy* (Surrey, British Columbia, 1995), p. 24.
54. The *New York Times*, 24 January 1906, p. 1.
55. The *New York Times*, 26 January 1906, p. 4.
56. Clarence H. Baily, 'The Wreck of the Valencia' in the *Pacific Monthly*,
March 1906, pp. 281–92, p. 281.
57. Baily (1906), p. 281.
58. Baily (1906), p. 281.
59. Baily (1906), p. 281. The extract is from the first verse of 'Nearer, My
God, to Thee'. One wonders, of course, how the 'strains' of the women
and children could be heard across the waters so thunderously
described.
60. Baily (1906), p. 282.
61. Wade notes a possible *Titanic/Valencia* connection in a (unreferenced)
sentence in Wade (1979), p. 58. Wade gives the date of the *Valencia*
sinking as 1905. This is not correct. His point was, however, worthy of
further investigation. A detailed account of the *Valencia* incident itself is
given in Neitzel's (1995) history of that disaster.
62. Neitzel (1995), p. 90.
63. Lifeboat number five. Personal visit, September 1997.
64. Stevenson (1914), p. 31.
65. In the popular texts, one or more of the verses is frequently omitted.
Verse, four, for example, was omitted from the Royal Albert Hall programme and concert.
66. Gibbs (1912), p. 1.
67. The *Daily Graphic* (1912), p. 8.
68. This was clearly an old photograph. Helen is shown as an 'infant child',
but was actually ten years old in 1912.
69. Gibbs (1912), p. 19.
70. Gibbs (1912), p. 28.
71. Stevenson (1912), p. 16.
72. Gibbs (1912), p. 14.
73. Gibbs (1912), p. 28.
74. Stevenson (1912), p. 27.
75. Stevenson, (1912), p. 15.
76. Stevenson, (1912), p. 14.
77. Stevenson, (1912), p. 23.
78. Owen Chadwick, *The Secularization of the European Mind in the
Nineteenth Century* (Cambridge, 1975, reprinted 1977), p. 262.
79. Young (1912), pp. 15–16.

7 'THE UNSINKABLE SHIP'

1. Cameron (1997), dialogue from the film.
2. Bainbridge (1996), p. 189. Bainbridge's account places her invented central characters in a generally faithful historic context. This example provides a rare but significant error.
3. Publicity leaflet for 'Titanica' (directed by Stephen Low, Imax Corporation, Canada, 1992) in repertoire at the National Museum of Photography, Film and Television, Bradford, England, from 22 September 1993.
4. Publicity leaflet for 'Titanica' (directed by Stephen Low, Imax Corporation, Canada) in repertoire at the CN Imax Theatre, Vancouver, Canada, Summer, 1997.
5. Lord (1956), p. 99; also (illustrated and revised edition, 1976), p. 139.
6. Lord, (1956), pp. 28–48; and Lord (1976), pp. 63–81.
7. Lord (1976), p. 8.
8. Lord (1976), p. 55; and Lord (1956), p. 23.
9. Lord (1976), p. 73; also Lord (1956), p. 38.
10. Marcus (1969), pp. 28–31. Versions of this anecdote are frequently related in the secondary material.
11. Marcus (1969), p. 39.
12. Coleman (1977), p. 71.
13. Charles Pellegrino, *Her Name: Titanic* (London, 1990), p. 2.
14. Heyer (1995), p. 23. To be fair, Heyer modifies this claim somewhat in the following paragraph, but ultimately believes that the *Titanic* was billed as 'unsinkable'.
15. Biel (1996), p. 37.
16. Philip Howard, 'That Old Titanic Sinking Feeling' in *The Times*, 13 February 1981, p. 14. Howard is presumably referring to *The Times* leading article the day after the sinking, which opined: 'Everything had been done to make the huge vessel unsinkable, and her owners believed her to be so. It may perhaps be doubtful whether any precautions could ensure that a ship shall be unsinkable by such a terrific shock as that caused by the impact upon a huge iceberg ...' *The Times* 16 April 1912, p. 9. Interestingly, there is no reference to the *Titanic*'s 'unsinkability' in the news coverage.
17. See, for example, Hamilton (1982), p. 10.
18. Personal visit to Titanic Historical Society, Indian Orchard, Massachusetts, 18 August 1992. See also John M. Groff and Jane E. Allen, *The Titanic and Her Era*, Philadelphia Maritime Museum (Philadelphia, 1982), p. 29. The wording is very similar: their booklet was published by the Philadelphia Maritime Museum, which at that time held much of the THS collection.
19. Ken Longbottom, 'Twelve Popular Myths Concerning the Titanic Disaster' in *The Atlantic Daily Bulletin* (Journal of the British Titanic Society), no. 3, 1993, pp. 14–15, p. 14. To be fair, this is not a scholarly article, but the contribution of an 'enthusiast' to an enthusiasts' magazine. Nevertheless, the point still stands: there remains a large body of

opinion (many of whom are in a position to know better) that the *Titanic* was never claimed to be unsinkable.

20. 'The White Star Liners "Olympic" and "Titanic" in *The Shipbuilder*, 6 (1911), Special Number, Midsummer, pp. 1–130, p. 26.

21. Lord (1976), p. 55; Marcus (1969), pp. 28–31.

22. Ballard (1989), p. 10; Thomas E. Bonsall, *Titanic* (second edition, New York, 1989), p. 14.

23. Wade (1980), p. 297; Bonsall (1989), p. 36.

24. Gardiner and Van Der Vat (1995), p. 4. See also: Davie (1986), p. 20; David F. Hutchings, *Titanic: A Modern Legend* (Blandford Forum, Dorset, 1993), first published as *RMS Titanic – 75 Years of a Legend* (1987), p. 6.

25. Lord (1987), pp. 27–9. It will be noted that Lord has changed his views since *A Night to Remember*. His 1987 account is, I believe, the most persuasive among the existing literature, but remains incomplete.

26. On 1 June 1911, both the *Irish Times* and the *Belfast Morning News* referred to the *Titanic*'s safety features 'practically making the vessel unsinkable'. The articles tied in with the ship's launch at Belfast, and are also cited in Lord (1987), p. 28. I have not included these articles in my discussion because they did not appear in nationally available publications. The reasons for this were explained in my introduction.

27. This publication date has been deduced both by the owner of the only known copy, Geoff Robinson, and by Don Lynch, the historian of the Titanic Historical Society. I concur.

28. White Star Line leaflet, not dated and no publication details given, but believed to be September 1910. Collection of Geoff Robinson.

29. Don Lynch, 'The "Unsinkable" Titanic, As Advertised: Another Great Myth Dispelled' in *The Titanic Commutator*, volume 16, no. 4, February–April, 1993, pp. 4–6. I first noticed the leaflet in Geoff Robinson's collection of *Titanic* memorabilia in April 1992, and it was the subject of correspondence between the two of us before the appearance of Lynch's article the following year. The *Commutator* article is subsequently cited by Heyer (1995), p. 23.

30. The possibility has, of course, occurred to me that his leaflet is a forgery aimed at the growing and lucrative market in *Titanic* collectibles (see, for example, James Brown, 'Caveat Emptor' in *The Titanic Commutator*, volume 16, no. 1, May–July, 1992, pp. 24–30. However, a forger would presumably have produced more than one document. Additionally, Peter-Boyd Smith (meeting with me, February 1993), a reputable dealer in ocean memorabilia in Southampton, believes the document to be genuine.

31. Publicity brochure: 'White Star Line Royal and United States Steamers "Olympic" & "Titanic" 45,000 Tons Each The Largest Vessels in the World' (Liverpool, 1911), 72pp.

32. Publicity brochure: 'White Star Line Royal and United States Steamers "Olympic" & "Titanic" ...' (1911), pp. 8–9.

33. Publicity brochure: 'White Star Line Royal and United States Steamers "Olympic" & "Titanic" ...' (1911), p. 31.

34. I have raised this question in correspondence with Michael McCaughan of the Ulster Folk and Transport Museum, which has one of these

brochures and prints a facsimile version of it. He, too, is unable to give a circulation figure.

35. I have studied six other publicity publications describing the *Titanic*, together with four other publications (such as price-lists, booking information, etc.) giving information to the public about the ship and her facilities. Additionally, I have examined every published and available advertisement for the *Titanic*. None has made any claim for unsinkability.

36. *The Shipbuilder*, Volume VI, Special Number Midsummer 1911, 'The White Star Liners "Olympic" and Titanic"', 130pp.

37. *The Shipbuilder* (1911), p. 25.

38. *The Shipbuilder* (1911), p. 26.

39. Nine other articles and supplements were consulted, in various editions of both *The Shipbuilder* and *The Engineer*. Each is listed under 'Technical Journal Articles' in the bibliography. Gardiner and Van Der Vat (1995), p. 4, claim that *The Shipbuilder*'s modifier 'practically' was dropped by 'less sober journals' and that this led to the legend of the 'unsinkable' *Titanic*. They neither specify nor quote from the journals in question, however. No example has yet emerged to support their claim.

40. Gibbs (1912), p. 2.

41. Gibbs (1912), p. 4.

42. Young, (1912), p. 102.

43. Young (1912), p. 117.

44. The *Daily Graphic* (1912), p. 3.

45. Gibbs (1912), p. 12.

46. Gibbs (1912), p. 10.

47. The following argument is informed by my personal experience of working as a journalist before entering academe.

48. Heyer (1995), p. 83, describes exactly such a process taking place in the *New York Times* archives early on 15 April as first reports of the *Titanic* disaster began to arrive. Editor Carr Van Anda sent an employee to the paper's archives 'to gather all known facts about the ship.'

49. Gibbs (1912), pp. 2–3; The *Daily Graphic* (1912), p. 9.

50. The wording corresponds most closely to the publicity brochure version rather than to that in the *Shipbuilder*. The differences between the two are slight, but nevertheless observable. It is entirely possible, of course, that one of the papers copied the description from the other, but the original source remains the brochure.

51. Franklin's first name is variously spelled as containing one or two 'l's in the secondary material. In the primary sources, only his initials are given.

52. Quoted in Lord (1976), p. 177; Lord (1987), p. 29; Eaton and Haas (1992), p. 204; Wade (1980), p. 30. Young reports Franklin as having issued a statement on the morning of 15 April: 'We ... are perfectly satisfied that the vessel is unsinkable... We are absolutely certain that the *Titanic* is able to withstand any damage.' Young (1912), p. 182.

53. The *New York Times*, 16 April 1912, p. 1.

54. The *New York Times*, 16 April 1912, p. 2. The extent to which the White Star Line as a whole would have agreed with Franklin at the time is a matter of conjecture. The only real insight we have is provided by

J. Bruce Ismay's evidence to the British inquiry on 4 June 1912. A. Clement Edwards, MP, representing the Dock, Wharf, and Riverside Workers' Union, asked Ismay if it was the view of his company – that the *Titanic* was 'unsinkable'? Ismay replied, simply: 'We thought she was.' Edwards continued: 'What was the ground upon which you based that belief?' Ismay: 'Because we though she would float with two of the largest compartments full of water, and that the only way that those compartments were at all likely to be damaged was in the case of collision ...' Edwards: ' ...you based the belief of her unsinkability upon what was said to you by building experts?' Ismay: 'Absolutely.' British Inquiry Evidence (1912), minutes 18825, 18826 and 18827, p. 427. It should be noted, however, that Ismay was speaking some six weeks after the disaster. We cannot be sure, therefore, that this reflected his or his company's opinion before the myth of unsinkability took hold. Certainly, it took until the sixteenth day of the inquiry for the notion of 'unsinkability' to come under formal consideration, and it then merits only a three-paragraph exchange as part of an investigation which took a total of 36 days. Clearly, the question of 'unsinkability' was not taken seriously in the sober atmosphere of the official inquiry, even after the event.

55.   The *Daily Mirror* of 16 April 1912, paraphrased the now familiar account of the bulkhead system and concluded that the *Titanic* was 'indeed, practically unsinkable' (p. 5), suggesting the source to have been *The Shipbuilder*. Additionally the *Mirror* quoted Franklin in reported speech as stating 'that the Titanic is unsinkable' (p. 3). The *Mirror*, at this stage believed the *Titanic* to be safe and reported (memorably, in retrospect): 'Every One On Board World's Greatest Liner Safe After Collision With Iceberg In Atlantic Ocean' (p. 3).

56.   Gibbs (1912), p. 24.

57.   Young (1912), pp. 182–3.

58.   Nemesis is the name of the Greek goddess of retribution, and so the word can also be used as a proper noun.

59.   Françoise Graziani, 'Discoveries' in *Companion to Literary Myths, Heroes and Archetypes*, edited by Pierre Brunel (London and New York, 1992), pp. 317–24, p. 318.

60.   Yves-Alain Favre, 'Narcissus' in *Companion to Literary Myths, Heroes and Archetypes*, edited by Pierre Brunel (London and New York, 1992), pp. 867–71, p. 867.

61.   Favre (1992), p. 871.

62.   Quoted by Raymond Trousson, 'Prometheus' in *Companion to Literary Myths Heroes and Archetypes*, edited by Pierre Brunel (London and New York, 1992), pp. 968–81, p. 970.

63.   Trousson (1992), p. 970. This summary of the Prometheus myth draws on Trousson's lucid article.

64.   Trousson (1992), p. 970.

65.   See Trousson (1992), p. 970. Trousson continues his article by tracing the Prometheus myth up to the twentieth-century.

66.   The descendants of the 12 original Titans were themselves known as Titans.

67. Of all these terms, 'Titan' alone appears in Stephen Phillips' poem 'In Memoriam' in the Covent Garden benefit programme (1912, unpaginated). There are some, brief references to these terms in the secondary material: hubris is mentioned by Davie (1986), p. 4; Marcus (1969), p. 298; and Wade (1980), p. 299. In each case, however, they are referring to the overall significance of the sinking today rather than interpreting the primary sources. There is no mention of nemesis, but the Titans are noted by Lord (1987), pp. 25–6.; Pellegrino (1990), p. 20; and Wade (1980), p. 39.
68. The *Daily Graphic* (1912), p. 8.
69. Gibbs (1912), p. 2.
70. Young (1912), p. 5.
71. Gibbs (1912), p. 22.
72. Young (1912), p. 53.
73. Young (1912), p. 157.
74. Young (1912), pp. 88–9.
75. The *Daily Graphic* (1912), p. 8.
76. Gibbs (1912), p. 2.
77. Memorial paper handkerchief (1912).
78. Gibbs (1912), p. 4
79. The fact that the *Titanic* texts, in keeping with convention, refer to the *Titanic* as 'she' adds further to the mythical personification of the characters in this story.
80. Gibbs (1912), p. 25.
81. Young (1912), p. 17.
82. The *Daily Graphic* (1912), p. 8.
83. The *Daily Graphic* (1912), p. 8.
84. The *Daily Graphic* (1912), p. 8.
85. Young (1912), p. 157.
86. Gibbs (1912), p. 27.
87. Young (1912), p. 192.
88. The *Daily Graphic* (1912), p. 8.
89. The *Daily Graphic* (1912), p. 8.
90. Gibbs (1912), p. 27.
91. The *Daily Graphic* (1912), p. 8.
92. Gibbs (1912), p. 25.
93. The *Daily Graphic* (1912), p. 8.
94. The *Daily Graphic* (1912), p. 8.
95. Gibbs (1912), p. 25.
96. Young (1912), p. 16.
97. Gibbs (1912), p. 8.
98. Young (1912), p. 48.
99. Clifford Geertz, 'Thick Description: Toward an Interpretive Theory of Culture' in *The Interpretation of Cultures* (New York, 1973, London, 1975), pp. 412–53, p. 5.
100. Coleman (1977), p. 84.
101. The ensuing summary of the building and similarities between the *Olympic* and the *Titanic* is non-controversial and would be known to experts in the field. Following academic convention, then, it is not my

intention to endnote every point. What is unusual is the emphasis: of all the secondary texts, only Bonsall (1989) has, in my opinion sufficiently emphasized the importance of thinking of the *Olympic* Class of liners as a group. The argument, and especially the idea of a control experiment, is, of course, my own.

102. See Bonsall (1989), p. 7.
103. The *Gigantic* was built later as planned, but in the light of the sinking of the *Titanic*, its name was changed to *Britannic*.
104. 'The Olympic and Titanic' in *The Engineer*, 111 (1911), pp. 209–15.
105. 'The White Star Liners Olympic and Titanic' in *The Engineer*, 109 (1910), p. 231; 110 (1910), p. 38; and 110 (1910), p.196.
106. 'Electric Lifts on the Olympic and Titanic' in *The Engineer*, 109 (1910), p. 640.
107. 'The White Star Line', supplement in *The Engineer*, 109 (1910), June 24, pp. iii–xvi.
108. Op. cit.
109. *The Shipbuilder* special (op. cit.), p. 43.
110. Op. cit. Four others shared very similar titles, as detailed in my bibliography.
111. See, for example, the White Star brochure of 1910 (op. cit.). There is an artist's impression of just one ship, but it is captioned: 'R.M.S. "Olympic" and "Titanic," each 45,000 tons, as they will appear when completed'.
112. Internal differences were very slight, too. These were mainly on 'B' deck, where small private promenades were added to the grandest of the first class suites.
113. See, for example, the postcards reproduced in Bown and Simmons (1987), pp. 73–7.
114. Christie's auction catalogue 'Titanic Memorabilia and Maritime Pictures, Ephemera and Models' (London, 14 April 1992). To be fair, Christie's do acknowledge in a small caption inside that the photograph is in fact of the *Olympic* the 'sister ship of the "Titanic"'. But the point is made: the two ships were so similar that the *Olympic* can even grace the cover of a Christie's *Titanic* catalogue.
115. Gardiner and Van Der Vat (1995), passim. It is not clear how seriously the authors (as opposed to their publicists) actually took the theory, which they appear to discount on p. 261.
116. *The Shipbuilder* (1911), p. 26.
117. *The Engineer*, 110 (1910), p. 196.
118. 'White Star Line' publicity brochure (op. cit.), *circa* September 1910.
119. 'The Launch of the Titanic' in *The Engineer*, 111, (1911), p. 575.
120. *The Times* reported that: 'The launching arrangements for the Titanic were similar to those in the case of the Olympic last October.' 'Launch of the Titanic' in *The Times*, 1 June 1911, p. 9.
121. *The Shipbuilder* special number (op. cit.), p. 129.
122. Captain Smith was master of the *Olympic* until he took command of the *Titanic*. As Commodore of the White Star Line, it was customary for Smith to captain new ships on their maiden voyage. The *Olympic*, at the time of the *Titanic*'s demise, was commanded by the improbably named Captain Haddock.

123 For the full story of the *Olympic,* see Simon Mills, *RMS Olympic: The Old Reliable* (Blandford Forum, 1993).

CONCLUSION

1. A portion of this conclusion was previously published as 'Re-sinking the *Titanic*: Hubris, Nemesis and the Modern World' in *Symbiosis*, volume 1, no. 2, October 1997, pp. 151–8.
2. Ronald Reagan (attributed to), 'The Future Does Not Belong to the Fainthearted' in *The Penguin Book of 20th Century Speeches*, edited by Brian MacArthur (Harmondsworth, 1993) pp. 448–50, pp. 449–50.
3. Reagan (1993), p. 450.
4. Theodore 'Ted' Sorensen was the best-known among Kennedy's writers, contributing both speeches and articles under Kennedy's name. Thomas C. Reeves observes: 'historians have difficulties in distinguishing Sorensen's consistently gifted rhetoric from Jack's.' Thomas C. Reeves, *A Question of Character* (London, 1992), p. 117.
5. For Noonan's own account of the writing of this speech, see Peggy Noonan, *What I Saw of the Revolution* (New York, 1991), pp. 261–71.
6. Reagan (1993), p. 540; Noonan (1991), p. 266.
7. John Magee, *The Complete Works of John Magee: The Pilot Poet* (Cheltenham, 1989), p.79.
8. There is, of course, no question of impropriety here. Noonan freely admits her debt to Magee.
9. Stevenson (1914), p. 16.
10. Reagan (1993), p. 449.
11. This and all subsequent biblical references are taken from the King James version of the Bible.
12. For more on the influence of Kant and Hegel on Grierson, see Ian Aitken, *Film and Reform: John Grierson and the Documentary Film Movement* (London and New York, 1992), especially pp. 39–40.
13. Geertz (1973), p. 30.
14. Geertz said of the Balinese cockfight: 'Its function, if you want to call it that, is interpretive: it is a Balinese reading of Balinese experience, a story they tell themselves about themselves.' Geertz (1973), p. 448.
15. Thomas Nagel, *Mortal Questions* (Cambridge, 1979), pp. 129–30.
16. Nagel (1979), p. xiii.
17. R.G. Collingwood, *An Autobiography* (Oxford, 1939), p. 147.
18. T.W. Adorno, 'On Resignation' in *The Culture Industry*, edited by J.M. Bernstein (London, 1991), pp. 171–5, p. 173.
19. Adorno (1991), p. 175.

Bibliography and Sources

BOOKS AND JOURNAL ARTICLES

Adorno, T.W., 'On Resignation' in *The Culture Industry*, edited by J.M. Bernstein (London, 1991), pp. 171–5.

Adorno, T.W. *Notes on Literature*, Volume II (New York, 1992).

Adorno, T.W. and Horkheimer, M., 'The Culture Industry as Mass Deception' in *The Dialectic of Enlightenment*, translated by John Cumming (London, 1979).

Aitken, Ian, *Film and Reform: John Grierson and the Documentary Film Movement* (London and New York, 1992).

Archbold, Rick and McCauley, Dana, *Last Dinner on the Titanic: Menus and Recipes from the Great Liner* (London, 1997).

Bainbridge, Beryl, *Every Man for Himself* (London, 1996).

Ballard, Robert D., *The Discovery of the Titanic* (London, 1987, revised edition, 1989).

Barthes, Roland, *Mythologies*, translated by Anette Lavers (New York, 1972, 23rd printing, 1990).

Beesley, Lawrence, *The Loss of the RMS Titanic: Its Story and its Lessons* (London, 1912), also (Boston, 1912).

Benedict, Ruth, *Patterns of Culture* (London, 1935, fifth impression, 1952).

Benjamin, Walter, *The Origin of German Tragic Drama*, translated by John Osborne (London, 1977).

Biel, Steven, *Down With the Old Canoe* (New York, 1996).

Bloch, Ernst, *The Principle of Hope*, three volumes, translated by Neville Plaice, Stephen Plaice and Paul Knight (Oxford, 1986).

Boas, Franz, *Tsimshian Texts (New Series)*, American Ethnological Society, Volume III (Leyden, 1912), pp. 71–146.

Bonsall, Thomas E., *Titanic* (second edition, New York, 1989).

Bown, Mark, and Simmons, Roger, *RMS Titanic: A Portrait in Old Picture Post Cards* (Loggerheads, Shropshire, 1987).

Brown, James, 'Caveat Emptor' in *The Titanic Commutator*, volume 16, no. 1, May–July 1992, pp. 24–30.

Brunel, Pierre, *Companion to Literary Myths, Heroes and Archetypes*, edited by Pierre Brunel, translated by Wendy Allatson, Judith Hayward and Trista Selous (London, 1992).

Burke, Peter, 'History as Social Memory' in *Memory*, edited by Thomas Butler (Oxford, 1989), pp. 97–113.

Butler, David, and Anne Sloman, *British Political Facts 1900–1975* (London, 1975).

Cannell, Fenella, 'Concepts of Parenthood: The Warnock Report, the Gillick Debate and Modern Myths' in *American Ethnologist*, volume 17, no. 4 (Washington, DC, 1990), pp. 667–686.

Chadwick, Owen, *The Secularization of the European Mind in the Nineteenth Century* (Cambridge, 1975, reprinted 1977).

Chartier, Roger, *Cultural History* (Cambridge, 1988).

Christie's, *Titanic Memorabilia and Maritime Pictures, Ephemera and Models*, auction catalogue (London, 1992).

Cohen, Percy S., 'Theories of Myth' in *Man*, volume 4, (1969), pp. 337–53.

Coleman, Terry, *The Liners* (Harmondsworth, 1977).

Collingwood, R.G., *An Autobiography* (Oxford, 1939).

Conrad, Joseph, 'Some Aspects of the Admirable Inquiry' in *The English Review*, 11 (1912), pp. 581–95.

Conrad, Joseph, 'Some Reflections, Seamanlike and Otherwise, on the Loss of the Titanic' in *The English Review*, 11 (1912), pp. 304–15.

Cooper, Gary, *The Man Who Sank the Titanic? The Life and Times of Captain Edward J. Smith* (Alsager, Stoke-on-Trent, 1992).

Crapanzano, Vincent, 'Hermes' Dilemma: The Masking of Subversion in Ethnographic Description' in *Writing Culture*, edited by James Clifford and George E. Marcus (Berkeley, 1986), pp. 51–76.

Cunningham, John, 'National Daily Newspapers and their Circulations in the UK, 1908–1978' in *Journal of Advertising History* volume 4, February 1981, pp. 16–18.

Cupitt, Don, *What is a Story* (London, 1991).

Cupitt, Don, *The Time Being* (London, 1992).

Cussler, Clive, *Raise the Titanic* (London, 1977, reprinted 1978).

Darnton, Robert, *The Great Cat Massacre and Other Episodes in French Cultural History* (London, 1984).

Davie, Michael, *The Titanic: The Full Story of a Tragedy* (London, 1986).

Dunn, John 'Practising History and Social Science on "Realist" Assumptions' in *Political Obligation in its Historical Context* (Cambridge, 1980), pp. 81–111.

Eagleton, Terry, *The Crisis of Contemporary Culture* (Oxford, 1993).

Eaton, John P. and Haas, Charles A., *Titanic: Triumph and Tragedy* (Sparkford, Somerset, 1986 and 1992).

Eaton, John P. and Haas, Charles A., *Titanic: Destination Disaster: The Legends and the Reality* (Wellingborough, Northamptonshire, 1987).

Eliot, T.S., *Notes Towards the Definition of Culture* (London, 1948).

Favre, Yves-Alain, 'Narcissus' in *Companion to Literary Myths, Heroes and Archetypes*, edited by Pierre Brunel (London and New York, 1992), pp. 867–71.

Finley, M.I., 'Myth Memory and History' in *The Use and Abuse of History* (London, 1986), pp. 11–33.

Fussell, Paul, *The Great War and Modern Memory* (Oxford, 1975; first paperback edition, 1977).

Galbraith, John Kenneth, *A Tenured Professor: A Novel* (London, 1990).

Gardiner, Robin, and Van Der Vat, Dan, *The Riddle of the Titanic* (London, 1995).

Geertz, Clifford, 'Deep Play: Notes on the Balinese Cockfight' in *The Interpretation of Cultures* (New York, 1973 and London, 1975), pp. 412–53.

Geertz, Clifford, 'Thick Description: Toward an Interpretive Theory of Culture' in *The Interpretation of Cultures* (New York, 1973, London, 1975), pp. 3–30.

198   *The Myth of the* Titanic

Geertz, Clifford, 'Found in Translation: On the Social History of the Moral Imagination' in *Local Knowledge* (New York, 1983), pp. 36–54.

Geoghegan, Vincent, *Utopianism and Marxism* (London, 1987).

Gibbs, C.R. Vernon, *British Passenger Liners of the Five Oceans* (London, 1963).

Gilovich, Thomas, *How We Know What Isn't So: The Fallibility of Reason in Everyday Life* (New York, 1991).

Girouard, Mark, *The Return to Camelot: Chivalry and the English Gentleman* (New Haven and London, 1981).

Gracie, Archibald, *The Truth About the Titanic* (New York, 1913). Reprinted as *Titanic: A Survivor's Story* (Chicago, 1986).

Graziani, Françoise, 'Discoveries' in *Companion to Literary Myths, Heroes and Archetypes*, edited by Pierre Brunel (London and New York, 1992), pp. 317–24.

Groff, John M., and Allen, Jane E., *The Titanic and Her Era*, Philadelphia Maritime Museum (Philadelphia, 1982).

Hall, Stuart, ed., *Representation: Cultural Representations and Signifying Practices* (London, 1997).

Hall, Wayne, 'Social Class and Survival on the S.S. Titanic' in *Social Science and Medicine*, volume 22, no. 6, pp. 687–90.

Hawthorne, Nathaniel, *The Scarlet Letter* in the collected novels edition (New York and Cambridge, 1983).

Heyer, Paul, *Titanic Legacy* (Westport, Connecticut, 1995).

Hill, Jonathan D., 'Myth and History' in *Rethinking History and Myth*, edited by Jonathan D. Hill (Urbana and Chicago, 1988), pp. 1–17.

Homer, *The Iliad*, translated by Richard Lattimore (Chicago, 1951).

Howells, Richard, 'And the Band Played on ...' in *The Times Higher Education Supplement*, 24 April 1992, p. 17.

Howells, Richard, 'Re-sinking the *Titanic*: Hubris, Nemesis and the Modern World' in *Symbiosis*, volume 1, no. 2, October 1997, pp. 151–8.

Hutchings, David F., *Titanic – A Modern Legend* (Blandford Forum, 1993), first published as *RMS Titanic – 75 Years of a Legend* (1987).

Hyslop, Donald, and Jemima, Sheila, 'The "Titanic" and Southampton: The Oral Evidence' in *Oral History*, volume 18, no. 1 (1991), pp. 37–43.

Inglis, Fred, *Media Theory* (Oxford, 1990).

Jackson, John Brinkerhoff, *Discovering the Vernacular Landscape* (New Haven, 1984).

Jay, Martin, *The Dialectical Imagination* (London, 1973).

Kazantzakis, Nikos, *The Last Temptation of Christ*, translated by P.A. Brien (New York, 1960).

Keneally, Thomas, *Schindler's Ark* (London, 1982).

Kracauer, Siegfried, *From Caligari to Hitler* (Princeton, NJ, 1947, fifth printing, 1974).

Larabee, Ann E., 'The American Hero and His Mechanical Bride: Gender Myths and the Titanic Disaster' in *American Studies*, volume 31, no. 1, Spring 1990, pp. 5–23.

Leach, E.R. *Political Systems of Highland Burma*, London School of Economics, Monographs in Social Anthropology, no. 44 (London, 1954, reprinted 1964, this edition 1970).

Lévi-Strauss, Claude, 'The Story of Asdiwal' in *The Structural Study of Myth and Totemism*, translated by Nicholas Mann, edited by Edmund Leach (London, 1967), pp. 1–47.

Lévi-Strauss, Claude, 'The Structural Study of Myth' in *Structural Anthropology*, translated by Claire Jacobson and Brooke Grundfest Schoepf (London, 1968), pp. 206–31.

Lévi-Strauss, Claude, *The Savage Mind*, The Nature of Human Society Series (London, 1972).

Lévi-Strauss, Claude, 'The Comparative Religions of Nonliterate Peoples' in *Structural Anthropology II*, translated by Monique Layton (London, 1978), pp. 60–7.

Lightoller, C. H., *The Titanic and Other Ships* (London, 1935).

Longbottom, Ken, 'Twelve Popular Myths Concerning the Titanic Disaster' in *The Atlantic Daily Bulletin* (Journal of the British Titanic Society), no. 3 (1993), pp. 14–15, p. 14.

Lord, Walter, *A Night to Remember* (London, 1956); also illustrated and revised edition (London, 1976).

Lord, Walter, *The Night Lives On* (Harmondsworth, 1987).

Louden-Brown, Paul, *The White Star Line: An Illustrated History 1870–1934* (Coltishall, Norfolk, 1991).

Lowenthal, Leo, *The Arts in Society* (Englewood Cliffs, New Jersey, 1964).

Lowenthal, Leo, 'On Sociology of Literature' in *Literature and Mass Culture*, Communication in Society, Volume I (New Brunswick, New Jersey, 1984), pp. 257–71.

Lowenthal, Leo, 'The Triumph of Mass Idols: Rise of Biography as a Popular Literary Type' in *Literature and Mass Culture*, Communication in Society, Volume I (New Brunswick, New Jersey, 1984), pp. 203–28.

Lynch, Don, 'The "Unsinkable" Titanic, As Advertised' in *The Titanic Commutator*, volume 16, no. 4, pp. 4–6.

Lynch, Don and Marschall, Ken, *Titanic: An Illustrated History* (London, 1992).

MacCabe, Colin, 'Defining Popular Culture' in *High Theory/Low Culture: Analysing Popular Television and Film*, edited by Colin MacCabe, Images of Culture (Manchester, 1986), pp. 1–10.

McCann, Graham, 'Ernst Bloch, The Utopian Function of Art and Literature' in *Radical Philosophy*, Autumn, 1988, p. 47.

McCann, Graham, *Marilyn Monroe* (Cambridge, 1988).

McCann, Graham, 'Biographical Boundaries' in *The Body: Social Process and Cultural Theory*, Theory Culture and Society, Edited by Mike Featherstone, Mike Hepworth and Bryan S. Turner (London, 1991), pp. 325–38.

Malinowski, B., 'Myth in Primitive Psychology' (1929) in *Magic, Science and Religion and Other Essays* (New York, 1954), pp. 93–148.

Maranda, Pierre, *Mythology* (London, 1972).

Maranda, Pierre, 'The Dialectic Metaphor: An Anthropological Essay on Hermeneutics' in *The Reader in the Text*, edited by Susan Suleiman and Inge Crossman (Princeton, NJ, 1980).

Magee, John, *The Complete Works of John Magee: The Pilot Poet* (Cheltenham, 1989).

Marcus, Geoffrey, *The Maiden Voyage* (London, 1969).

Mills, Simon, *RMS Olympic: The Old Reliable* (Blandford Forum, 1993).
Monaco, James, *How to Read a Film* (New York and Oxford, 1981).
Nagel, Thomas, *Mortal Questions* (Cambridge, 1979).
Nagy, Gregory, *The Best of the Achaeans* (Baltimore, 1979).
Neitzel, Michael C., *The Valencia Tragedy* (Surrey, British Columbia, 1995).
Noonan, Peggy, *What I Saw of the Revolution* (New York, 1991).
Pace, David, *Claude Lévi-Strauss* (Boston, 1983).
Padfield, Peter, *The Titanic and the Californian* (London, 1965).
Pellegrino, Charles, *Her Name: Titanic* (London, 1990).
Rappaport, Joanne, *The Politics of Memory*, Cambridge Latin American Studies (Cambridge, 1990).
Raskin, Marcus, 'JFK and the Culture of Violence' in *The American Historical Review*, volume 97, no. 2, pp. 487–99.
Reade, Leslie, *The Ship That Stood Still* (Sparkford, 1993).
Reagan, Ronald, (attributed to), 'The Future Does Not Belong to the Fainthearted' in *The Penguin Book of 20th Century Speeches*, edited by Brian MacArthur (Harmondsworth, 1993) pp. 448–50.
Reeves, Thomas C., *A Question of Character* (London, 1992).
Riffenburgh, Beau, *The Myth of the Explorer*, Polar Research Series (London and New York, 1993).
Rose, Jonathan, *The Edwardian Temperament, 1895–1919* (Athens, Ohio, 1986).
Sperber, Dan, 'Claude Lévi-Strauss' in *Structuralism and Since*, edited by John Sturrock (Oxford, 1977), pp. 19–51.
Stape, J.H., '"Conrad Controversial": Ideology and Rhetoric in the Essays on the Titanic' in *Prose Studies* volume 11, no. 1, pp. 61–68.
Taylor, Philip M., and Sanders, Michael, *British Propaganda During the First World War 1914–18* (London and Basingstoke, 1982).
Ticehurst, Brian *The Titanic: Southampton's Memorials* (Poole, Dorset, 1987, revised and reprinted, 1992).
Trousson, Raymond, 'Prometheus' in *Companion to Literary Myths Heroes and Archetypes*, edited by Pierre Brunel (London and New York, 1992), pp. 968–81.
Turner, Terence, 'Ethno-Ethnohistory: Myth and History in Native South American Representations of Contact with Western Society' in *Rethinking History and Myth*, edited by Jonathan D. Hill (Urbana, Illinois and Chicago, 1988), pp. 235–81.
Wade, Wyn Craig, *The Titanic: End of a Dream* (London, 1980).
Wadsworth, A.P., 'Newspaper Circulations 1800–1954', a paper of the Manchester Statistical Society, (Manchester, 1955).
Warshow, Robert, *The Immediate Experience* (New York, 1962).
Weber, Eugene, *France: Fin de Siècle* (Cambridge, Massachusetts and London, 1986).
Wittgenstein, Ludwig, *Culture and Value*, translated by Peter Winch (second edition, Oxford, 1980).
Wolin, Richard, *Walter Benjamin: An Aesthetic of Redemption* (New York, 1982).
Young, Filson, *Titanic* (London, 1912).
Žižek, Slavoj, *The Sublime Object of Ideology* (London and New York, 1989).

TECHNICAL JOURNAL ARTICLES

'Electric Lifts on the Olympic and Titanic' in *The Engineer*, 109 (1910), p. 640.
'The Launch of the Titanic' in *The Engineer*, 111 (1911), p. 575.
'The Laundry of the White Star Liner, Titanic' in *The Engineer*, 111 (1911), p. 567.
'The Olympic and Titanic' in *The Engineer*, 111 (1911), pp. 209–15.
'The White Star Line' in *The Engineer*, 109 (1910), supplement, 24 June, pp. iii–xvi.
'The White Star Liners Olympic and Titanic' in *The Engineer*, 110 (1910), p. 196.
'The White Star Liners "Olympic and Titanic"' in *The Shipbuilder*, 6 (1911), Special Number, Midsummer, pp. 1–130.
'White Star Liners Olympic and Titanic' in *The Engineer*, 109 (1910), p. 231.
'White Star Liners Olympic and Titanic' in *The Engineer*, 110 (1910), p. 38.
'The White Star Liner Titanic' in *Engineering*, 91 (1911), pp. 678–81.

None of the above articles was credited to any individual author.

NEWSPAPER AND PERIODICAL ARTICLES AND LETTERS

Baily, Clarence, 'The Wreck of the Valencia' in the *Pacific Monthly*, March 1906, pp. 281–92.
Conan Doyle, Sir Arthur, letter to the *Daily News and Leader*, 20 May 1912, p. 9.
Conan Doyle, Sir Arthur, letter to the *Daily News and Leader*, 25 May 1912, p. 9.
Duval Smith, Alex, 'Survivors Sail into Titanic Row on Disaster Spin-Offs' in the *Guardian*, 5 April 1997, p. 16.
Hamilton, Alan, 'Sunk at Last: Some Myths About the Titanic' in *The Times*, 15 April 1982, p. 10.
Harrington, Michael, 'Dead to the Truth' in the *Sunday Telegraph*, 22 November 1992, p. 31.
Howard, Philip, 'That Old Titanic Sinking Feeling' in *The Times*, 13 February 1981, p. 14.
Letts, Quentin, 'Six Narrow Slits That Sank the Titanic' in *The Times*, 9 April 1997, p. 16.
McAdams, Clark, 'Enough Said' in the *St Louis Post-Dispatch*, 22 April 1912, p. 10.
O'Brien, R. Barry, 'Inquiry Captains all on Different Courses' in the *Daily Telegraph* 3 April 1992, p. 8.
O'Brien, R. Barry, 'Titanic Inquiry Fails to End Row Over Rescue That Never Came' in the *Daily Telegraph*, 3 April 1992, p. 8.
Radford, Tim, 'Titanic Iceberg is Innocent' in the *Guardian*, 17 September 1993, p. 1.
Shaw, George Bernard, 'Some Unmentioned Morals', letter to the *Daily News and Leader*, 14 May 1912, p. 9.

Shaw, George Bernard, letter to the *Daily News Leader*, 22 May 1912, p. 9.
Wagner, Erica, 'Dinner as the Ship Went Down' in *The Times*, 14 April 1997,
    p. 16.

Additional articles from the *Daily Mirror*, the *Daily Telegraph*, the *New York
Times*, *The Times* and the New York *Evening Sun* were published without by-
lines and are detailed in the end-notes which conclude the relevant chapters.

NEWSPAPER SPECIAL EDITIONS

The *Daily Graphic* 'Titanic In Memoriam Number', 20 April 1912.
'The Deathless Story of the Titanic' (by Philip Gibbs for *Lloyds Weekly News*),
    1912.

PAMPHLETS, BROCHURES, PROGRAMMES,
MEMORABILIA, ETC.

Adamson, Jas. (ed.), 'Institute of Marine Engineers Vol. XXIV Memorial to
    the "Titanic" Engineering Staff' (London, 1912).
Anon, 'In Memory of the Captain, Crew and Passengers...' (memorial paper
    handkerchief) (Wigan, 1912).
Anon, 'List of First Class Passengers Royal and U.S. Mail S.S. "Titanic"',
    White Star Line (April 1912).
Anon, 'Steamers of the White Star Line, The' (publicity brochure) (nd, but
    dateable to *c*. 1909).
Anon, 'White Star-Dominion Canadian Service' (publicity brochure) (nd, but
    dateable to 1909).
Anon, 'White Star Line' (publicity brochure) (nd, *circa* September, 1910),
    possibly a printers' proof, collection Mr. G. Robinson.
Anon, 'White Star Line First Class Passage Rates' (New York, January, 1912).
Anon, 'White Star Line The Largest and Finest Steamers in the World
    Olympic Titanic Some Interesting Views' (publicity brochure) (n.d., prob-
    ably American, *c*. 1911).
Anon, 'White Star Line Plan of First Class Accommodation R.M.S. Titanic'
    (December, 1911).
Anon, 'White Star Line Royal & United States Mail Steamers "Olympic" &
    "Titanic"' (publicity brochure) (Liverpool, 1911).
Anon, 'White Star Line Second Class Rates, 1912 Olympic Titanic' (New
    York, January 1912).
Anon, 'White Star Line Titanic Olympic' (publicity brochure) (New York, nd,
    but dateable to 1911).
Anon, 'White Star Line Triple Screw Steamers Olympic and Titanic' (public-
    ity brochure) (nd, probably 1910–11).
Anon, 'The World's Largest & Finest Steamers The New Triple Screw S.S.
    "Olympic and Titanic"' (publicity brochure) (nd, but dateable to 1911).

Royal Albert Hall, 'The "Titanic" Band Memorial Concert' (programme) (London, 24 May 1912).
Royal Opera, Covent Garden 'Dramatic and Operatic Matinée in Aid of the "Titanic" Disaster Fund' (programme) (London, 14 May 1912).
Scott, B. 'Stand to Your Post' (78 rpm record 'In remembrance of the "Titanic"'), sung by Ernest Gray, The Winner label (UK, 1912).
Stevenson, F.S. (ed.), *'Be British' Captain E.J. Smith Memorial A Souvenir of July 29th, 1914* (Lichfield, Staffordshire, 1914).
Wright, L., 'Be British' (78 rpm record 'In remembrance of the "Titanic"'), sung by Ernest Gray, The Winner label (UK, 1912).

SHEET MUSIC

Augarde, Haydon, 'The Wreck of the Titanic', The Lawrence Wright Music Co. (London, 1912).
Donnelly, Robert, 'The Band Was Playing as the Ship Went Down', Rossi & Spinelli, Ltd (London, nd, presumably 1912).
Moore, E., 'Carpathia Grand March', A.W. Perry & Sons' Music Co (place of publication not given, 1912).
Pelham, Paul, and Wright, Lawrence, 'Be British!', The Lawrence Wright Music Co. (London, 1912).
St. Clair, F. V., 'The Ship That Will Never Return', E. Marks & Son (London, 1912).

GOVERNMENT PUBLICATIONS

Formal Investigation into the Loss of the S.S. "Titanic". Evidence, Appendices and Index. (London, 1912).
'Shipping Casualties (Loss of the Steamship "Titanic.") Report of a Formal Investigation into the circumstances attending the foundering on 15th April, 1912, of the British Steamship "Titanic," of Liverpool, after striking ice in or near Latitude 41° 46' N., 50° 14' W., North Atlantic Ocean, whereby loss of life ensued.' Parliamentary Command Paper cd. 6352 (London, 1912).
'"Titanic" Disaster Report of the Committee on Commerce United States Senate Pursuant to S. Res. 283 Directing the Committee to Investigate the Causes Leading to the Wreck of the White Star Liner "Titanic"'. Senate Report No. 806, 62nd Congress, 2nd Session (Washington, 1912).

FILMOGRAPHY

'Atlantic', directed by E.A. Dupont, British International Pictures/Süd Film, UK, 1929.

'A Night to Remember', directed by Roy Ward Baker, The Rank Organization, UK, 1958.

'Raise the Titanic', directed by Jerry Jameson, Martin Starger Productions for ITC, USA, 1980.

'SOS Titanic', directed by Billy Hale, EMI Films, UK, 1979.

'Time Bandits', directed by Terry Gilliam, Handmade Films, UK, 1981.

'Titanic', directed by Herbert Selpin and Werner Klinger, Tobis Films, Germany, 1943.

'Titanic', directed by Jean Negulescu, Twentieth Century Fox, USA, 1953.

'Titanic', directed by James Cameron, Twentieth Century Fox/Paramount Pictures, USA, 1997.

'Titanic', directed by Stephen Low, Imax Corporation, Canada, 1992.

SPEECHES

Gore, Al (Vice-president of the United States of America), address to National Press Club Luncheon, Washington, DC, 21 December, 1993. Transcript via Federal News Service.

INTERVIEW

Hart, Eva (*Titanic* survivor). I interviewed Miss Hart at her home at Chadwell Heath, Essex, on 21 October 1990. The interview was video-taped, and extracts from it are included in the video-documentaries 'The Story of Captain Smith and the *Titanic*' (Ray Johnson Productions, 1990) and 'Titanic' (Ray Johnson Productions, for Castle Communications, for WH Smith, 1993).

Index

Index